Edward Bond is considered one of Britain's most important, innovative, and controversial playwrights writing today. In this book, Jenny Spencer examines Bond's contribution to contemporary dramatic literature, uncovering the cultural and theoretical issues that make his work so challenging. With an in-depth examination of the plays, Spencer identifies and discusses the dramatic strategies that are key to understanding Bond's diverse and wide-ranging body of drama. Spencer's fascinating analysis calls upon the work of Brecht, Freud, Bahktin, and others to better define and clarify the interconnected political and aesthetic issues Bond's plays invariably raise.

This book will be of interest to the theatre-goer, as well as to scholars and students of contemporary British literature and drama.

DRAMATIC STRATEGIES IN THE PLAYS OF EDWARD BOND

DRAMATIC STRATEGIES
IN THE PLAYS OF
EDWARD BOND

JENNY S. SPENCER

CAMBRIDGE
UNIVERSITY PRESS

Published by the Press Syndicate of the University of Cambridge
The Pitt Building, Trumpington Street, Cambridge CB2 1RP
40 West 20th Street, New York, NY 10011-4211, USA
10 Stamford Road, Oakleigh, Victoria 3166, Australia

© Cambridge University Press 1992

First published 1992

Printed in Great Britain at the University Press, Cambridge

A catalogue record for this book is available from the British Library

Library of Congress cataloguing in publication data
Spencer, Jenny S.
Dramatic strategies in the plays of Edward Bond / Jenny S.
Spencer.
p.   cm
Includes bibliographical references and index.
ISBN 0 521 39304 3
1. Bond, Edward – Technique.   2. Drama – Technique.   I. Title.
PR6052.05Z92   1992
822′.914 – dc 20   91-45931   CIP

ISBN 0 521 39304 3 hardback

For those who have not survived,
and those who remember them

Contents

Illustrations

xi

Acknowledgments

My first encounter with the plays of Edward Bond was in a graduate
student classroom at the University of Iowa. The course, Brecht and
Contemporary English Drama, was taught by a visiting German
film specialist, on leave from a British University, to American
students with no experience of a live theatre culture, and little
knowledge of the history and politics informing contemporary
Anglo-European literature. Reading *Lear* and *Bingo*, the assigned
Bond texts, did not inspire great love: the dialogue seemed difficult,
the range of allusion complex, the impact of stage images hard to
imagine. Bond's prefaces, I remember thinking, were irritatingly
didactic and not very helpful to understanding the plays. Like many
of Bond's early reviewers, my responses were almost predictable –
the plays seemed at once presumptuous, unnecessarily violent,
deliberately obscure, or maddeningly simplistic. But, unlike the
other playwrights we read that semester (whom I quickly forgot),
Bond nagged on in my mind. I was disturbed – not as much by these
plays I had never seen, as by the feeling I was "missing something,"
and that it was the way in which I had been taught to read and think
about literature that prevented me from seeing it. Months later, I
bought a second-hand paperback and read *Saved*, *The Pope's Wedding*,
and *Early Morning*. Outside the classroom, something clicked. Despite initial resistance, or perhaps because of it, the plays worked a
powerful change in my thinking about the possibilities of contemporary political theatre.

Much time has since passed, but some things have not changed.
Bond has persisted, for example, in writing plays and in writing them
his own way despite unpredictable support from the British theatre
establishment, continuing derision from the popular press, and an
economic climate that has severely limited the number of venues for
new, and overtly political writing. Because Bond's plays *can* be read –

he is one of few playwrights who have more scripts published than have been produced – his potential influence is widespread. Although his work is now taken seriously by a growing number of students, theatre practitioners and drama scholars, his plays are performed and written about far more infrequently than one would expect for a contemporary writer of his stature, a situation that I hope this book helps to change. Indeed, the plays discussed in this volume can sustain the kind of reading and rereading, staging and restaging, discussion and argument that we expect of dramatic "classics," modern or not. But, unlike literature that has survived from the past, these plays were written for us. At the moment, the work of producing Bond does not involve a recovery of relevance or false claims of universality; rather, Bond's plays immerse actors and audiences in questions involving history and politics that more popular playwrights may prefer not to face.

I would like to thank Edward Bond for his permission to use unpublished material. For permission to use photos and illustrations, I thank Chris Davies, Zoë Dominic, Günter Englert, Gerry Goodstein, Yale University, and the New York Metropolitan Museum of Art. Sections of this book previously appeared in the following articles by the author: "Edward Bond's Dramatic Strategies," *Contemporary English Drama*, ed. by Christopher Bigsby, Stratford-upon-Avon Studies (London: Edward Arnold, 1981), pp. 123–138; "Edward Bond's *Bingo*: History, Politics and Subjectivity," *Themes in Drama*, vol. 8 (Cambridge University Press, 1986), pp. 213–221; "Rewriting 'Classics': Edward Bond's *The Woman*," *Modern Drama* (Dec. 1989), pp. 561–573. Thanks to Hodder and Stoughton Publishers, Cambridge University Press, and *Modern Drama* for permission to reprint.

I gratefully acknowledge the financial support of the American Association of University Women (AAUW) that allowed me to begin this project, and the support of the Graduate Research Council and English Department of the University of Massachusetts at Amherst that allowed me to finish. Acknowledgments are more than due the following people: Thomas Elsaesser, who introduced me to Bond's plays, and whose own thinking on the subject made this book possible; Frederick P. W. McDowell, who generously directed an earlier version; Miriam Gilbert, who helpfully commented on the manuscript and on whose mentoring skills I still constantly rely. My thanks to Philip Roberts, who read the entire manuscript, supported the book, and made final revisions almost painless; and to Sarah Stanton and Victoria Cooper, who managed the book through production. My deep appreciation to Susan Carlson, whose joyful enthusiasm and own research in the area inspires mine, and to Eugene van Erven, whose energy and political attitudes have served as a model. Thanks also to Herb Blau, Chris Bigsby, Joe Donohue, Ray Heffner, Enoch Brater, Janelle Reinelt, Mary Swander, Simon Lyster, Charles Arthur, Ceci McGee, Robert Cooper, and Steven Gooch, all of whom contributed, in ways they may or may not remember, to the research, writing, or revision of this book. Melanie Almeder and Elizabeth Merica assisted with research in the face of original deadlines; Christine Lyall Grant offered valuable aid in the preparation of the manuscript. A special thanks to Edward and Elisabeth Bond, whose personal kindness and unexpected generosity during the final stages of the project made my job much easier. I remain most grateful to my husband, Edwin Gentzler, whose intellectual and emotional support manifested itself in the most practical of ways. To Megan, I apologize for time spent in the study that in a different world, would have been spent with you.

CHAPTER I

Introduction

In 1965, Edward Bond's *Saved* made legal history as the last play to be successfully prosecuted by the Lord Chamberlain before his powers of censorship were rescinded by Parliament. At that time, *Saved* aroused the kind of controversy one associates, especially in drama, with the "revolutionary" qualities of avant-garde literature. As with Ibsen's *Ghosts* before him, and Brenton's *The Romans in Britain* more recently, Bond's play confronts the audience with a profoundly disturbing image of its own world. Such examples suggest that in the theatre formal innovations may first be recognized as challenges in subject-matter – that to a work's content audiences most easily and vociferously respond. By shaping the viewers' horizon of expectation, the institutional context of a performance further contributes to the play's meaning. Productions by state-subsidized or national theatres, for example, can lend more immediate and powerful authority to a script than can other venues. In addition, plays that directly challenge the views of reality an audience brings to the theatre invite a different kind of response than plays which do not. The uproar over *Saved* involved what could (and should) be shown on the public stage. If nothing else, the divided and outspoken response to Bond's earliest plays made the complex relations of cultural production at a particular moment in history unusually visible. A number of converging factors were highlighted: the Royal Court's artistic policies under George Devine and his successor William Gaskill, the favorable working conditions provided by the English Stage Company, a newly educated class of London theatre-goers, an archaic theatre censorship law, the dominant conventions of narrative and stage naturalism, and the barely submerged issues of a politically charged decade.[1] More sensitive to struggles outside the theatre than admittedly apolitical playwrights, Bond's plays often thematically incorporate the very social and cultural contradictions that the strategies of plays, and their formal innovations, address in different ways. By constantly bringing into question the function of literature, Bond's work can uncomfortably challenge an audience's unexamined habit of attending the theatre.

Bond's contribution to theatre history did not end with *Saved*, nor has the controversy he engendered entirely died. Though Bond's reputation as one of Britain's most important living playwrights is now relatively secure, critics still feel compelled to take sides about his work, and from play to play little consensus of opinion reigns. The terms of debate often reveal as much about the conventions and constraints of contemporary drama criticism as they do about the plays themselves. On the one hand, students of postmodernism may feel justifiably uncomfortable with a playwright who defines his artistic activity as "telling the truth."[2] The contemporary qualities of Bond's work owe nothing to the anti-textual aesthetics of performance art nor to the dislocated verbal gymnastics of self-consciously scripted postmodernist work. Indeed, the more self-reflective theatre becomes, the more difficult the problem for the politically committed playwright. In order to "truthfully" represent onstage the forces affecting reality offstage, Bond must avoid the impasses of an increasingly hermetic, "high modernist," literary practice. His plays tell stories about a world that really exists in language that still communicates to audiences who don't need critics.

On the other hand, Bond is not reticent about his work. By 1982, more than a hundred interviews and discussions with the playwright had seen print, not to mention letters, program notes and play prefaces written by Bond himself. The extent to which the use of Bond's statements can reveal a critic's own political stance makes the difficulty of "objective analysis" more than usually apparent. In the face of such risks, many have chosen to ignore Bond's work altogether, while the more sympathetic rely heavily on Bond's own explanatory information in their approach to the plays. Regardless of the attitude taken toward the playwright, Bond's own statements usually provide the starting-point for discussion of his plays.[3] Understanding how easily production choices can undermine the intentions of an author, Bond has also become increasingly involved in the production and direction of his own plays. Among English theatre-folk, such concerns have earned him, perhaps unfairly, a reputation as a difficult author; but the problems point to issues more fundamental, and more political, than are usually indicated in struggles over interpretive latitude. Bond's relationship to his public is equally affected by the status ceded him as a "literary heavyweight" – that is, a playwright whose works are intellectually demanding, require more economic and artistic resources than usually available, do not have broad appeal, and rarely pay for themselves. The self-fulfilling nature of such prophecies should be apparent.

Since the commentary that accompanies the published texts is necessarily part of reading the scripts (and permission to perform a play must still be granted), Bond has successfully managed some control over the production and critical "consumption" of his work. For actors and readers alike, the useful context he provides is always one in which politics and aesthetics cannot be disengaged. Although Bond's critical writing may limit the plurality of meanings otherwise to be found in the plays, his writing has also generated political discussion outside the theatre – often within the institutions that define and legitimate what passes for "literature" in the first place. Bond's critical writing, continued productivity, and notable generosity towards students, scholars, and would-be directors has in fact facilitated his embrace within a European literary establishment and by an international network of theatre practitioners. But what pose as "critical keys" to the plays are far more frequently political and social analyses of the world to which the plays ultimately refer. Despite the depth and quality of Bond's writing for the stage, textual analysis is rarely his concern; and the abstract, philosophical arguments of his polemical essays can as easily confuse and confound a reader as provide illumination. The belief that Bond is his own best explicator not only short-cuts critical analysis, but may unnecessarily inhibit the production of his work. In order to adequately describe or properly theorize Bond's dramatic practice, a different kind of critical discourse is needed – one that neither ignores Bond's stated intentions, nor simply appropriates his own theoretical vocabulary. In this regard, the plays themselves prove richer than any single perspective can possibly reveal.

Despite virtual neglect in the US and perennially mixed reviews in Britain, Bond's plays found immediate and enthusiastic acceptance on the continent, especially in Germany, where his profound influence on a generation of contemporary German playwrights is readily acknowledged. Again, the fact may have less to do with the quality of playwriting than with national arts policies and politically embedded cultural biases that the plays themselves often address.

Bond is, after all, a firmly committed socialist playwright who fully acknowledges his debt to Brecht. By both necessity and choice, his international reputation has been earned outside both American and commercial theatres in independent, state-subsidized, or university funded sectors where art can claim a certain autonomy from the economic forces of the culture industry. More significantly, perhaps, Bond's work is often East European in its perspective. Unlike his American counterparts, Bond assumes that the stage is an appropriate and serious forum for the discussion of cultural issues. In addition, the vocabulary and concerns of Bond's essays signal a deeper connection to the premises and methods of Marxist theoreticians than one might otherwise suppose. If we can say that postmodern (or high modernist) literary texts incorporate critical consciousness in regard to their own operation, then the consciousness that Bond's work displays is of a distinctly dialectical turn. Without belaboring the question of influence, it is important to point out here a difference between playwrights who haphazardly borrow from the Brechtian legacy, and those who seriously and substantially build upon it. In the final analysis, Bond's contribution to modern drama will lie in his development of a dialectical theatre along Brechtian lines, in the creation of a materialist poetic that addresses the most significant political issues of his time.

Bond may have first called his theatre a "rational theatre" in response to the apparently irrational reaction provoked by the violence of *Saved*'s scene in the park.[4] Like most critical labels, the usefulness of the term lies in economy rather than precision, inviting audiences to see broad similarities of intention across a corpus of stylistically diverse work. But the term "rational theatre" also places Bond in a tradition of realistic literature with its own history of struggle since the nineteenth century. In one sense, all of modern drama can be seen as a history of formal experimentations aimed at providing a more adequate representation of social, psychological, or existential "truths." But the Brecht–Lukács debates of the 1930s gave shape to theories of realism that, however defined, depended on a dialectical definition of reality. Recent developments in psychoanalysis, semiology, and popular culture have further complicated the terms and issues of that debate by focusing on the functioning of ideology in the construction of the subject. Thus Brecht has been frequently called upon to foster the distinction between "classic" and "critical" realism. Both denote a reflection of reality that produces recognition, but classic realism naturalizes (or conceals) the conventions on which it depends, obscuring dynamic contradictions that could lead to radical change. Classic realism may support the dominant ideology by (a) posing problems too limited or too easily resolved to be significant, (b) presenting social contradictions in terms of psychological conflicts, metaphysical dilemmas, or symbolic oppositions, (c) representing reality and human nature as ahistorical, eternal, or essentially unchanging. To prevent the audience from immediately perceiving this constructed reality, classic realism depends on narrative continuity and audience identification. In film and drama, such techniques produce a readable discourse with an entirely appropriable meaning addressed to an audience fixed, unified, and rendered immobile in the act of seeing.[5]

The aesthetics of Brecht's epic theatre took shape against the illusions of classic, "culinary" realism as described above. But despite the formal characteristics associated with Brecht's drama, "critical" realism is defined in terms of its overall project and political stance rather than by strictly formal criteria. In response to Lukács' narrower definition of realism, Brecht wrote:

Our conception of *realism* needs to be broad and political, free from aesthetic restrictions and independent of convention. [. . .] Realism is not a pure question of form. [. . .] Reality alters; to represent it the means of representation must alter too.[6]

Brecht's insistence that "time flows on" and "methods wear out" not only recuperates the experiments of modernism for the "realistic" project, but should historicize for us his own epic models. What sometimes gets lost in such a formulation is the implicit assumption that if reality alters, so too do audiences. Any discussion of the effects upon an audience of formal, stylistic strategies needs also to recognize that audiences themselves are not a unified, undifferentiated whole, but vary in gender, over time, and across cultures.[7]

To expose, in theory, the limits and effects of certain naturalistic conventions is not the same as constructing a more adequate artistic account. Moreover, a literary practice that exists – through alienation-effects, parody, or quotation – by virtue of what it opposes, rarely attempts nor often achieves the kind of aesthetic power we associate in the theatre with the "classical" repertory. When such power *is* achieved, as Brecht noted with chagrin, it is often for the wrong reasons.[8] While Bond writes in critical opposition to his own society and its dominant aesthetic practices, he also writes as a confident member of an emerging social class whose "classics" have yet to be written. In other words, Bond writes consciously artistic plays (fictional, structured, and participating in a tradition of literary forms) in behalf of a society that does not yet exist. The desire to speak *for* a society rather than always and only *against* one is increasingly present in Bond's work. That Bond's drama must address audiences in the process of change within a society that urgently needs changing may help to account for both the distinctiveness and the so-called contradictions of his aesthetic practice.

Although Bond shares with Brecht his critical aim and several of his "epic" methods, their thematic concerns differ with their historical situation, and their strategies are not identical. Like Brecht, Bond attempts to orient the audience toward action with plays that demand active interpretation in lieu of passive consumption. Both view reality as historical, contradictory, and subject to human intervention; and they write in order to change it. Both are centrally interested in the relation between history and the individual, a concern that manifests itself in the choice of subject-matter, the internal dynamics of the plays, and the relationship of the plays to their audiences. Both acknowledge that lived experience of reality is mediated by ideology in ways that affect the capacity for action, and both incorporate a "critical" stance in the formal structures of their plays. The most important distinctions between Bond's theatre and Brecht's lie in the specific, material reality of the plays themselves, in the different rhythms and references that Bond constructs for his audience. Indeed, Bond's wide choice of genres and rich theatrical idiom have a particularly British inflection. It registers in the colloquial accuracy of Bond's working-class figures and the epigrammatic wit of his mannered aristocrats; in the literary precedents of *Lear*, *The Woman*, and *Restoration*; and in the historical referents of *Early Morning*, *Bingo*, and *The Fool*. Whether the cultural and artistic codes are aggressively foregrounded or contextually implicit, the recognition that they are being consciously and adeptly manipulated for "rational" ends is one of the social pleasures both Brecht and Bond offer their audiences.

Claiming "human consciousness is class consciousness,"[9] Bond pinpoints a central problematic shared with Brecht, one affecting character development, narrative construction, and theme. Thus conflicts and relationships between characters frequently arise from, and in turn illuminate, the contradictions of a society based on class. But Bond shares with most latter-day Marxists the belief that history does not move automatically toward socialism or any other pre-determined end. Because social progress often depends upon acting against the very forces that have determined one's mental and physical life, it can be neither easy nor inevitable. Nor are the difficulties limited to a particular class. Bond's plays implicitly acknowledge the complexities involved in the historically deter-mined subject as the location of political practice. Although all of Bond's characters are in some way victims of an unjustly ordered society, their subjective responses to it notably differ. In *The Pope's Wedding* and *Saved*, the narrative itself is woven from the subtly differing responses of characters who come from the same social class, speak the same language, and face the same environmental conditions. In *Bingo*, class position separates Shakespeare and the Son, but both find their situations intolerable. Shakespeare intern-alizes his anger in guilt, despair, and suicide while the Son extern-alizes his rage in self-righteousness, paranoia, and murder. In *The Fool*, Patty adapts and survives, Darkie resists and is killed, Clare observes and goes mad; yet all three share the same class perspective toward enclosure and industrialization. In *The Sea*, Evens isolates himself from society in order to save his sanity, and Hatch loses his in the effort to fit in. In *Jackets II*, one working-class youth joins the army while the other struggles against it; but the divided society results in pain, loss, and deep personal sacrifice to both. The list of examples could include figures from each of Bond's plays. Clearly, Bond's concern is not only with how individuals perceive and understand their historical situation, but with the ways in which that perception affects their capacity for political action.

As the damaging effects of a class-structured society are reiterated from play to play, Bond's analysis of appropriately "human" responses becomes increasingly focused, clarified, and developed. Variations of fear, apathy, remorse, and despair plague Bond's most articulate characters (Clare, Shakespeare, Lear, Evens, Trench), draining their energies and distorting their vision. Anger, on the other hand, allows Darkie, the Son, the Dark Man, and Tiger to become, however temporarily, energetic forces of protest and change. Ineffective as isolated figures, and rarely the focus of the narrative, their gut-level class-consciousness positively affects other characters and directs the audience's attention to stark social contradictions in the play. While the actions of Bond's "dark forces" always serve a crucial narrative function within the plays, they also provide a radical measure of the limits and consequences of other characters' actions. Through them Bond encourages a political reading of events without resorting to traditional methods of empathetic identification.

Indeed, the dynamic between play and audience is at least as complex as the internal dynamics of each play. All of Bond's plays provide narrative contexts that call for social change, situations which demand some moral action from the characters, and by extension, the audience as well. But none of Bond's characters are automatically endowed with an enlightened perspective; they come to it through the concrete social interactions recorded in the plays. The dialectical learning process involved begins and ends in action, and is similar but not identical to the process experienced by the audience. If objective conditions change faster than subjective consciousness – if there is always a lag between external stimuli and the responses dictated by habit and ideology that make one's objective assessment of oppression more difficult – then there is some justification for the sense of urgency Bond writes into the tempo of the plays. The calm, analytical pace that gradually builds to isolated moments that seem shocking, intensely emotional, or naturalistically compelling has become an identifiable Bondian strategy. The baby-stoning sequence in *Saved*, the torture scenes of *Lear*, the velvet-cutting or corpse-stabbing scene in *The Sea*, the parson-stripping scene in *The Fool*, Trench's murder of the chauffeur in *The Worlds*, the body identification scenes of *Jackets* all provide protracted moments of threatened or explicit violence remembered by the audience long after the performance. What compels is the disturbing imagery and real menace involved in the experience – when a character the audience understands, or a clearly recognizable situation, is viewed "on the brink" of destruction or increasingly out of control in a moment etched in memory with powerful stage imagery. Fully playing Bond's extreme images is crucial to the vision inscribed in the plays, which may explain one difficulty in getting them more widely produced. Bond calls such deliberately choreographed moments "aggro-effects" as opposed to Brechtian alienation-effects, but both fulfill a didactic function. Often they represent the character's own subjective experience of history as an inexplicable concatenation of events, an overwhelming flow of experience. As one might expect, such traumatic events are "determining" for the audience, and lead characters to various kinds of reflective assessments (more or less adequate, depending on the play), which foster further action. In later plays, Bond uses the term theatre event, or "TE," to mark the complex, deliberately non-naturalistic social analysis upon which such moments depend. While a viewer's own analysis may relieve a scene's nightmarish qualities, the sense of urgency remains. The resulting rhythm provides a constant pull on the movement toward abstraction, even in plays that reflect a structure of logical argument.

Since the beginning of his career, Bond has questioned, examined, and extended the perimeters of theatre after Brecht, developing a body of dramatic work that is both politically engaged and aesthetically complex. What follows is an attempt to define and describe the nature of Bond's contribution more closely and critically than an overview usually allows. Without being inclusive (Bond has written more than twenty plays and shows little sign of slowing down), this study considers together plays that share similar dramatic strategies. Though roughly chronological within chapters, the analysis of particular plays should lead to insights that work in both directions across the corpus of Bond's work – prefiguring later "problematics" as well as forcing reexamination of earlier plays. Chapter 2, "Violence and voyeurism," begins with the reception of Bond's earliest work and looks closely at the possible psychodynamic operations these productions made visible. Here a discussion of the scopophilic drive and its relationship to curiosity, the acquisition of knowledge, and the theatre situation itself provides an approach to the complex issue of violence and its relationships to the passive or appropriative gaze of the viewing subject. While *Saved* and *The Pope's Wedding* work on conscious and unconscious levels to involve and implicate their audiences, the question of what the stage should make us "see" gets thematic elaboration in *The Sea*. Likewise, Bond's brief and reluctant work in film, with its different economy of the look, may suggest the importance of the theatre situation itself in any reading of Bond's scripts.

Chapter 3, "Rereading history," takes up the issue of Brechtian historicization in two plays that construct their narratives from historical fact. The psychosexual realm explored in Bond's earliest plays is in *Bingo* and *The Fool* more explicitly connected to the social and economic ground that gives it meaning. With the development of the multi-focused stage, Bond invites the audience to fill in with discursive analysis what these plays only structurally suggest, to actively "read" the gaps and contradictions exposed by the knots of epic narrative. Whereas the 1970s revival of interest in revisionist history provides a context for the writing of *Bingo* and *The Fool*, *Lear* and *The Woman* return to literary classics during an era in which the parody and dismemberment of the classical texts has become as common as their recuperation for nostalgic purposes. Both plays use and examine the tragic genre, but their strategies of adaptation differ to reflect in interesting ways the politics of their own production. Chapter 4 hardly exhausts the discussion of tragedy and adaptation to which *Lear* and *The Woman* can contribute, but an examination of their formal techniques may prove useful to understanding plays written within and against other genres (comedy, Noh, farce) and to those like *Restoration* and *Jackets* with different "counter-texts" behind them.

Since Bond's plays are usually described, and often judged, with pointed reference to their didactic impulse, chapter 5, "Political parables," discusses Bond's use and development of the parable form in relation to Brecht's experimental *Lehrstücke*. Here *The Bundle*, more so than in its earlier version, *Narrow Road to the Deep North*, provides evidence of Bond's appropriation of Brechtian concerns and techniques, while self-consciously didactic parables like *Stone* prove to be more complex and interesting than their overt political stance may suggest. Clearly an audience member's own political tendencies must be considered in gauging the effect of the play's formal strategies. The importance of the position taken up by the viewer proves central to the examination of the "Social pleasures" provided by Bond's comedy. In chapter 6, Freud's definition of "*Witz*" and Bakhtin's notion of "carnival" contribute to a discussion of the characters' humor in *Saved*, the "class-inflected" satire of *Early Morning*, and the comic techniques of *Derek*. *The Sea* and *Restoration*, on the other hand, offer an opportunity to look more closely at Bond's use of the comic genre for specific political ends.

Chapter 7, "Reading the present," considers Bond's appropriation of the popular, naturalistic forms through which current events are made familiar to their audience in order to reanalyze and reformulate contemporary issues. Whereas *The Worlds* critically responds to a news-saturated public world, *Summer* works within and against inward-looking, psychologically focused dramatic forms. In chapter 8, "Remembering the future," both *Human Cannon* and *The War Plays* trilogy extend and ultimately undermine the notion of isolatable dramatic strategies on which this book is organized. Given the scope and complexity of the trilogy, the focus on dramatic strategies delimits the discussion and provides some sense of closure to what must surely be the ongoing project of assessing Bond's contribution to modern drama.

The premise on which this book takes shape is that Bond's political project, historical position, and dramatic talent combine to provide the scholar and theatre practitioner a unique position from which to survey the problems and potential of post-Brechtian, political drama. While Brechtian strategies may prove an appropriate entry to an understanding of Bond's plays, they are not enough. Certainly the "epic" vs. "illusionist" terminology introduced earlier limits the use to which Bond's plays can be put, as well as the kind of interpretation those plays can sustain. Without further development of a critical discourse appropriate to Bond's drama, and without closer, more subtle readings of actual plays, scholars run the risk of repeating the mistakes of popular reviewers and of reproducing the very divisions between politics and aesthetics that so many playwrights since Brecht have tried to move beyond.

While Bond describes his work as the creation of a "rational theatre," I would describe his plays as experiments in poetic materialism. Fredric Jameson has warned that "materialisms" always seem to end up projecting a determination by matter/body/organism rather than by mode of production, a warning echoed in Terry Eagleton's criticism of Bond – that in writing about his own plays, Bond dangerously confuses nature/culture issues with those of economics, failing to think through the logic of his position carefully enough.[10] Without a doubt, Bond's stage images evoke an ecological realm in which nature and culture, individual and species, history and subjectivity inseparably collude. Yet Bond's appeal as an artist, rather than a philosopher or theorist, may lie precisely in this merging of terms. In his most recent plays, Bond suggests that the category of "the human" cannot simply be jettisoned – that without a better definition, we may ultimately forfeit the right, as a species, to exist. Given the scope of the problem and the speed of change, older socialist categories of analysis may or may not prove useful. If what distinguishes Bond from many of his socialist contemporaries is an insistence on writing "literature" in the first place, and of keeping his eye on posterity, what distinguishes his plays from the literary norm is their passionate concern for the future, and the revolutionary vision they impart on its behalf, for audiences now.

CHAPTER 2

Violence and voyeurism

Both blessed and burdened by the moment of his arrival, Edward Bond first gained wide public notice as the author of *Saved* (1965). The furious critical response that first production provoked may now be more familiar to theatre audiences than the play itself.[1] Original reviewers were especially quick to link sexuality to the play's violence; Herbert Kretzmer's remarks in the *Daily Express* were not atypical: "From first to last, Edward Bond's play is concerned with sexual and physical violence. It is peopled by characters who, almost without exception, are foul-mouthed, dirty-minded, illiterate and barely to be judged on any recognizable human level at all." Penelope Gilliatt, who wrote one of the few favorable reviews of the first production, noted "I have had more vehement reactions about this play and what I wrote about it, pro and con, than about any other opening in the last year. The objectors mostly deny, with frightening violence, that such violence exists. Two people sent torn-up programmes. One enclosed a newspaper photograph of my child with her head cut off and daubed with red ink."[2] Hostile reviewers who reversed their opinion at the play's revival a few years later must have wondered at the intensity of their original reaction; yet subsequent explanations rarely venture beyond notions of the playwright's misunderstood intentions. While *Saved* fuelled debate about the use of violence on the stage, the issue of violence becoming an obsessive concern of Bond's own writing as well as his critics', the connections between the play's violence, its social picture, and its psychosexual themes remain relatively unexamined.[3] Like many of Bond's later plays, *Saved* and *The Pope's Wedding* work on both conscious and unconscious levels to involve, implicate, and provoke the audience in ways that may challenge their own theatre-going activity.

Dramatic strategies

The Pope's Wedding

Despite obvious similarities between Bond's first two plays, reaction
to the Royal Court's single Sunday-night performance of *The Pope's
Wedding* (1962) provided little to prepare for the critical storms
ahead. Indeed, *The Pope's Wedding* was deemed by most critics an
auspicious beginning for a new playwright,[4] and George Devine
commissioned a new play on the basis of its success. If anything
provoked the audience, it was the meandering tempo and the length
of time accorded scenes not directly related to the strange relationship between Scopey and Alen, who do not meet until halfway
through the play. Several reviewers implied that the photographic
portrayal of rural life was itself to blame. As one put it "the young
are overcome by a deadening boredom which cannot be dissipated
by sex, sport, violence or filth: but it is unfortunate that the handling
of the story gradually causes that boredom to spread among the
audience."[5] Kenneth Tynan begins a favorable notice with similar
reservations about a play that may be "too long, too portentous, too
elliptical," but his accompanying accolade of "born mood evoker"
was quickly taken up by Bond defenders as the very mark of Bond's
theatrical genius.[6] The stark surface verisimilitude and unhurried
pacing of scenes highlighted Bond's ear for the rhythms and nuances
of working-class dialogue – dialogue that accurately conveys the feel
of "hanging out," dead tired after work, too broke for a beer, passing
time until the next payday. As in *Saved*, the dialogue of *The Pope's
Wedding* roots the action in a working-class community whose
members are bound and limited by their language, desires, and
shared sense of time – Scopey's very individuality shaped and
informed by the society from which he grows estranged. But such
surface naturalism, focused as it is here on a single social class,
separates *The Pope's Wedding* and *Saved* from nearly all of Bond's
subsequent work.

So convincing is the naturalistic illusion of Bond's two earliest
plays that analysis of the action may easily be short-circuited. Unlike
the political drama that audiences tolerated in the plays of Osborne
and Wesker, for example, Bond offers no set speeches from highly
articulate characters as a key to understanding the plays' issues. In
both subject-matter and tone, *Saved* and *The Pope's Wedding* more
closely resemble the work of early Pinter than any socially conscious
inheritor of a Shavian tradition.[7] The marginally articulate charac-

ters, plotless interactions, elliptical dialogue, and menacing under-currents of barely repressed violence that characterize Pinter's *The Caretaker*, *The Birthday Party*, *The Room*, and *The Dumbwaiter* (all written before 1962) have clear analogues in Bond's first two plays. But while Pinter and Bond both aim at a total theatre experience to which the language of the script only partially contributes, Bond's project is to examine and clarify the situations he depicts onstage, not to intrigue or mystify his audience with them. Indeed, Bond envisioned the hermit figure of *The Pope's Wedding* in conscious opposition to the kind of theatre with which Pinter quickly became identified:

The important thing is not to be intrigued or puzzled by images but always to understand them. So that what I wanted to do was to try and get inside the image, and see what it was all about. That is what Scopey does in the play, and in the end he kills a man and wears his clothes in order to find out. And of course there's nothing there. The truth about this man's charisma, you see, is that it's based on nothing.[8]

As a response to the real questions with which the audience is left at the end of the play, Bond's comment reminds us that the meaning of *The Pope's Wedding* is not self-evident. But what does it mean to say a man's charisma is "based on nothing"? In psychoanalytic terms, the "nothing" Alen represents is not devoid of content. Scopey's curiosity has both sadistic and homoerotic overtones; the disappointment that leads to Alen's murder is in fact unintelligible without taking into account the unconscious motives that fuel Scopey's interest in the old man. Rather, Alen's charisma is based on Scopey's own projections, needs, and desires – and by extension, the audience's as well.

Bond intimates such a connection between Scopey and the audience when he notes:

Scopey doesn't understand his situation at all, not at all, but I wanted the audience to understand the way it could happen to Scopey, who I suppose is a typical member of the audience in a sense.[9]

But Bond's "typical" audience member would not share Scopey's educational background, social class, or situation. Rather, the detailed and intimate view of the community that the audience is invited to observe and vicariously experience is analogous to the one exposed, through Alen, to Scopey. Although in every way typical of the community from which he emerges, Scopey's questions and eventual obsession with Alen as an enigmatic presence will mirror the audience's own growing fascination with the strange relationship that evolves between the two characters onstage. As the narrative unfolds, distinctions between observation and action, means and end, voyeurism and violence become gradually blurred for Scopey and the audience alike.

Unlike *Saved*, which it in other ways resembles, the centrally violent episode of *The Pope's Wedding* occurs offstage and is not revealed until the final scene. Although Scopey briefly describes Alen's murder, only circumstantial evidence remains in the stolen coat that Scopey wears and the decaying bundle of a body lying on the floor. Pat, whose limited perspective is one of the problems addressed by the play, finds the situation frightening and incomprehensible. But the audience has been privy to scenes between Scopey and Alen that prepare us to understand, on some broader level, what has happened. The startling brevity of the final tableau should force us back through the play to consider the broader social relationships that Scopey's actions illuminate. As reviews indicated, however, many viewers *did* find the play enigmatic and had difficulty making the connection between Scopey's psychologically "strange" (but interesting) relationship to Alen and the sociologically "typical" (but, for them, less interesting) sections of the play. As in *Saved*, the sociological facts conveyed through Bond's insistently naturalistic dialogue cannot fully account for the characters' actions – nor the audience's reaction to them – without consideration of the psychological reality to which the plays also refer.

In both *The Pope's Wedding* and *Saved*, the sense of enclosure, limitation of possibility, frustration, and restlessness as well as the movements of desire that propel the narrative are elaborated through references to a libidinal economy that rests just below the consciousness of characters and audience alike. Deliberately alerted to the psychological issues of *Saved* with the subtitle *An Oedipal Comedy*, Bond draws attention to the psychic economy of *The Pope's Wedding* in different ways, beginning with its title. Bond's own explanation, that "the pope's wedding is an impossible ceremony – Scopey's asking for an invitation for something that isn't going to happen, that can't happen,"[10] helps locate the title as an image of Scopey's own unarticulated longing; but it does not exhaust the train of associations such a title calls up. The image of a "pope's wedding" resonates with references to male authority, institutionalized sexuality, and forbidden desire; but does so in a potentially comic and self-deflating way. With its apparent *lack* of relation to the real characters and action of the play, the title seems to withhold meaning with the very gesture through which it invites interpretation. By provoking curiosity that the play itself does not satisfy, the title provides the first figure for the audience-play-playwright dynamic that Scopey's own inquisitive path will parallel.

As in *Saved*, the action and relationships of *The Pope's Wedding* are structured by Oedipal configurations difficult to ignore. In the course of his encounters with Alen, Scopey tries out a number of positions fraught with Oedipal significance: he cooks for Alen, spoonfeeds him, wears an apron, and complains about his habits. By taking over Pat's original responsibility for Alen, Scopey self-consciously plays the role of both wife and mother as he attends to housekeeping duties in the hut; and with Scopey's deliberate exclusion of Pat from the intimate, private life he establishes with Alen, Bond lends a homoerotic quality to their relationship which Scopey himself would undoubtedly deny. Scopey's gradual identification with Alen as a surrogate father is revealed in countless details – from Scopey's suggestion that Alen is a "crafty owd sod" in his sexual exploits, to Scopey's expression of jealousy and suspicion about Alen's real relationship to Pat, to Scopey's desire to "inherit" both the secrets of Alen's past and the safety of his hut. In their first meeting, Scopey suggests that Alen might be Pat's father and they "could be in the same family" (279); in their final encounter, Alen elicits from Scopey the strange confession that he doesn't have a "dad" (286). Bond reinforces the domestic quality of Scopey's relationship to Alen and the sexual needs for which it compensates by alternating Scopey's housekeeping sessions at the hut with scenes of domestic intimacy and increasing unrest between Scopey and his wife. At the end of the narrative, Scopey abandons his various positions as Alen's "wife," "mother," and "child" to become, in a startlingly literal way, the "father" that Alen had replaced. Such a conspicuous use of Freudian structures does not explain Scopey's behavior, but the constant referral to a level of reality of which the characters themselves are unaware keeps constantly before us the possibility of reading the action in psychoanalytic terms.

Without distancing the audience from the stark social reality depicted onstage, Bond's set and lighting cues further indicate an interest in the examination of subjective experience in a way that

1 Scopey and Alen share an intimate moment in Alen's hut, *The Pope's Wedding*

links (without merging) the experience of the audience to that of the characters. In the opening stage note, Bond suggests that Scopey's psychological evolution should correspond in some way to a development in audience understanding:

In these sixteen scenes the stage is dark and bare to the wings and back. [...] The objects are very real, but there must be no attempt to create the illusion of a "real scene". In the later scenes the stage may be lighter and Scene Fifteen may be played in bright light.[11]

Because detailed, naturalistic sets tend to call attention to themselves, such a note may allow for the more effective creation of stage illusion. But the darkness of the set also promotes an unreal, dreamlike quality that the audience's eventual understanding is intended to dispel. Discussing the play's first production, Bond likewise noted that Alen should first appear to the audience as tall, somber, and as mysterious as he does in Scopey's imagination, only at the end becoming the "techy" man he really is.[12] Both instances suggest a Brechtian-like clarification of what might otherwise be understood as the expressionistic examination of Scopey's subjective experience. By grounding the play in the life of a rural community, Bond does show that Alen, despite first impressions, and Scopey, despite final revelations, are representative rather than deviant characters – socially conditioned, not psychotically inclined. Equally important, however, the gradual focus on Scopey's private life and the secret relationship he shares with Alen suggests that the unconscious itself is a material force constructed *in* and *by* society, having real (not merely private) consequences.

The meaning of *The Pope's Wedding* thus rests on two inseparable "levels" of reality: the social and the psychological. The very accuracy of the social depiction lends psychological plausibility to the plot, but original viewer ambivalence toward this play suggests that some connections between Scopey and the audience may be discomforting. Not simply does the character with whom we most easily identify eventually murder an innocent man, but, as the following analysis suggests, the sadistic and potentially violent impulses that underlie Scopey's desire to see and understand Alen call into question the normal scopophilic impulses that underlie our own desire to see and understand the play.

In *The Pope's Wedding*, the connections between violence, voyeurism, knowledge, and desire are made primarily through Scopey, whose very name is a combining form meaning to view, observe, or examine. But Scopey is individualized only insofar as his development determines the story. More episodic than narrative, the play gradually shifts its focus from the public gatherings of friends and co-workers to the intimate duologues between Scopey and Pat and Scopey and Alen. The movement from social integration to individual alienation suggests the pattern of a *Bildungsroman* (by following a character's growth and maturation within a specific social context) or a case study (by investigating a character's psychological development to determine the causes of deviance), yet the play does not yield the kind of answers expected of either form. Indeed, the questions themselves remain unfocused until the play's final scenes, and even then the viewer may be disappointed to find no more knowledge about Scopey than any other character in the play.

In retrospect, Scopey's curiosity seems to distinguish him from his crowd of friends and to account for the play's movement and outcome; and the voyeuristic overtones of that curiosity are apparent from the first. Scopey's opening lines refer to watching Bill's encounter with Old Man Bullright's wife ("I seen yoo back a Farrin field sarternoon," 230); though Scopey rarely speaks in the scene, he seems the only one interested in Bill's sexual escapades. Noticeably silenced by the entrance of Pat and her friend June, Scopey provokes their interest by lifting Pat's skirt, looking underneath, and announcing that her knickers are white. Later in the play, Alen reveals to Pat the sense of being secretly watched, uneasy about Scopey's presence before they ever meet: "Someone snoopin'. [. . .] Listen. [. . .] Someone's tryin' t' be quiet" (258). Nor does Scopey's eventual involvement with Alen end his night-time vigil:

SCOPEY: [. . .] I was outside last night.
ALEN: I ont 'eard yoo.
SCOPEY: Yoo were asleep.
ALEN: I'd always woke up afore.
SCOPEY: I kep' quiet. (286)

Scopey's revelations indicate the obsessive nature of his attraction to Alen while highlighting the voyeuristic character of earlier actions. As one of the few links to the unusual behavior of later scenes, Scopey's "normal" curiosity helps prepare the audience for what is to come.

The frustration that leads to Alen's murder builds slowly and circuitously, linked to some need or desire that Scopey himself cannot articulate. Thus while Scopey looks at things throughout the play, he is never entirely satisfied with what he sees. At first disappointed that Pat is wearing knickers at all, he later sniffs and tosses out the contents of her purse. At the end of Scene Six, Scopey pretends to look for Pat, but doesn't find her; nor does he get a look at old Alen, crouching panic-stricken under the bed. In Scene Eight, Scopey uses a similar pretext, pretending to retrieve Pat's purse in order to get inside Alen's hut and have a look around. As prelude to the scenes that follow, Alen refuses to answer Scopey's questions about what he sees there. In similar fashion, Scopey looks at the postcard Pat shares with her friend, interested, yet dissatisfied with what it shows:

JUNE: I like it.
SCOPEY: Yoo need more than that. Yoo'd 'ave t' see more.
JUNE: It's nice.
SCOPEY: Yoo need more.
JUNE: I know what I like – they keep the streets swep'.
SCOPEY: Where yoo seen streets like that?
JUNE: Only count a people drop dirt all the time. People are pigs.
SCOPEY: Nothin's like that. No more yoo ent seen sky like that.
JUNE: Never said I 'ad. I just said I like it.
SCOPEY: Yoo can't tell. Where's the people an' the corners? (264)

Scopey not only distrusts the surface appearance of the picture and what it promises, but desires to see more than such a postcard can possibly reveal. Moments later he wants to plaster his entire room with postcards, a desire June attributes to erotic motivations ("I know what 'e's after. Dirty owd man," 265), the explicitly sexual nature of which Scopey promptly denies.

The potentially neurotic character of Scopey's curiosity is perhaps best illustrated when he insists on cutting open the sewn pockets of Alen's greatcoat, a coat that makes Scopey "feel bigger": "Ent yoo 'ad a look? [...] There might be somethin' inside [...] Chriss yoo might 'ave anythin' in 'ere" (290). By this point in the play, Scopey has repeatedly indicated his wish to look inside and underneath the coat that Alen never takes off, a desire that bespeaks as well as any other the nature of Scopey's fascination ("What 'e wear under that owd coat? PAT: Nothin', that wouldn't surprise me," 283). Scopey's involvement with Alen manifests itself as a desire to look through his "things," to discover "something" he assumes throughout that Alen has. Although Alen knows Scopey "'on't find nothing" (287), he is helpless in the face of his persistent desire to find it. Indeed, Scopey's curiosity survives Alen: in Scene Fourteen, the audience watches Scopey pry at Alen's watch, gradually realizing, with the gang's harassment outside and offstage, that Scopey has replaced the old man.

On one level, the manifest content of the "lack" generating Scopey's desire can be found in the carefully articulated economic details of the play. There is never enough money, not to mention beer, cigarettes, sex, or free time. Pat is unable to afford a white wedding, to fix up the flat they are renting, or to keep the electricity on. The dialogue circles around characters' irritation with not having enough and a related frustration with the things they have: Pat's purse gets broken, Bill's grandmother has a washing machine on the blink, Len's television set doesn't work, Scopey's fuse-box blows. The accumulation of such details culminates in Scene Eleven: when Scopey returns from the kitchen to find Pat smoking his last cigarette, he stamps it out in a gesture so close to hitting his wife it creates tension for Pat and the audience alike. In the potentially violent moments of the following scene, Alen likewise worries that Scopey may simply be asking for money ("Yoo ont get no money out a me," 294). Scopey's behavior cannot finally be understood outside the social and economic world of the play and the cycle of frustration it engenders.

But for Scopey to find what he is looking for, he must know what it is; and the very ambiguity involved in the search is indicative of the ambivalence with which he looks. Scopey not only pries into Alen's life, but forces Alen to keep his activity a secret; and when Pat unexpectedly comes looking for him in Scene Twelve, Scopey hides behind the couch. Indeed, Scopey's disappointment in finding the pockets empty is loaded with the conscious and unconscious associations that Pat's visit inspires. In his essays on sexuality, Freud connects the pleasure of looking to the child's first sexual investigations and explains the voyeuristic mechanisms of adult life as attempts to circumvent the threat of castration that such early investigative activity may produce.[13] As film critic Laura Mulvey has pointed out in another context, "the look, while pleasurable in form, may be threatening in content,"[14] and Scopey's probing curiosity is balanced by the fear, guilt, and denial of desire that his view of Alen also arouses.

Scopey himself cannot grasp the unconscious motives that provide an underlying logic to the action of this play. On the one hand, his naive questions, and the sexual inexperience they suggest, establish an innocence about his character that makes the end more shocking. Just as a reader is unable to discriminate between Scopey's willingness to fix Pat's purse and his desire to see what's inside it, it is impossible to distinguish between Scopey's willingness to help out his wife with Alen and his desire to manipulate her out of the picture. In a manner associated with fetishistic behavior, Scopey knows and does not know what he is doing, acknowledges and denies his sexual curiosity ("I 'ont never been out 'ere an' yoo 'ont seen nothin' of me," 268), is both attracted and repulsed by the figure onto which he projects his own wishes and needs. Pat's intrusion in Scene Twelve further complicates our understanding of Scopey's behavior. Foreshadowing the discovery on which the play ends, her visit provides the play's climax (if such traditional dramatic categories could be applied to Bond's play) by upsetting the tenuous, unspoken relationship that Scopey and Alen have established. Scopey's discovery (or recognition) that the greatcoat pockets are empty ends an emotionally charged sequence of accusation, threat, confession, and denial that began with Alen's comment "I like gals," Scopey's "disillusionment" with what Alen represents thereby connected to the fear, anger, jealousy, and sense of personal betrayal that Pat's visit (and Alen's response to it) provokes. The sexual ambivalence that underlies Scopey's probing curiosity and can explain his behavior with Alen is reinforced by the apparent ambiguity of the play's dialogue and the kind of emotional subtext for which such ambiguity allows. The surface "undecidability" of the script permits the audience to take up a position similar to Scopey's in the play, knowing and not knowing what is to come, "innocently" watching action that stimulates viewer curiosity in deliberate ways.

The power and effect of *The Pope's Wedding* hinge not simply on Scopey's simultaneously innocent and disturbing relationship with Alen, then, but on the audience's relationship to it. This Bond establishes in two early scenes that are as different from each other as they are from the rest of the play. Scene Three, from which Scopey is entirely absent, offers the audience its first view of Alen, mentioned moments earlier as the cause of everyone's bad luck ("I reckon owd Alen's put 'is curse on us," 243). Requiring two pages of detailed stage notes, the scene shows Alen alone in his hut, doing nothing in particular, periodically listening for sounds from outside, at one point "*With his back to the audience* [. . .] *his ear against the wall*" (245). The darkness of the set, the lack of accompanying exposition, the intensity with which the character listens, and the length of time accorded a scene played in total silence all contribute to a scenario linking the audience's gaze to Freud's primal eavesdropping fantasy – an unconscious fantasy wherein the pleasure of looking and listening is repressed and projected into the fear of being discovered.[15] Indeed, except for the labored breathing such a semi-invalid old man might make, the shuffling of papers, and Alen's own movements, the only sounds to be heard are those by which an actual theatre audience might betray its own presence.

A startling "*bang on the door*" interrupts (and ends) the episode. Although we assume it is Pat, who in Scene One had money for the old man's shopping, the door is not opened and the identity of the visitor remains unknown. Alen's reaction to the knock ("*a sigh – gasp*") combines the relief of Pat's expected visit with the panic he later shows towards strangers. Thus Alen's withdrawal from society, expressed as a fear of being seen (and discovered), is counterpointed to his dependence on Pat and desire to be seen (and tended to) by her. Earlier in Scene Three, Alen stands on a stack of old papers with his ear to the wall, seems unsatisfied with the arrangement, then shifts the table and tries to lift himself up. The meaning of these movements is later clarified when we see (long before Scopey does) that Alen uses the stack of papers to peer out of a hole in the wall. Despite his overwhelming fear, Alen (like the audience) wants to know who's outside; and he hopes it is Pat, not the menacing intruder it could as easily be. The abrupt ending of Scene Three thus sets in motion the audience's desire not only to see who is there, but to watch the undisclosed interchange between Alen and the person behind the door – a desire Bond accommodates with later scenes. Scopey expresses a similar wish in his ambivalent desire to know (and to watch) what goes on between Alen and Pat, as well as to know what Alen does when Scopey is not around. The unmediated view of Alen's private life leaves us curious, wondering what to make of it. Later we discover that Scopey also spends time secretly watching the old man. Rather than initiating our interest in Alen and what he represents, then, Scopey merely takes up a position already established by the audience's view of Scene Three.

While the private glimpse of Scene Three arouses curiosity about the old man, the public cricket match that immediately follows promotes attachment to Scopey. In tempo, subject-matter, mood, and effect, the difference between the two scenes could not be more marked. Creatively staged with bowler running in from stage left, batsmen running off stage right, umpires' calls and spectators' voices heard to the sides, the audience finds itself positioned in the middle of the cricket field as Scopey, almost miraculously, hits the winning runs. Since Bill, the team's best player, has been assigned to work on the day of the match, none of the characters expects to win; and although Scopey promised to practice, it is unlikely such last-minute training could turn the twelfth man into the figure who ends a sixty-year losing streak. For both audience and characters, knowing the unfair advantage taken by the opposing team only heightens the pleasure of the victory. Thus Scopey emerges as the hero of the day in a realistically improbable but narratively desirable manner, claiming the audience's attention and the romantic interest of Bill's girl, Pat. Orchestrated by the owners on one level and the play-wright on another, the match provides "strategic" relief for both audience and characters from the frustrating and seemingly mean-ingless action it follows for each. The manipulation of the game's outcome and the sharp contrast between Scenes Three and Four not only renders visible the playwright's shaping hand, but accentuates the very issues of difference with which the play is concerned.

Like Scopey, the audience that quietly watches Alen alone in Scene Three is unacknowledged and presumably uninvited, whereas the audience of the sporting event is directly recognized in the shouts, groans, and applause written for it in the script. Scene Three imitates the active, potentially sadistic desire involved in subjecting an unknowing or unwilling victim to a controlling and curious gaze, a voyeuristic activity the implications of which are fully dramatized through Scopey's relationship to Alen later in the play. Scene Four, on the other hand, involves the narcissistic pleasure of passively identifying with the practiced, deliberately exhibitionist perfor-mance of trained athletes. By marking out Scopey as a "hero" of sorts, Bond also acknowledges the audience's desire (based on habit) to experience the action through some controlling point of view, one that does not radically disturb its own attitudes or self-image. If the desire to look actively reverses the desire to be seen, however, then the kinds of looking that seem to separate these two scenes are closely linked. Scopey, for one, will discover an unsettling similarity to the figure whose very "otherness" was the original source of attraction: "Chriss, yoo don't know anythin'. [...] Yoo owd fake! [...] Yoo're at that crack all day! Starin' out! It all goos on outside an' yoo just watch!" (294), a recognition that ultimately provokes him to action. In terms of the story, Scopey moves from the position of the observer to that of the observed, from the questioning subject to the object of our gaze. Just as Scopey "becomes" Alen, eliminating by violence the distance that separates them, so too does Pat "become" Scopey by taking up, in the play's final scenes, the actively curious position that Scopey's absence has inspired. As Scopey puts it, "Snoopin'. That's all she's after" (294). Likewise, the sensitivity that distinguishes Scopey from his peers is erased by a crime that far surpasses the muted violence of the gang's harassment. As the "differences" set up by the play's narrative gradually collapse into the final tableau, so too do some distinctions between Scopey's curiosity and our own.[16]

To briefly summarize, Scopey replaces Pat, in a relationship from which he had previously been excluded, to establish an imaginary relationship with Alen, which Pat's return from the "real" world will disrupt. Scopey then resolves – in a violent and self-destructive manner – the contradiction that Pat's uninvited presence unwittingly exposes, by murdering and replacing the man with whom he most identifies. Scopey's interest in what Pat "does" with Alen, and in what Alen "knows," provides the recurring subtext for his questions; and the actions accompanying them, the increasing urgency with which they are asked, and Scopey's complete ignorance of their origin makes him the first of a series of Bondian characters who are both violent aggressors and helpless victims of their own libidinal economy.[17] While sexually repressed characters in Bond's later plays often provide a comic caricature of socially rooted psychic damage, Scopey's sexual ambivalence is not symptomatic of social ills. Rather, Scopey's ambivalence naturalistically (or psychologically) grounds his curiosity – itself a normal and healthy characteristic. Despite its voyeuristic nature, only in retrospect can Scopey's curiosity be grasped as an aggressive, sadistic, and latently violent impulse as well. Indeed, with his inspired athletic performance and ordinary attitudes, Scopey embodies the positive aspects of the collective from which he emerges. Until the end of the play, his active curiosity suggests the possibility of breaking through the cyclical, imprisoning patterns represented by the weekly payday, seasonal work, annual sporting event, and daily domestic routine. But if Scopey's questions lead nowhere, if his apparent activity is revealed as an obsessive repetition, if the liberating knowledge he seeks is simply not to be had, then what is to be said of the audience's own fascination with Alen as an enigmatic presence on the stage, and of the aroused curiosity that the end of the play does not entirely satisfy?

Clearly the voyeuristic impulses which seem to drive the narrative, those which Scopey acts out and represents, those experienced by the audience watching the play, and those which drove them to the theatre in the first place are not the same; but their connections are worth considering. In "Instincts and Their Vicissitudes" (1915), Freud identifies scopophilia (the pleasure of looking and its reversal in the pleasure of being seen) as a primary drive subject to the same bilateral polarities (active/passive, subject/object, pleasure/pain) that govern other sexual instincts.[18] Because sexual gazing and self-display (or voyeurism and exhibitionism in the language of the perversions) emerge with the child's first sexual investigations, they are associated in psychoanalytic discourse with the desire for knowledge. As in sadism and masochism, which Freud discusses at the same time, their relative detachment from (originally autoerotic) organic sources results in their ambivalent form. Freud's description helps clarify Scopey's behavior in terms of sexual ambivalence, and illuminates both the oscillating pattern of narrative and the elliptical dialogue that Scopey's ambivalent desire seems to generate.

Moreover, in both the language of the instincts and the dynamics of *The Pope's Wedding*, voyeurism has sadistic overtones as an "active" pleasure. Scopey's gaze is not simply "erotic" and timeless (symbolic); Scopey specifically desires to know who Alen is, what he knows, and what he has done – a detective-like stance that feeds the audience's own investigative curiosity. If Scopey's gaze is murderous and his investigation self-destructive, what then of our own, or, for that matter, the playwright's? As an observer, Scopey is the figure through which we are invited to position ourselves in relation to the action, but a character with whom it is hard to identify. In this regard, the final scenes are particularly telling: Scopey has replaced the object of his investigation with himself, the object of ours; and Pat's discovery of what has happened to Scopey does not begin to answer the questions with which we are left.

Scopey's own story, however, is what original audiences found

most compelling about *The Pope's Wedding*. Indeed, the more Scopey
and Alen engage the viewers' interest, the less likely the contemplation of the end to which that curiosity will lead. For some, Bond's
narrative fell short, leaving only "sex, sport, violence and filth."[19] Of
the 1973 production, one reviewer noted the effect of directing the
play at "the unplanned snail's pace of real life. To begin with, this
was eerie and faintly irritating but gradually the action takes on an
unstoppable inevitability."[20] Even sympathetic reviewers felt
uncomfortable with Bond's hyper-realistic style, the desire to "get on
with it" expressed as the disagreeable memory of the play's "slow
start." Not only does Bond introduce the narrative threads slowly,
but he deliberately withholds a story that can incorporate the entire
play, that retrospectively orders and organizes the experience into a
unified whole. Because no play can "show everything," we expect
only action and dialogue required by the narrative. Bond, on the
other hand, shows more than one feels the need, even retrospectively, to see. However unpatronizing, the intimate view of the
community might itself be considered voyeuristic, the verisimilitude
extending from rough language and crude jokes to characters having
sex and even urinating onstage – and in 1962, such moments would
have been censored from a licensed performance. For the audience,
the potential embarrassment live performance makes possible
renders visible our "look" from the outside.[21] In *The Pope's Wedding*,
unlike *Saved*, the audience is rescued from such potential discomfort
by the gradually absorbing story.

The anticipatory structure of narrative itself (with its promise of
an end to grant order and meaning to what comes before) mitigates
the "threat of seeing" that theatre-goers must surely experience
more intensely than other kinds of audiences. According to film
theorist Christian Metz, the very presence of live actors makes the
voyeurism of the theatre closer to its exhibitionist counterpart than
that found in cinema, where "the economic regime of the primal
scene and keyhole reign."[22] Even today, what commonly and
comfortably can be seen on the screen may seem entirely inappropriate in a staged performance. The pleasure of film relies on an
awareness that the object being watched is no longer present (and is
thus unaware of being watched), the filmic state inviting a state of
lessened wakefulness in which distinctions between perception and
hallucination begin to disappear. The pleasure of theatre, on the
other hand, is associated with a *heightened* sense of perception, with a

tension that derives from the presence of live actors and perhaps with the possibility (safeguarded by theatre conventions) of ourselves being "seen." As Metz writes, "True exhibitionism is always bilateral, in the exchange of phantasies if not in concrete actions [. . .] the exhibited partner knows that he is being looked at, wants this to happen, and identifies with the voyeur whose object he is, but who also constitutes him as subject."[23] In film, the actors have left before any viewing begins; in theatre, the viewing exchange is fully acknowledged. Thus theatre is by its very nature "authorized" scopophilia, something epitomized in the actors' final bow and institutionalized until 1968 in the Lord Chamberlain's censorship office. What keeps the scopophilic impulse from being a sadistic perversion is precisely the community oriented nature of the event, which is always at some level based on consent.

Some notion of mutual consent might be a necessary precondition for aesthetic pleasure of all kinds; indeed, a case could be made that dramatic and literary forms and conventions serve a function similar to the rules and conventions of spectator sports – providing an unspoken compact that regulates and thus makes possible the pleasurable indulgence in looking and self-display. In *Bingo*, Bond's Shakespeare compares his own theatre to the bear-baiting with which it competed, finding the openly sadistic character of the latter analogous to the pleasure audiences found in his own plays. In *The Pope's Wedding*, the gang comments at some length on a televised boxing match in a scene that immediately precedes the revelation of Scopey's crime.

JUNE: Why can't they wear white shorts?
JOE: Don't know.
RON: Count a they'd show the blood.
JUNE: I 'eard it's so's yoo can't see what they got underneath when it get all sweaty. (*She giggles.*)
JOE: It's traditional. (297)

In this case, "tradition" distances the audience from the sadomasochistic nature of their own spectating pleasure. But Pat does not enjoy the event like the others precisely because she has been made aware of something wasteful and inappropriate about the activity:

PAT: I felt sorry for that dark fella.
JUNE: Shouldn't come over 'ere.
PAT: Blood everywhere. Must a got splashed if yoo was sittin' close. Waste.

JUNE: What is?
PAT: That blood.
RON: Why?
PAT: They could use that in 'ospitals. (298)

However comic her suggestion, Pat withholds her consent from the
uses of all "that blood" in a manner that marks her as more sensitive
than her friends. The viewers' objections to the staged violence of
Bond's subsequent plays may in fact be understood in similar terms,
as a socially responsible and thus entirely appropriate reaction.

While Scopey's story forces to consciousness the violent nature of
Freud's symbolic narrative, the structural similarities are more
suggestive than informative. The apparent openness of the script, its
stance of never quite revealing (in visual or thematic terms) its
own meaning, provokes a varied and potentially puzzled audience
response. But Bond's depiction of the Scopey–Alen relationship
should not finally suggest some unfathomable depth of character, a
general break-down of language and communication, or a world that
is ultimately unknowable. Rather, the knowledge to which our
curiosity leads is always, as Scopey's own path suggests, elsewhere.
For the theatre audience following Scopey to this particular dead-
end, that "elsewhere" is offstage – presumably in the world the play
can only represent, in actions the plot can only imitate, and in
answers the stage can never provide. If such a revelation is precisely
the aim of Bond's plays, we are left with a contradiction that accounts
in part for Bond's peculiar relationship with audiences and critics
alike. For if Bond is successful and his plays really work, then the
spectating audience, whose motives have been exposed and pleasures
have been challenged, will not find them easy to like.

Saved

The vocabulary of "liking" or "disliking" seems particularly inappropriate for *Saved*, a play from which British audiences, at least
temporarily, withheld their collective consent. The sharp difference
between original reactions to the two plays (ambivalence vs. rage)
should now be easier to understand. Compared to *The Pope's
Wedding*, *Saved*'s narrative is more episodic and less focused on a
single relationship – the sense of inevitability that arises from the
gradual focus on Scopey's destiny absent in the later play. Moreover,
the killing in *Saved* occurs mid-play, with the act graphically

depicted on the stage. While the pram prevents the audience from actually seeing the victim, it also makes possible a more forceful visualization of the crime, the reality of which a cruder representation would inevitably deflate. Scene Six (the longest of the play) builds slowly, deliberately, logically; "seeing" the crime is not nearly as horrifying as the gradual realization of how easily it happens. Nothing is suddenly revealed, nothing obliquely stylized; no particular moment alerts the squeamish to cover their eyes. Rather, the play invites us to watch a series of actions the consequences of which are so horrendous it is hard to imagine just letting it happen. Of course we do, since the stage assures us these actions are not real, and dramatic conventions lead us to expect some appropriate frame to cathartically manage the emotions that events onstage arouse. Nor is the violence (both here and in the domestic fight of Scene Eleven) the only thing that makes *Saved* uncomfortable to watch. The offstage crying of the neglected baby throughout Scene Four, the sexually explicit joking, Len's onanistic tendencies, and the very length of the play may all have contributed to the vociferous responses of original audiences.

As in *The Pope's Wedding*, the sexuality and violence of *Saved* are not separate issues. Both the "Author's Note" and subtitle (*An Oedipal Comedy*) reveal Bond's deliberate use of Oedipal configurations to structure the action of the play; and from the joking of the gang to the arguments and encounters between the family, the sexual undercurrents of the dialogue are unrelenting. *The Pope's Wedding* and *Saved* are based on the assumption that characters' actions have unconscious sources, that the unconscious itself is shaped and determined by social conditions, and that the audience shares the impulses that the characters onstage act out or represent. *Saved* may unwittingly tap unconscious sources as well: the baby-stoning sequence publically stages the apparently common private fantasy Freud reported and analyzed in "A Child Is Being Beaten" (1919).[24] Freud's study links the beating fantasy to a feminine (passive) attitude toward the father for whom the subject has an incestuous attachment; the subject evades his homosexual feelings by first repressing and remodelling the original fantasy in a masochistic direction, then substituting another for himself. In the heavily censored and pleasurable version, of course, no one is hurt. The strong impression of physical injury that Scene Six produces must inevitably suggest the absence of the censor – in its psychological as

well as institutional form.[25] The "atavistic fury"[26] released by the
gang, the scene's nightmarish quality, and the range of displeasure
evoked may all be related to an action too closely imitating sadistic
and sexually ambivalent instincts that have undergone repression in
the psyche of individual audience members. Attributing the charged
response of original audiences entirely to unconscious sources – like
Bond's remark that one policeman saw the production five times –
can be pushed too far. However, the way in which Freud's description of the beating fantasy links sado-masochism, voyeuristic
pleasure, and sexual insecurity can illuminate Len's character and
help make sense of his actions in the play.

In psychoanalytic terms, Len offers the passive, potentially masochistic obverse of Scopey's active and sadistic line of development.
Although Len is saved from Scopey's particular fate, he shares with
the earlier protagonist an inquisitiveness that troubles the surface
complacency of other characters and generates much of the play's
action and dialogue. Like Scopey, Len's incessant questioning
reveals a basic insecurity about his sexual identity, an insecurity
established in the opening scene as Len's sexual encounter with Pam
is delayed, first by Len's own questions and then by the interruption
of Pam's father, Harry. Most subsequent scenes involve Len's more
or less successful attempts to secure or defend his position within the
surrogate family Pam's household provides. When Len is caught in a
compromising situation with Harry's wife later in the play, Bond
deliberately avoids what he calls the "Oedipus outcome [...] a row
and a death" to make the play, formally, a comedy.[27] But the play's
real challenge to the viewer is located in the uncomfortable relationship established between Len and the audience.

Whether as an outsider asking questions, an observer making
comments, or an insider offering unwanted but usually decent
advice, Len is the likeable character through whom the viewer is
introduced to this world. In this regard, the conventions of audience
identification prove useful to the play. But the angle of vision Len
(our lens) provides is one that, for several reasons, must implicate the
viewer. As with Scopey before him, Len's actions are charged with
ambivalence, the subtextual nuances of the script left open and
ambiguous. On the one hand, Len appears throughout *Saved* want-
ing only to help: he carries Mary's groceries and helps pay the rent;
he offers Pam his tickets to the Crystal Palace to help her win back
Fred; he accepts responsibility for Pam's baby, refusing to desert the

situation even when begged to do so; he brings Fred cigarettes in jail and offers him his own room when he gets out; at the end of the play he is mending a chair. But given the grief Len gets for his efforts, we may begin to suspect the passive–aggressive nature of his initiatives. At least for Pam, Len's presence is a constant source of irritation both before and after the death of her baby. More than once, she begs Len to leave; and in Scene Ten she tries to enlist Fred's aid: "'E won't let me alone. [. . .] 'E follers me everywhere. [. . .] Tell 'im for me! 'It 'im! 'It 'im! [. . .] Somebody's got a save me from 'im" (114–115). While it is possible to read Len's actions as positive, his decision to "stay put" at the end a measure of his humanity,[28] one might also find his actions self-serving and complacent. Len, after all, caused the row in which the chair got broken and may well have been the father of Pam's baby; his economic support of the household is balanced by the emotional stress and discord his very presence seems to cause. In Scene Eleven, Pam's accusation hits home: "'E's killed me baby. Taken me friends. Broken me 'ome" (122). Len is far from being the innocent martyr that some may see in the play's final tableau.

A more disturbing side of Len's "innocence" is revealed in his questioning of Fred, his real sexual rival, and Harry, his symbolic one. In Scene Six, Len not only badgers Fred to talk about his sexual experiences and to explain the source of his luck with Pam, but he tells Fred (and later Harry) that he listens to them "on the bash" all night in the room below. Fred is both surprised and disturbed by the fact that Len never let on, suggesting that if it bothered him, he should have done something about it: "I reckon it was up t'you t'say. Yer got a tongue in yer 'ead" (64). Later Len questions Harry about everything, from what it was like with Mary "in bed" (127) to what it was like in the war, the entire scene framed by Len's silent eavesdropping on Pam's activities below. By directly recalling the tone of earlier conversations in which Len badgers Fred to reveal to him the secrets of his sexual successes, Len's questions in Scene Ten are perhaps most troubling of all: "What was it like?" he repeats, "Wass it feel like when yer killed it?" (113).

While both inexperience and ambivalent desire may explain Len's sexual curiosity, the sadistic component that underlies Len's eavesdropping activity is most fully revealed when we discover at the end of Scene Seven that Len watched the baby being stoned to death and did nothing:

2 The audience watches Harry, watching Len, listening to Pam in
the room below, *Saved*

LEN: I saw. [. . .]
FRED: Yer ain't grassed?
LEN: No.
FRED: O.
LEN: I was in the trees. I saw the pram.
FRED: Yeh.
LEN: I saw the lot.
FRED: Yeh.
LEN: I didn't know what t'do. Well, I should a stopped yer.
FRED: Too late now.
LEN: I juss saw.
FRED: Yer saw! Yer saw! What's the good a that? That don't help me! I'll
    be out in that bloody dock in a minute! (86)

Under the circumstances, Fred's inappropriate response is typical of
the displacement of responsibility revealed elsewhere in the joking
banter of the gang. But here Len's difference from the gang is
sharply qualified by his own self-incriminating statements. Unlike

Scopey, Len watches rather than commits the most violent act of the play. Like Len, the audience of the play may be disturbed by the view, but stays put nonetheless. Len cannot act at the time without alienating himself from the group; later he cannot blame others without reminding himself of his own responsibility. Like the audience, the essence of Len's action in Scene Six is "to watch and do nothing," and whatever his misgivings or intentions, he is judged with the others in terms of it. Such criminal negligence helps explain Bond's epigraph from William Blake's *The Marriage of Heaven and Hell* for the program note of the first production: "Sooner murder an infant in its cradle than nurse unacted desires." As the audience looks to the rest of the play to explain, frame, or make sense of such a crime, they must do so through Len – with his disturbing questions, troubling presence, and limited repertoire of responses.

In *The Pope's Wedding*, Pat's question "why?" is left hanging, like her call for "elp!" on which the play ends. *Saved* goes further, asking what is considered unacceptable, obscene, and/or immoral in our society and why? At what point does the accumulation of actions that are essentially the same become something qualifiably different? And who, in the last analysis, is responsible? Bond's use and displacement of the Oedipal story does not in itself provide an answer to the issues raised. The relationship established between Len and Harry may present a positive variation upon the potentially murderous father–son dialectic represented by Scopey and Alen; or it may simply reinscribe the impasse both reach. Near the end of *Saved*, Harry advises Len to let things remain as they are, to bide his time, to wait – and in doing so, reinforces the stasis that the play's violence only momentarily unsettles. Earlier, Colin asks what Len's been doing, and his response – "Waitin'" (41) – is both accurate and telling. Despite the feigned disbelief of the gang, Len *is* waiting – for Mary to come with the groceries, for Pam to change her mind, for things to change – and will do so for the rest of the play. Waiting is a key to Len's character: in Scene One, he waits for Harry to leave, in Scene Four, he waits for the baby to stop crying, in Scene Nine, he waits for Fred to show up, and at the end, he puts off leaving. But the passive position that links Len to the audience is not unique to his character. Pam waits for Fred with as much persistence as Len does for her, and Harry is waiting to leave Mary ("I'll go when I'm ready. When she's on 'er pension. [...] Then see 'ow she copes," 129). Even more to the point, the murder of the baby and the voyeuristic non-interference that makes Len an accessory to the crime occur when Fred and the gang are made to wait for its mother. Fred is not the only character who "does time" in the play; he is simply the one singled out for it. In *Saved*, as in *The Pope's Wedding*, the lingering of scenes in which nothing much seems to happen, the alternating repetition of narrative scenarios, the cyclical rhythms of domestic quarrelling, and the young men's rounds of insults and innuendos, all contribute to an oppressive sense of stasis in the lives of the characters. Given the well-articulated social context, the violence that erupts in Scene Six is not unusual but symptomatic, not a cause but a consequence. If the stoning of the baby seems both plausible and unnecessary, accurately portrayed but difficult to accept, so too is Len's passivity, Harry's silence, Pam's indifference, and ultimately the audience's own. Through the figures of both Scopey and Len, Bond invites the audience to look closely at the problem of violence while questioning the means and motives for doing so. Because the view of each play remains within the single social class depicted, the answers are not forthcoming.

While Bond's work grows increasingly familiar to British and European audiences without garnering broad popular support, something like a positive critical consensus has formed about the play that first so angered its public. Viewed as a masterpiece in its own right, *Saved* also seems to characterize the skills and concerns of a generation of Royal Court writers. Indeed, some of the respect now accorded this play, at least by Anglo-American critics, may rest on the way in which Bond's two earliest plays can be seen to occupy – through ambiguity, elliptical dialogue, working-class subjects, sexual innuendo, and unresolved tensions – the same critical space staked out by a playwright like Pinter. In *The Pope's Wedding* and *Saved* Bond's own point of view seems more submerged than in any later play; and one wonders what direction Bond's work might have taken had *Saved* not been the focus of such misunderstanding and intense debate. As it turned out, Bond's subsequent career has offered audiences of the early plays substantial evidence of his overriding social concern, and further development of the images with which he began. That the theatrical revival of both *The Pope's Wedding* and *Saved* lags far behind their current critical reputation pays tribute not only to the alternately ambivalent and explosive responses of original audiences, but perhaps to the inherently unpredictable ways in which these plays may still affect their viewers.

From Bond's own vantage point, the surprising "irrationality" of initial audience reaction may have encouraged a more explicit connection of the psychosexual realm to historical and political themes in later plays. Indeed, the subtextually established relationship between voyeurism and violence that challenges audiences in *The Pope's Wedding* and *Saved* finds far less problematic treatment in a comedy like *The Sea* (1973). Dominated by images of watchfulness and distraction, by characters observing and being observed, and by caricatures of both, *The Sea* observes a small, seaside community at the turn of the century. The implicit moral of both *Saved* and *The Pope's Wedding* – that society is responsible for its violence and the audience is responsible for its society – gets explicit demonstration through the broader social picture of *The Sea*, the psychological sufferings and bizarre actions of characters more easily traced to the tensions caused by the economic and social conditions of a class-ridden society. When Mrs. Rafi, the town autocrat, rehearses a version of *Orpheus and Eurydice* to hilarious effect, Bond challenges the theatre audience's own motives in viewing, participating in, and supporting particular kinds of stage productions. Despite the shift in strategy and dramatic technique separating this play from his first, two characters reappear in slightly altered form. Evens, a hermit by choice (and a man who does, in fact, know something) provides a more articulate and optimistic version of Alen, and Willy provides a more helpful and capable version of both Scopey and Len.

Opening on Willy's call for "help!" *The Sea*'s narrative involves establishing responsibility for the death of Colin at sea. Hatch is "on watch" but mad; Evens sees what happens, but is drunk; Willy, who tries to save his friend, is a helpless observer of both his friend's death and the rest of the play's action. (Characteristically, Mrs. Rafi and the rest of the town are sleeping soundly at the time.) Hatch, believing Willy to be a dangerous alien from another planet, organizes his men to "keep an eye" out; and through his actions in the play, Bond links observation to socially conditioned ignorance and aggression. Yet Evens, who provides the sensible alternative to Hatch's madness, is as culpable as a wise and passive "coast watcher" as Hatch is as an actively deluded "spy." Evens thus joins a series of Bondian figures (Basho, Lear, Shakespeare, and Trench among them) whose education, wisdom, or enlightened vision is made suspect through passive or variously inappropriate responses to real suffering. Rose's observations, in a town that relentlessly observes her, provide (with Willy's help) the strength that makes a new life possible. Throughout the play, Willy remains a questioning outsider; and, through him, Bond explicitly comments on the relationship between watching and acting that he would like his own audiences to adopt. Moments before Hatch hacks up the corpse of his friend Colin, who has washed up on the beach, Willy describes the attitude that will allow him to view calmly the same action Rose will find "so violent," and to judge it as an "innocent murder":

If you look at life closely it is unbearable. What people suffer, what they do to each other, how they hate themselves, anything good is cut down [...] It is all unbearable but that is where you have to find your strength. What else is there? [...] So you should never turn away. If you do you lose everything. Turn back and look into the fire. Listen to the howl of the flames. The rest is lies.[29]

Understood as playwright's advice to the audience, the speech justifies Bond's use of "aggro-effects" by linking them with a socially responsible vision.

Bond's challenge to theatre audiences and theatre institutions gets played out differently in later plays. But it might be interesting to reflect for a moment upon the relevance of Bond's work at the time in and for another medium. One of Bond's first projects after *The Pope's Wedding* and *Saved* was to write the dialogue for Michaelangelo Antonioni's film *Blow-Up* (1966); and although Bond claims to have simply needed the money, the collaboration appears particularly fortuitous given the similarities in theme and style that link such different texts. On the one hand, Antonioni's film concerns the artist's moral and aesthetic obligations to society, an issue that Bond later develops in plays like *Narrow Road to the Deep North*, *Bingo*, and *The Fool*. On the other hand, *Blow-Up* comments on the nature of filmic pleasure in ways that parallel Bond's own challenge to the passively gazing position of his theatre audience, whose disturbed consciences are so often managed and contained by the artistic medium through which they are aroused.

Blow-Up

In *Blow-Up* the main character's profession as a photographer, the lengths to which he will go to get the right shot, and his unwitting collusion in the violent episode he pieces together provide self-conscious comment on the illusion created by the film director's camera – an illusion created for the passive, literally helpless, enjoyment of the film audience. In photographic sessions with his models, Thomas' artistic activity explicitly substitutes for the sexual act, highlighting in a quite literal way the actively voyeuristic nature of Thomas' profession, of filmmaking and of audience pleasure. The heavily made-up (almost clown-like) faces of the fashion models Thomas "shoots," as well as the passive, rigidly unnatural, and overtly exhibitionist poses into which they are arranged for the photographic eye, offer further visual comment on the dehumanizing and potentially sadistic character of photography as "trade" and, by extension, film as commodity. The process of objectification appears before our eyes as both deliberately erotic ("good" pictures eliciting desire, which sells products) and violent (distorting the human body into grotesque death masks and physically unnatural positions). Thus the pleasure of the film spectator's passive consumption of images complements and completes the active sadism of the filmmaker, the audience's consent to this process cemented through identification with the film's successful, technically proficient (though morally suspect) detective-photographer.

In a photographic session midway through the film, Thomas arrives late and leaves early while the models are shown ready and waiting both before and after the sequence:

Thomas (to his models): I can't see your eyeballs anymore, they're just slits. Close your eyes. Close your eyes and *stay* like that. Its good for you. Close your eyes. (He leaves.)[30]

In a film marked by minimal dialogue, Thomas' repeated imperatives stand out, metaphorically alluding to the visual themes of the film as they metonymically underscore the use and abuse, exploitation and concern, sexual pleasure and playful betrayal within the scene. Thomas, certainly, seems to work too hard and need more sleep; his obsession to piece together what he "sees" in the park is fraught with social and political potential that ultimately proves detrimental to his own self-interest.

Because *Blow-Up* both privileges and questions its own methods of visual communication, the film's use of the spoken word is both minimal and telling. Bond's contribution to the script is unmistakable. But here the elliptical interchanges cannot simply be attributed to Bond's ear for the speech patterns of barely articulate working-class youths. Thomas' restless, easily distractable character, his focus on the present moment, his ruthless "professionalism" and his working-class background are all characterized through his speech, while the photographic quality of the film camera visually connects his action and character to the broader socio-economic sphere that conditions his behavior. In several scenes, the camera pans the monotonous suburban setting of row houses, pubs, shops, and alleys – Thomas' flashy sports car one indicator of his intent to escape the tedium suggested in other ways by the set. Interestingly, the single "set speech" of the film is not by Thomas, but by his wife's lover, an abstract painter whose material success is an ironic comment on the values of the society that buys his work. He says to Thomas:

I must be five or six years old. I don't mean anything when I do them. Just a mess. Afterwards I find something to hang on to. Like that. [gestures toward painting] Then it sorts itself out. Its like finding a clue in a detective story.

Such lines clearly foreshadow the single, oversized, barely readable print with which Thomas is left at the end of the film. While the speaking artist may unwittingly condemn the abstract tendencies of his own art (and the contemporary market for it), the lines also remind us that even the most "meaningless" artworks are humanly produced, and may thus be read and understood (like the film itself) symptomatically. At the other extreme, the truth-capturing possibilities of the photographic medium are illustrated in the park scenes, where Thomas seems to be aesthetically rather than economically motivated. But Thomas' aesthetic response to the murder he "witnesses" (with the aid of his camera) beneath the surface of the park incidents seems inappropriate, and disturbingly so. The motivation for Thomas' pursuit of the truth is never made clear; how involved in or how distanced he remains from the incident and its aftermath is never resolved.

The final sequence of *Blow-Up* visually reiterates the thematic issues of the film in a kind of musical coda: in the park where a "real" corpse has disappeared, costumed court jesters, oblivious to the drama we have witnessed, mime a game of tennis; Thomas watches and then self-consciously participates in the charade by returning an invisible stray ball. Thus the audience is left with a deliberately constructed image to frame a complex discourse on the relationship between image and truth, art and reality, pleasure and profit. The form itself – a narrative ending on a coda or complex poetic image – is characteristic of all Bond's early plays. *Saved*'s ending, played in total silence, is perhaps most similar in technique; but the final image of *The Pope's Wedding*, *Narrow Road to the Deep North*, *Early Morning*, and *Bingo* all work in much the same way. As in Antonioni's film, the meanings of Bond's plays are not to be found in the dialogue, nor in the consciousness of a single character, but rather in the complex relationship *between* character, action, visual image, and audience positioning that the notations of the script merely orchestrate.

CHAPTER 3

Rereading history

The texture and detail of everyday life, the relationship between observation and action, and the interwoven dynamics of family and social life prove as crucial to *Bingo* and *The Fool* as they do to Bond's earliest plays. Despite the apparent focus on a single central character, both plays defy a psychological perspective. But with Shakespeare in *Bingo* and eighteenth-century poet John Clare in *The Fool*, issues of naturalistic authenticity give way to questions of historical truth. Given Bond's political commitments, the turn to historical subject-matter is less surprising than the relative infrequency with which he does so. Though playwrights have used history as a source of inspiration long before Aristotle examined the activity, Brecht's example of ransacking history in pursuit of raw material for epic representation has specifically influenced the shape and uses of history for a recent generation of British playwrights. Nor has the interest in historical subjects and epic techniques been confined to playwrights on the left: John Osborne, Robert Bolt, Peter Shaffer, and Tom Stoppard have all written history plays that tout the use of Brechtian devices.[1] But the most thoroughgoing appropriation of epic methods has come, not surprisingly, from those sharing Brecht's politics and using historical subjects to serve critical rather than conservative ends. In some cases, the turn to historical subjects has involved the recovery and validation of marginalized figures or incidents from the past; in others, well-known events and famous people get presented unheroically, from the critical perspective of their victims. Often the return is to particular moments of history where class antagonisms are close to the surface, economic injustices apparent, and working-class consciousness sharply defined.[2] Thus plays like John McGrath's *The Cheviot, the Stag, and the Black, Black Oil* (1974) or John Arden and Margaretta D'Arcy's *The Non-Stop Connelly Show* combine popular, agit-prop, and documentary techniques for their political ends. Yet Howard Brenton's deliberately provocative history play *The Romans in Britain*, staged at the National Theatre in 1980, seems closer to Bond than to the work of McGrath's 7:84 Company. Using the graphically depicted metaphor of homosexual rape to represent the British occupation of Ireland, Brenton's large-scale epic is more complex in its analysis of an historical process than critics, irritated by Brenton's language, imagery, and aggressive political stance, generally allowed. And the play triggered a revival of interest in censorship issues that provoked Bond to a public defense.[3] However different their methods and particular aims, Brenton, McGrath, Arden, and Bond have all written history plays that deliberately work against the aesthetic expectations and political sympathies of the audiences of traditional, West End theatre. All have faith in the revitalizing and potentially energizing effects of the theatre, and like Brecht, they write for a particular social class and from an engaged, political stance. Their decision to write about historical figures and to stage historical events is but part of their self-conscious desire to be engaged in the making of history, to have some effect on struggles outside of the playhouse.[4] Bond's own contribution to the genre thus takes shape against the practice of his contemporaries.

Despite the apparent irrelevance of the charge, each of the aforementioned plays have been charged with "historical inaccuracy," an accusation that pays tribute to the power that rests in the interpretation and revision of history. Yet staged history inevitably makes the audience aware of the irrecoverable nature of the past and the constructed nature of any historical account. Since Aristotle, plausibility has been the measure of dramatic truth, not strict verifiability, even for plots based on actual events. Plays "based on" history employ certain liberties: changes are made for dramatic economy, exaggeration used for rhetorical purposes, dramatic metaphors found for abstract ideas, action and dialogue created in the absence of historical record, and much gets left out. On the other hand, "true stories" can provide an aura of authenticity even to the most incredible rendition. The issue is of some importance as we turn to Bond's treatment of both Shakespeare and John Clare.

Bingo

Unlike Bond's second "history play" *The Fool* (1976), *Bingo* (1974) enjoyed sparse praise, even from critics favorably disposed to his earlier work – despite the fact the National, the Royal Court, and the Royal Shakespeare Company all vied for its initial production.[5] Something about the subject-matter and its treatment left audiences "cold": and indeed, *Bingo* is a play that strongly resists popular appropriation. Unlike the history plays of Bond's socialist contemporaries, *Bingo* is neither epic in size nor specifically addressed to a working-class audience – nor is it meticulous in its use of historical fact. In a mere six scenes, the play traces the social and economic changes besetting Stratford-upon-Avon in the final year of Shakespeare's life, changes that in this play intrude upon Shakespeare's retirement, demand his unwilling response, and force him to reflect on the meaning of his success as a writer and its effect on both his family and the larger community in which he lives. The portrait of Shakespeare as a shrewd and practical businessman easily emerges from the historical record of Shakespeare's financial and legal dealings with his contemporaries.[6] More disturbing, however, is Shakespeare's decision at the end of *Bingo* to take his own life. Whether interpreted as an act of resignation, despair, or responsible self-criticism, the view of Shakespeare that emerges is undeniably critical.

Reviewers faulted the play on several counts: a presumptuous and unfair treatment of Shakespeare, poetic prose that lacked the depth and intensity of Shakespearean language, a loose and uncompelling episodic structure, a self-indulgent preoccupation with "writers' problems," and, as expected, historical inaccuracy.[7] Such a list reveals more about the expectations audiences brought to the play than it does about the play itself. Clearly audiences were made uncomfortable by the nagging suspicion that Bond was comparing himself to Shakespeare, or worse, presuming to pass judgment. Since so little is known about Shakespeare's life, no doubt audiences were further disappointed by a play not entirely dominated by the character they came to see. Given the brevity of the play, the amount of historical and literary material Bond manages to incorporate is impressive, to say the least. Historical documents show that Shakespeare did purchase rent-producing real estate and collect tithes; that William Combe advanced a scheme (which eventually failed) to enclose public lands; that Shakespeare secured a deed of indemnity from Combe against any ensuing personal loss; and that the town's resistance to enclosure was not formally endorsed by Shakespeare. The play also acknowledges the growing presence of Puritanism, the laws governing vagrants, public executions,

Shakespeare's last drinking bout with Jonson (from which he reputedly caught a fever and died), Shakespeare's reputation for generosity, his rather enigmatic will, and his father's previous bankruptcy. Ben Jonson's killing of a man, his various jail sentences, his problems with the theatre management, his walk to Scotland, the fire at the Globe Theatre, and the two writers' lack of male heirs all have a firm basis in historical record. Most deletions and additions are made in the interest of dramatic economy, and Bond defends himself against inaccuracy by noting that he is "not really interested in Shakespeare's true biography in the way a historian might be."[8]

Ironically, perhaps, audiences may find as many allusions to Shakespeare's plays as to historical facts. Combe is as smooth and sinister as Claudius, Judith as acquisitive and self-interested as Lear's daughters. Shakespeare's movement toward self-knowledge recalls that of Shakespeare's Lear, the staggering journey home in the snow an effective counterpoint to Lear's ranting on the heath; while Shakespeare's self-doubt has many analogues in *Hamlet*. Given the scope of Shakespeare's work, the signaling presence of Shakespeare on the stage, the culture-conscious audience the play may attract, and Bond's own elliptical style, far more allusions might be cited than ever were intended by the playwright. The point is simply that Bond's fleshing out of facts is made without regard to the demand of documentary or other traditional narrative forms that contribute to the plausibility of staged action. What finally separated Bond from his audiences was not the play's historical accuracy, but rather its "truth."

Though notions of "truth," "accuracy," and "plausibility" are central to the history play genre, an important distinction must be made between plays that take historical figures and events for their plots (which may be plausible yet blatantly untrue) and plays in which history itself (its movement and interpretation) is the playwright's foremost concern. While the former is characteristic of costume drama and the ever-popular television "history series," the latter is both the challenge and the problem of a socialist theatre practice. Occasionally, the same criticism can be levelled against both. In the film *Reds*, for example, Trevor Griffiths complained that despite the best intentions of its historically knowledgeable and politically committed producer, history is collapsed, "then" is seen as "now," and historical differences are glossed over to emphasize the contemporary relevance of the material.[9] Indeed, of much

"historical drama" we could say that history is not the subject-
matter, but merely the set. Griffiths' criticism echoes Brecht's
caution to socialist playwrights over thirty years earlier:

We must drop our habit of taking the different social structures of past
periods, then stripping them of everything that makes them different; so
that they all look more or less like our own, which then acquires from this
process a certain air of having been there all along, in other words, of
permanence pure and simple. Instead we must leave them their distinguishing marks, and keep impermanence always before our eyes.[10]

The differences to which Brecht refers involve not simply those of
background and environment, but those of character as well. While
a person's thought and behavior may vary according to social class,
age, and personality (aspects with which audience members might
identify), in a "history play," differences should also result from the
particular social and economic organization of the period in question. According to Brecht, a play that encourages its audience only
to share the responses of its characters "may allow that such a thing
as history exists, but it is none the less unhistorical."[11]

Brecht's injunction provides a way of understanding the initial
response to *Bingo* and to perceiving the play's importance. While
maintaining some audience distance from the past, *Bingo* nevertheless reaches forward in history – connecting without collapsing two
historical worlds. As a play that "reads history," *Bingo* is about a
particular historical moment and about reading history in a politically useful way. It is also as much about the culture hero who
haunts the present as the man who lived through the enclosures of
the early seventeenth-century, as much about the individual's
responsibility to her society as about the unique responsibilities of
the artist. However circumscribed by their historical moment,
however, Bond's characters are still capable of (therefore responsible
for) meaningful political action. Since the way in which individuals
(both then and now) perceive their situation affects and limits their
capacity for changing it, *Bingo* focuses not simply on the need for
social change, but on those subjective elements that may help or
hinder it. By the end, the audience is put in the uncomfortable
position of neither sharing the response nor identifying with the
behavior of a single character. Understanding the action in terms of
historical difference allows for a less simplistic judgment of the play's
relevance to contemporary life.

Bingo finally resists the question–answer (cause–effect) structure of simple narrative just as strongly as it resists the multiply determined depths of psychological realism. Without the hero/ine or narrator typical of Bond's later plays, *Bingo* must rely almost entirely on the structuring of relationships to make its connections between history, politics, and subjectivity. As the characters interact, responding to the same situations according to their differing interests, a portrait of society emerges that, however distant, is disturbingly similar to Bond's own. Thus Combe's lawful violence, Judith's petty greed, and Jonson's self-lacerating hatred – as well as the Son's religion, the Old Man's mental handicap and Shakespeare's obsessive self-doubt – are symptoms of a particular economic organization of society (nascent capitalism) that dehumanizes its members through the continual conversion of human needs into monetary ones.[12] Acquisitiveness and aggression are linked as qualities necessary for survival in such a society; and no character is immune to its effects. Judith fears that her father will become a financial burden just as Shakespeare fears the precedent of his own father's bankruptcy; Jonson comes to Stratford hoping to scout the investment futures for his London employers and to touch Shakespeare for a loan. Even the beggar-woman prefers money to Shakespeare's offer of food and clothing.[13] Equally important, nothing that the characters do or say is without repercussion on the lives of others. Judith speaks and a woman is arrested, Shakespeare remains silent and the town loses its common lands, the Son arouses rebellion and a father gets shot, Jonson sells Shakespeare poison purchased for himself, and so on. The action of *Bingo* is constituted by the inextricably related (and mutually determining) social and economic exchanges that occur. However fragmented and elliptical, such action clearly *has* under-lying causes as well as multiple (and not always predictable) effects.

As the play's central figure, Shakespeare's character is "filled" by his interaction (or lack thereof) with the other characters in the play; what happens between them provides the audience with the basis on which he is judged. Although each relationship is important, per-haps the most significant and easily overlooked is that which exists between Shakespeare and the Son. Focusing on it may help to illustrate Bond's use and displacement of Oedipal configurations in the early plays, and to account for their abandonment or re-envisioning in later work.[14] Both characters are involved in a crisis of identity directly related to the outer contradictions of a quickly changing world; but, separated by age and social class, their searches follow different trajectories and yield strikingly different results. Their relationship not only calls attention to the metaphorically overdetermined father–son patterns in the play, but their separate actions comment on each other and in some sense direct the play's temporal movement.

In simplest terms, the Shakespeare of *Bingo* wants both to "know the truth" about himself and to die in peace; and the contradictory nature of these two objectives ends in suicide. The Son, on the other hand, wants to live; but his active maneuvering for survival leads ultimately to the murder of his own innocent father. These two actions – murder and suicide – are essential to the narrative structure of *Bingo*, since the events of the play lead us to them in the final scene where Shakespeare and the Son directly and privately confront each other for the first time. That meeting is, in fact, the belated fulfillment of one urged by the Old Woman in the opening scene of the play. With his mother's help, the Son would enlist the support of Shakespeare against Combe's plans; but Shakespeare's deliberate avoidance of that alliance, there and in subsequent scenes, forces the Son along a path of his own making.

The Shakespeare–Son connection is not sprung on the audience in the final scene, although its centrality may not appear until then. In Scene One, the Old Woman tries to draw out Shakespeare on the enclosure question as he sits in "the last of the sun" (17), but gains neither information nor reassurance for her pains. Shakespeare, silent through several pauses, avoids responding to her questions with an accusation: "Your son told you to question me" (17). During the beggar-woman's first arrest, Shakespeare speaks only one line, and that is to the Son ("Why were you in my orchard? SON: I come t'see yo'," 23), temporarily directing suspicion away from the accused to her ranting accuser. Already knowing the answer, Shakespeare's question is itself a response to the Old Woman's request and indicates not only his disapproval of the Son's actions but his unwillingness to grant an audience for his cause. In Scene Three, Shakespeare gets up and moves away during the Son's harangue (37), and although "his movements and face express nothing," the Son interprets Shakespeare's action correctly, as a personal betrayal. ("He were here," he tells Judith, "I sid a prayer but he turn away from the word. WALLY: Spurned lord god like the roman in the judgement hall," 38.) By Scene Four, Shakespeare and the Son seem to occupy entirely different worlds, even in the same room – the Son's energy and forward-looking thought counter-pointed by Shakespeare's drunken, backward-looking remorse.

Shakespeare's initial and continued avoidance of the Son is inextricable from his decision to remain silent on the enclosure issue. The suicide can be read as the very limit of Shakespeare's refusal to act: he takes the poison after his own admission of guilt and the Son's confession of murder ("A murderer telling a dead man the truth. Are we the only people who can afford the truth?" 63). Asking for the tablets when Combe enters, Shakespeare will refuse to tell Combe (or anyone else) what he knows. Ironically enough, Shakespeare's final silence is the very alliance the Son needs to escape arrest – though different from that originally sought. As the play unfolds, then, these two characters provide alternative methods of under-standing and coping with their world. By examining the limitations of both, the audience finds itself engaged in the critical and ultimately political activity of interpreting history with a view to changing it.

Bond sets up the thematic importance of interpreting events in several ways – inviting the audience to read symptomatically. Thus critics who found the argument of *Bingo* unconvincing generally sought for the play's meaning in Shakespeare's isolated moments of perception, a view necessarily distorted. Since an idealized image of Shakespeare, some notion of Shakespeare's capacity for both wisdom and wit, and/or the habit of character identification is precisely what an audience brings to this play, the power of *Bingo*'s opening three scenes rests on Shakespeare's silence, his expressionless face, his lack of response to those around him. Such a passive, inscrutable stance frustrates our desire both to know what Shakespeare is thinking and to see him act, if not heroically, at least "appropriately" – a desire that increases as the intensity of the action heats up around him and Shakespeare remains cold and impassive.

Without a cue from the central character whose physical presence so dominates the stage, the question of how to interpret events is kept constantly at issue. Shakespeare himself is worried how others interpret him. When Combe comments on their bargain (Shake-speare's silent assent to enclosure in exchange for financial assur-ances), Shakespeare complains "You read too much into it" (21); later he is amazed when Ben Jonson interprets his drunken, placid appearance as a sign of inner serenity; and in the play's final scene,

Shakespeare is appalled that the Son cannot read "truthfulness" in his face, but sees only sickness and old age (62). It is no surprise that when Shakespeare does speak, we are disappointed. Not simply are economic motives provided for his actions, but Shakespeare's thoughts and perceptions seem limited for a man of vision and cannot account for nor explain the social contradictions set up in the play. We can hardly be satisfied that the hero's glimpsed understanding dies with him in a Hamlet-like assertion of "the rest is silence" (*Hamlet*, V.ii.369). If it is Shakespeare's ego-centered and metaphoric reading of events which leads to suicide in lieu of progressive political action, then we are confronted with the particular limits of Shakespeare's imagination. Thus Bond's Shakespeare speaks not only against the idealized and ahistorical figure that haunts the present, but also against the bourgeois world view represented by the "timeless," richly metaphoric vision of the plays.

Fixated upon his past and professionally secure, Shakespeare is not prepared to understand the quickly transforming world he retires to, nor to perceive until late in the play his own implication in it. Even then, his reaction – guilt – is indicative of his class position: a politically harmless response that may destroy an individual but in no way threatens the prevailing social order. Simply put, Shakespeare sees nothing more than the contradiction between the identity he has created for himself and the outer experience he observes. As he tells the Old Woman: "I quietened the storms inside me. But the storm breaks outside. To have usurped the place of God, and lied ... " (41). One problem he faces is the realization that the symbolic and providential world he created in his plays is not relevant to the world in which he now lives, a realization the audience is expected to note as well. If there is no God within and no Providence without, Shakespeare's path to "truth" can lead only to the self, not to divine wisdom. As he states:

There's no higher wisdom in silence. No face brooding over the water. [...]
No hand leading the waves to the shore as if it's saving a dog from the sea.
[...] No other hand ... no face ... just these ... (40)

This recognition of the absence of God, a recognition made by the Son in Scene Five with much different consequences, leads Shakespeare back to his own reflection on the water, unable to break through the enclosure of self-consciousness and an obsessive feeling of guilt. The pattern of his thinking, his aesthetic and metaphoric reading of the world, works in the static categories of good and evil, innocence and corruption, love and hate, truth and falsehood – polarized absolutes ultimately inadequate for dealing with either the problems of the play or the movements of history.

Scene Three, visually dominated by the three-day-old corpse of the hanged beggar-woman, provides perhaps the clearest example of Shakespeare's thought in relation to others. In terms of the narrative, the dead body aptly represents Combe's law and serves as both warning and religious portent for the Son. Yet Bond historicizes the image for the audience by visually quoting Rembrandt's drawing, New York Metropolitan Museum of Art, inv. "76487" (34). The particular body from Rembrandt's drawing is thus reinscribed with the social relations that have determined it – wrested from the realm of the symbolic, and historically resituated as the result of human actions having socio-economic implications that only the audience of a later historical period can fully grasp. While characters come and go, interpreting the woman's death in variously inadequate ways, Shakespeare perceives its significance metaphorically. The depraved public hanging reminds him of the London playhouse crowds, and he is suddenly appalled to have (like his audiences) walked to the theatre under sixteen severed heads and heard the noise of bears suffering in the nearby pit. His graphic description of bear-baiting, with its reference to the issue of interpreting signs, provides in its double movement a remembrance of things past and a judgment of events that have occurred in the play:

[...] Flesh and blood. Strips of skin. Teeth scrapping bone. [...] Howls. Roars. Men baiting their beast. On and on and on. And later the bear raises its great arm. The paw with a broken razor. And it looks as if it's making a gesture – it wasn't: only weariness or pain or the sun or brushing away the sweat – but it looks as if it's making a gesture to the crowd. Asking for one sign of grace, one no. And the crowd roars, for more blood, more pain, more beasts huddled together, tearing flesh and treading in living blood. (39)

As the scene progresses, Shakespeare gradually displaces his pity for the beggar-woman and her indifferent torturers to himself. Feeling increasingly trapped (and baited) by the sight of human brutality everywhere he turns, he here begins to reckon the cost of his career in the suffering he has ignored ("What does it cost to stay alive?" 40).

But like the self-lacerating judgments of Jonson (Shakespeare's literary *alter ego*) later in the play, such insights remain static and

3 Rembrandt's drawing "Woman Hanging on Gallows"

4 Shakespeare, his back turned on the hanged woman in *Bingo*

self-implicating, unconnected as they are to larger social and economic issues.[15] Always reading the world in terms of himself, Shakespeare's metaphoric and self-reflective imagination yields a distorted kind of truth. Indeed, it takes some imagination to share Shakespeare's aesthetic response to the hanging corpse: "Still perfect. Still beautiful," a sentiment not shared by the Old Woman. "No. Her's ugly. Her face is all a-twist. They put her legs in a sack count a she's dirty. [. . .] She smell" (42). Projecting into the dead woman his own desire to be at peace, away from the "noise" and "dust" of social life, Shakespeare's death wish is expressed as a desire to be left alone in a totally natural environment. Perhaps because he is an artist, he sees that environment in symbolic rather than concrete terms; unlike any other character in the play, he reads Nature as a sign. "I went to the river yesterday. So quiet. They were all here. [. . .] Then a swan flew by me up the river. [. . .] I heard its breath when it flew by. Sighing. The white swan and the dark water" (41–42). Although Nature offers no higher wisdom, Shakespeare's movement in *Bingo* is an unflagging retreat from society and its demands, an attempt to transcend (both physically and spiritually) the sordid world that surrounds and entraps him. He retires from London to his garden, to be constantly interrupted and intruded upon. He walks to the river to avoid the Son's public harangue, and sees his own reflection in the water. Wandering in the clean, empty, traceless snow, he is faced again by his own death-bound image. Even on his deathbed, Shakespeare finds no peace.

As Bond's Shakespeare comes to question the truths of his own plays ("To have usurped the place of God, and lied," 41), Bond makes a connection between creative writing and narcissism with obvious debts to Freud's analysis of the artist.[16] Not only is Shakespeare's vision a subjective one, but as the play progresses, writing itself gets described with increasingly loveless, ugly, violent, and masturbatory images. Jonson accuses Shakespeare of "scrabbling it off in noisy corners," (44) and both speak of writing in other men's blood, the pen as a sword. The money-grubbing world of London come to haunt him in the flesh, Jonson's self-hatred works like a poison on Shakespeare's imagination. Jonson describes writing as, "Fat white fingers excreting dirty black ink. Smudges. Shadows. Shit. Silence" (45), lines echoed by Shakespeare in the last scene: "I must be quiet. White worms excreting black ink. Scratch. Scratch"

(61–62). The image is connected in turn to the writing of the will, his wife's desperate scratching outside the locked door of his bedroom, and to his own death. The cluster of images with its Freudian overtones (writing, wish-fulfillment, avoidance of the reality principle, narcissism, sterility, and death) economically expresses Shakespeare's disillusionment in a way that relates his position to that of the twentieth-century writer. Clearly the issue involves, on a general level, the kind of personal compromises that successful writing so often involves. For Shakespeare, the problem is most baldly stated near the end of the play: "[...] I howled when they suffered, but they were whipped and hanged so that I could be free. That is the right question: not why did I sign one piece of paper?" (62–63). Yet Freud's analysis may itself be symptomatic of the extent to which the artist's social role has been undermined and marginalized under capitalism. While the psychoanalytic dimension opened by the imagery appropriately coincides with Shakespeare's self-assessment, the inevitable trace of a later historical moment also makes the viewer sense some distortion. Not simply are we easier on Shakespeare than he is on himself, but rather the psychological focus itself seems inadequate to understanding the play's issues in the most productive and useful way. To *read* the personal as the political must involve an analysis that goes beyond the existential predicament of individuals acting alone – something the play, but not Shakespeare, is able to do.

Like Hecuba of *The Woman*, Trench in *The Worlds*, and Lear, Shakespeare's growth in self-consciousness is not necessarily a positive development. Indeed, the life and action of the play increasingly occurs around and outside Shakespeare's vision; and the audience that persists in Shakespeare's own psychological focus will be led to the same frustrating impasse at the end of the play. Shakespeare's subjectivity ultimately costs him his connection with the world and his ability to act at all. By the end of Scene Five, hate, money, property, greed, aggression, injustice, suffering, lying, guilt, writing, and death have all become connected in Shakespeare's mind by a metaphoric condensation that obscures the precise relations between them. His search for some unalterable truth in what he observes ends in a final question leading back to his own activity – to a painful irony faced with much difficulty. "Was anything done?" (62). The audience, not Shakespeare, is left to judge. World-weary, physically and emotionally drained, nearly dead, Shakespeare could be speaking of himself when in the first and final meeting with the Son he says, "Go and bury your father" (65).

As a character, the Son is a more problematic figure than Shakespeare in the play. He seems to change from scene to scene, his lines are often elliptical or incoherent, his energy very near hysteria, his actions desperate. He has no name and lacks the consistency of a firmly fixed identity because he lacks both Shakespeare's self-consciousness and a particular basis in historical fact. But unlike Shakespeare, the Son is constantly influencing, judging, and intervening in the events of his world. He represents not so much a crisis of identity as an identity in crisis, a difference that provides an alternative to Shakespeare's particular development. Both seek, with varying degrees of success, to escape the enclosures of *Bingo*, whether they be economic, political, psychological, or metaphoric. Both constantly read and interpret events, but while Shakespeare's crisis of identity distorts his vision, the Son's *lack* of identity distorts his. That one is a father, the other a son, is not the source of their contrast, but rather their point of relation in the play.

The Son's sanctimonious, Puritan zeal makes him far less sympathetic a character than Shakespeare. Yet the Son's religious fanaticism is a response to a society which, according to Bond's portrayal, has abandoned reason, is governed by money, and is basically immoral. Since it is within the family unit that such social structures are reproduced, the Son's rejection of the various father-figures offered by the play can be interpreted as a positive, if limited, movement. Bond here takes the Freudian notion of the religious experience as a substitute for the longing for the father and makes it a viable dramatic image with historical and political, rather than psychological, implications. For the Son, the desire for social change is a personal need – a lack or gap structured by the inadequacy of the play's father-figures. The Old Man, the Son's biological father, is incapable of supporting or educating his son, a blow on the head with an ax having rendered him senile. William Combe, on the other hand, is an unacceptable father. A father-figure in terms of his wealth and power, he controls the society of *Bingo*; but the society he ushers in is avaricious and dehumanizing.

At the end of the play, Shakespeare's comment to the Son "So you met. The son and the father" (63), resonates with meaning given that Shakespeare himself is the most over-determined fatherly presence onstage. Having taken in and supported the Old Woman's family, he is the Son's surrogate father; he is Judith's biological father; and both he and Jonson have buried a son. Shakespeare's literary success makes him a cultural father too – England's timeless poet laureate. To Jonson, Shakespeare is "Old Serenity," a god-like figure supported by Shakespeare's own self-conception ("to have usurped the place of god," 41). Bond calls attention to the father–child relationship from the beginning of the play with the recurring and conspicuously placed offstage shouts "Father!" by the Old Woman and Judith, who seem in constant search for men who remain elusive and indifferent to their concerns. Shakespeare is not only the dying father and the absent god, but in terms of his relationship to both Judith and the Son, an unwilling father as well. The Son's own religious reading of current events is phrased accordingly:

Rich thieves plunderin' the earth. Think on the poor trees an' grass an' beasts, all neglect an' stood in the absence a god. [. . .] Where there's no lord god there's a wilderness. [. . .] (*rocking slightly*). The absence a god, the wilderness . . . neglect . . . (49)

Even Jonson refers to the significant absence of his own father: "I know I'm not human. My father died before I was born" (45). The patriarchal mindset is an historical given, one measure of the limits of the characters' own reading of events – and thus, perhaps, of any interpretation dominated by images of inadequate fatherhood. But Bond's conspicuous use of the pattern also invites a positive reading of the Son's action, given the historical context. Not simply in search of a father or ego-ideal (a structural pattern familiar to literary narrative), the Son's actions suggest the possibility of intervening in a glaringly inadequate society, of "becoming" a father by rejecting in turn each of the play's father substitutes.

Because the Son's religious reading of events is both a symptom and a means of coping with his situation, it has Marxist as well as Freudian implications. In historical and political terms, the growth of fundamentalist Protestantism (the Son's brand of religion) can be understood as a measure of the atomization of society and the individual alienation that results. Thus religion becomes increasingly internalized, a matter of individual consciousness separate from the workings of the state, the more it becomes the refuge of the politically disenfranchised. According to Marx, at certain historical moments, religion can cease to be merely an "opiate of the people" by leading social movements against or away from a state they no longer control and which threatens their existence. While Shakespeare's metaphoric and aesthetic understanding leads him to incorporate the events he witnesses – to identify, connect, and relate things in ever-broadening categories – the Son's religious reading is always one that fixes him, for the moment, in a position from which to judge, to negate, or to act. Most often, the Son uses religion as a way of rationalizing or repressing his own guilt, or for projecting outward his own objectionable impulses. Such a process helps explain his hysterical reaction to the discovery of his father's sexual activity as well as his later interpretation of the events that result in the woman's hanging. Although implicated in both, he attributes the death of both the woman and his father to the "Lord's mysterious ways," bypassing the individualistic self-consciousness that debilitates Shakespeare.

As early as Scene Two, the Son's legitimate anger is linked to his religious fanaticism. The Old Man complains, "My boy's cross too. He rage up an' down all hours. [...] He's allus talkin' t'god – so stands t' reason he never listen to a word I say" (28). Confused as to the meaning of events and his own implication in the beggar's death, the Son uses his somewhat fanciful and often contradictory religious pronouncements in Scene Three to pass judgment: on the peasants ("A festival a dark. [...] Is that reverence?" 36), on Judith ("Dost matter t'him her beg when all eat out his yand? No. [...] Even the sinner's innocent," 38), and on Shakespeare ("Thou sent the whore t' the rich man's yate an' the poor man fell in her way but thou art not mocked," 36). While such judgments may seem peevish and self-serving, they can be mobilized in the interests of others (here, too late, for the beggar). The transference of guilt involved leaves the less reflective character freer to act in a collective and politically effective manner. By Scene Four, the Son has turned his religious vocabulary and prophetic intonation to powerful use – undermining the more rational-sounding arguments of Combe and inciting the peasants to an uprising. By the end of the play, the Son's religious reading of events has proved politically subversive as well.

The problem Bond leaves us with in *Bingo* involves how to understand the Son's final action – shooting his father. Before it occurs, the Son's interpretation of the moral and socio-economic implications of the new enclosure laws appears clear-headed and reasonable, despite his personality. After the shooting incident, the Son seems suddenly older and wiser: he confronts Shakespeare on his deathbed with a calm self-confidence, he out-maneuvers Combe to escape arrest, the hysterical edge to his character is gone, and he shows evidence of a new self-reflectiveness. Had the Son shot either Shakespeare or Combe, the positive political point would have been immediately apparent. In other words, had the shooting of the father been only symbolic, we could say that the Son, working through the Oedipal configuration, had entered society and adult social relations to become a father of a better sort than those around him. If nothing else, we have found in him the *energy* needed for social change. However, the context of the action makes it clear that the acting out of this Oedipal wish is both destructive and unnecessary. For, as noted earlier, the Son's real father is an innocent, child-like, sympathetic figure throughout the play. As the Old Woman describes him, "He weren't greedy for money loike some men. I yont know. [. . .] He wanted summat a child want. I yont know what" (59). Killing this particular father clearly signals the larger human cost of the social transformations represented in *Bingo*.

The Son's last words provide a final twist to the Oedipal drama, displacing with their ambiguity any closure to the events we have witnessed:

When yo' think on't, t'ent so sure I shot him neither. I fire a gun – I yont hide no truth. That yont mean I shot him. Someone else'n moight a fired. Death on an unarmed man – that's more loike the sort a think Combe'd get up to. That want sortin' out in my yead. I may have done meself a wrong. (65)

One can read the final lines of this speech as the Son's typical defensiveness giving way to genuine confusion, generated by vague feelings of remorse. This would indicate the Son beginning, at the very end of the play, to "count the cost," to interpret the effect of his act upon himself, and to resolve the question of his own identity (something Shakespeare does only too well). On the other hand, Combe's willingness to take responsibility for the murder may have planted genuine doubt in the Son's mind as to who is responsible for the murder, the "done meself a wrong" referring to an overly hasty admission of guilt earlier in the scene ("Everyone looked the same in the moonlight. I shot him," 63). Since the shooting itself occurs "far upstage" and outside the clear view of both Shakespeare and the audience, the doubt we are left with may be quite real. No matter how these lines are interpreted, however, the Son reaches neither Shakespeare's level of consciousness nor that of a revolutionary. To the end, the Son believes that "the yand a god's in it someplace" (65).

While the Son may use religion in practical, politically useful ways, his consciousness is limited by the same social structures that limit the responses of the other characters; he cannot, within the framework of the play, make the more radical move of displacing religion altogether. Bond invites us to understand the political problems of *Bingo* in the context of seventeenth-century England, which precludes the use of the Son as a left-wing hero or a model for contemporary political activists. For although the Son becomes, through his dealings with Shakespeare and Combe, class conscious (something Bond expects from his audience as well), it's a consciousness imprinted by the needs and events of a different historical moment. Allied momentarily to the needs of a laboring class, the Son's future rests with the entrepreneurial ventures of a rising merchant class. The Son simply wants what the others have; and as his own words suggest, he will go to America, as a Puritan father, to get it. Bond remains faithful to history on this point, not implanting in the Son an anachronistic political consciousness. Religion remains for him both the means of responsibly entering into and acting upon society, and the crutch which prevents any radically effective change; like the audience, the Son's subjectivity is shaped by the society he is attemping to transform. By making the shooting incident symbolically appropriate (in Freudian terms), historically necessary (in Marxist terms), and totally self-implicating (in humanist terms), the problem of correctly interpreting historical events is left open and urgent.

But Bond also remains oddly faithful to the present moment by suggesting that the desire for the father (or any historical account that depends on Freudian-based, psychological explanations) must itself be displaced if we are to escape the patriarchal aspects so clearly evident in the nascent capitalism of *Bingo*'s world. Thus the play ends not with the discussion between Shakespeare and the Son, but with the actions of Shakespeare's daughter Judith, desperately searching the room for a new will as her father lies dying on the floor. The moment is a profoundly disturbing one, and suggests that the social world of *Bingo* will go on according to its narrow set of principles, dehumanizing its members, and becoming our own. Indeed, in the figures of Combe, Ben Jonson, and Judith, economic greed and moral insensitivity have been carefully linked. But the most pitiable victims of the play are women. The beggar-woman is uprooted, beaten, and eventually hanged by the same law, and her death is a slow one. The severe beatings make her shake uncontrollably; the fires she sets are not rebellious, but the wretched result of previous punishment. The Old Woman survives, but loses both her husband and Son. Judith, the damaged product of her father's rejection, finds that nothing can rid her of the insecurity that his physical absence and emotional neglect have caused. And to what depths of misery and madness has Shakespeare's absent wife been reduced? Perhaps the most unnerving moments of the play are heard over Judith's pleas from the wings in the final scene. Bond's stage directions are explicit:

Outside the two women bang on the door. The crying is louder and wilder. Suddenly it becomes hysterical. The OLD WOMAN *gets up and slowly and methodically makes the bed.* (60)

The door is violently banged, kicked and shaken. Someone scratches it. Outside the OLD WOMAN *gasps and shrieks hysterically.* (61)

Throughout the scene Shakespeare remains unmoved, or faintly amused: "Thirty-five years. All like this" (61). The world is out of joint. Displaced to the margins of action in *Bingo*, the fates of these women are impossible to ignore; and through them, the play may most forcefully dramatize the need for social change – here, and now.

The Fool

In *Bingo, Scenes of Money and Death*, Bond contests the universal authority of Shakespeare's voice; in *The Fool, Scenes of Bread and Love*, he argues for John Clare's right to be heard. Written in sequence, the two plays share parallel subtitles, an historical topic, and an interest in writers that readily lends to their treatment as companion pieces.[17] More importantly, both plays are non-psychological in their approach, depending for their effect on the careful structuring of episodes; both assume a reciprocal relationship between the artist and society, made acutely visible against a period of historical transition; and both ground the differing subjective responses of individual characters in the material conditions that separate them. In neither play is the artist allowed to speak directly, through his art, to the audience of a later age – biographical rather than literary facts predominate. The problems besetting both Shakespeare and Clare, despite enormous differences in upbringing, temperament, material success, and literary reputation, are located in an historical moment when class tensions are particularly apparent and in economic interests that alternately enable and limit the vision of their work. By reminding their audiences that real history is imaginatively embodied and/or suppressed in works of art, both plays historicize issues facing the contemporary writer, offering an interpretation of history in which the artist plays a symptomatic role.

As a "history play," *The Fool* thus shares with *Bingo* broad similarities in theme, style, and use of historical material. But the historical material itself presents different problems for the playwright and assures a play unlike the one it follows. Enterprising and self-reliant, Shakespeare exploited the tastes of his audience to become a major, and well-paid, literary figure in his own lifetime; he owned stock in his theatre, invested in real estate, and died a gentleman. John Clare, on the other hand, was not so lucky. After a brief period of popularity with the fashionable London literati, the self-styled "peasant poet" was quickly dropped. Plagued by illness and unable to earn a living as an artist, he died impoverished and neglected in the Northampton lunatic asylum where he spent the last twenty-two years of his life. While Clare's reputation as a poet has varied over time, *The Fool* is not concerned with the relative merits of Clare's writing but with the conditions to which it was inseparably tied. In this, Bond's own treatment follows that of literary critics and historians since Clare's death in 1864.[18] Clare himself encouraged the connection in his letters, poems, and autobiographical writings, helping shape the myths through which his work became known to his own and to later generations. The story that generally emerges is of a rural, working-class poet driven mad by "accursed wealth" in its various guises: fickle friends and patrons, self-serving publishers, rapacious landowners, and the forces of the marketplace. For both characterization and incident, Bond could draw on Clare's own descriptions of Milton, Radstock, Mrs. Emmerson, Lamb, and even the local game-keepers; on Clare's record of escape from an asylum, an 80-mile trek home, and the hunger-induced hallucinations he experienced; and on letters that indicate

Clare's growing disillusionment with the good intentions of supposed admirers. Milton's unapproachability, Admiral Radstock's sailor-like bluntness, Mrs. Emmerson's tiresome sentimentality; the contrast between the parson's hypocrisy and the gypsy's truthfulness; Clare's obsessive attachment to his first love Mary; his despair over the Helpstone enclosures and the changes they inspired all find their source in Clare's own writing. Even the London boxing match and Clare's pugilistic hallucinations, perhaps the most "Bondian" images of the play, are not entirely original, but suggested by the published accounts of Clare's visitors.[19]

Although reviewers complained of a "cold" and "undramatic" treatment, the historical accuracy of Bond's depiction of Clare was not an issue.[20] Bond does use East Anglian dialect, with which he is more familiar, for his Northamptonshire characters; but for the unaccustomed ear of the audience, the dialect enhances rather than diminishes the sense of historical distance. Likewise, the Cambridge-shire food riots did not take place in Clare's own village, but the incidents based on them enable the play to cover, in eight remarkably condensed scenes, both the lifespan of the poet and the social climate of the age in which he lived. On the surface, at least, *The Fool* keeps linear chronology intact, following the trajectory of Clare's life as it is generally understood – from rural obscurity (Scenes One through Four) to literary fame (Scene Five), to relative neglect (Scene Six), and eventual madness (Scenes Seven and Eight). As with *Bingo*, *The Fool* works more powerfully for those familiar with the literary and social history of the protagonists.[21] But in the case of Clare, the facts themselves speak forcefully to the issues with which Bond is most concerned. In a discussion of the poet, Raymond Williams puts it this way: "Clare himself is a deeply significant figure, for in him there is not only the literary change but directly, in his person and his history, the inwardness of the social transformation [. . .] Clare marks the end of pastoral poetry, in the very shock of its collision with the actual country experience."[22] Precisely this notion of an historically and artistically representative life makes Bond's choice of subject appropriate to his goals.

Presenting an analysis of events that seems to arise from a straightforward dramatization of particular incidents from John Clare's life, *The Fool* resists the melodramatic, sentimental, or documentary treatment the subject might easily suggest. As in most of Bond's early plays, no individual or group of characters articulates the political thought of the play; and yet by the end, the political message seems virtually self-evident. The apparent simplicity in fact belies a carefully controlled, complex, and self-consciously structured play. As in *Bingo*, the perceptions of the characters, all observant in their way, are shaped by their historical moment, with the socio-economic laws governing their lives clearly visible to the audience of a later age. Strongly urged, on the one hand, to share the characters' subjective views of events and to empathize with their plight, *The Fool* simultaneously interprets and rejects their limited perspectives. Using the multi-focused stage and a studied sequencing of scenes, Bond forcefully wrests the focus and the point of view from the play's central character to avoid a psychologizing perspective, and make social analysis, rather than empathy, the final goal of the production. While the audience is led to interpret this historical moment in a particular light, to "read" the social transformation implicit in the concrete interactions between characters, and to make connections to present-day social issues yet unresolved, the analysis is "shown" rather than argued. Indeed, we are moved to accept the play's analysis of events precisely to the extent that we *need* it to make sense of them; by the end of the play, the social analysis and the counterpointed poetry of the play's staged incidents are virtually inseparable.

Like many of Bond's plays, *The Fool* falls into two distinct parts, with the relationship between the play's structure and politics most readily grasped in the connections between them.[23] As in *The Pope's Wedding*, the main character emerges slowly as the focus of interest. In Scenes One through Four, Clare is but one member of an entire rural community facing the break-up of their traditional way of life in the wake of nineteenth-century industrialization and the enclosure of common land. The class conflict, brought more clearly into view by the historical situation, is represented in the play's first half by the increasingly antagonistic relationship between Lord Milton, supported by the clergy and his own hired guns, and Darkie, who is hanged for his protest. One of few fictional characters in the play, Darkie not only represents those peasants most seriously affected by the enclosure, but a fate that Clare might easily have shared were it not for his artistic inclinations. Like the "dark figures" of later plays, Darkie's physical experience of class oppression counterpoints Clare's more enlightened perspective, providing a view of events that Clare alone will never adequately articulate. Offstage chasing

Mary when the Parson is humiliated by the rioting workers, Clare neither witnesses the event nor participates in the protest related to it. While historically accurate (neither Clare nor Patty took part in the Cambridgeshire food riots that resulted in the hangings at Ely), Clare's absence is crucial to Bond's narrative argument in other ways. Saved from the immediate consequences of the peasants' uprising and left free to pursue a literary career, the limits of Clare's vision remind the audience of his difference from the others, a difference for which he both is and is not responsible, a difference not always represented in the most positive light. By the end of Scene Four, an important connection has been established between Darkie, whose presence gradually dominates Part I, and Clare, who provides the focus of the play's second half.[24] With mental and physical labor equally (if not identically) affected by the relationship between landowner and laborer introduced in Scene One, Clare's cause as an artist comes to speak for that of the entire working class. Indeed, as the play progresses, Clare's scribbling is shown to be no less necessary to his health and survival than Darkie's own fieldwork; and, in linking the two characters, the distinction between labor and labor-value, between writing as a productive activity and art as a marketable commodity comes more clearly into view. Thus the objective social contradictions that Bond represents through Darkie's actions, and articulates most forcefully in the parson-stripping scene, are subjectively reinforced and developed through Clare's partial and belated understanding of those same contradictions later in the play.

The four condensed scenes of Part II trace the major turns of fortune in Clare's career: the early success that takes him to London, the difficulties that arise when his books don't sell, the temporary escape from Dr. Alen's sanitorium, and the final asylum secured by his somewhat bewildered former patron. Clare ends his life muttering "*in a bathchair, a shrivelled puppet*" (150), neither robbed of his life nor quite living it. Without narrowing the focus (more than fourteen new characters appear in the play's second half), the play gradually shifts in focus from the rural community to one of its members, from a communal perspective to an individual one, reflecting a change in the value system of Clare's society as it sets about its historical task of accumulating capital. Given the focus on working-class characters, the *Fool*'s particular blend of the social and the psychological may recall Bond's earliest plays – the subjective force of powerful stage images (murder, madness, suicide) preceded, framed, and ultimately contained by the careful detailing of social conditions, which grant to those images a realistic logic. By the end of the play, the audience shares Clare's feeling of powerlessness over events – the final scene a deeply moving one that captures, in its understated way, the pathos of Clare's story as it is generally told. Yet Clare's madness is grounded in the objective social conditions detailed in the play's first half; only after witnessing the harsher fate of others can the audience fully focus on Clare. The resulting critical viewpoint cuts another way: Clare is not only a poet, but a "fool," whose knowledge of the world comes too late. What *The Fool* provides that Bond's earliest plays do not is the class analysis of a broader, more distant, and more balanced social picture. Without denying Clare a central and sympathetic role, the wider social picture requires the viewer to make sense of Clare's individual fate in political, rather than psychological, terms.

In *The Fool*, the narration of events cannot easily be separated from their political analysis. The "prison" scenes that end both Parts (Scene Four and Eight), provide the most obvious example. Not only does the earlier scene, played in darkness against the sporadic and hysterical laughter of the unseen prisoners, foreshadow Clare's own end in the madhouse, but the calm and brightly lit sanitorium room, replete with chess-playing inmates and Dr. Skrimshire's straitjacket, seems as prison-like in atmosphere as Darkie's dimly lit cell. Even the pacing of the two scenes is similar, both involving a confrontation between victim and survivor that results in awkward silences and uneasiness among the characters. Clare in the final scene, confined to a wheelchair, his head nodding *"like a doll's"* (150), presents a stark visual contrast to the self-confident and jubilant youth of Part I, who, having escaped Darkie's fate by sheer luck, laughs happily during the visit. And yet the spectacle of the older survivor also incorporates the wisdom and point of view represented by Darkie's raw energy earlier in the play. A vision of human strength and unnecessary waste emerges in both portraits.

A similar contrast occurs between the real meeting between Clare and Mary in Scene Two and the hallucinated encounter of Scene Seven. When the formerly young and healthy couple meet again in the woods, not only is Clare dirty and starving, but his former love has degenerated into a cruel, coarse, raggedly dressed tramp. The Mary who openly and cheerfully gratifies the sexual appetite of the young Clare in Scene Two viciously rejects his later overtures: "Cut you open doo you bother me" (143). Likewise, the ever-hopeful, conciliatory Patty of Part I appears in Part II as a nagging, unreasonable wife. Such studied contrasts reinforce connections between the play's two parts; and at the very least, the audience is invited to "read" the scenes in light of each other. Not simply ironic, the contrasts give rise to questions as to the underlying causes of the situations depicted, the kind of justice revealed, and the appropriateness of the characters' responses. If abstracted from the contexts provided within each scene, the "falling" movement of the action as a whole might reinforce the Parson's own assessment of the human condition:

How small and impotent we are. We clear a few fields, build a few houses, twist a few rods of iron, and think our laws are everlasting. [...] Abandon this bitter hope. Hope! – it is a tide that goes in and out and grinds men together till they wear each other down. (111, 114)

But such a "unified" reading of the play's experience denies the logic of Bond's structural parallels. The Parson's despair is contextualized by his earlier confrontation with (and humiliation by) the peasants – a subjective reaction to objective social contradictions that cannot, within the constraints of his own beliefs and historical moment, be grasped by him in any other way. As with Clare's own visions near the end, *The Fool* manages to present the "psychological truth" of each character's point of view; but by grounding those perceptions in the concrete conditions of life dramatized onstage, the audience is granted a perspective from which to interpret the experience in ways the characters cannot.

With the subtle shift in focus from the community to Clare (from conditions to consequences) comes an increasing concern with Clare's own perception of events. Caught in the crossfire of conflicting demands, Clare is finally overwhelmed by events, his occasional glimpses of understanding distorted by the pressing immediacy of his situation. The plot structure, insofar as it is bound by Clare's biography, reinforces this apparently linear progression from youth to old age, health to sickness, virility to impotence, hope to despair. Clare's powerlessness (and not his alone) is further highlighted by a narrative in which the most important actions and decisions of the play, those that affect the course of history and individual plights, occur offstage. In Scene Two, men have already been hired to drain the fens and Mary has been sacked from her job; Clare's belated discovery of both events foreshadows the logic of action to follow. With Patty's worried maneuverings ("Wish I had a kid. We'd hev t'git wed then," 92) Bond suggests, as does Clare's autobiography, that Clare was manipulated in the matter of marriage. In Scene Six, the publisher's decision is revealed through a letter and an uninvited visit by Mrs. Emmerson. Unbeknownst to Clare, Patty has already given Lord Milton permission to commit Clare for treatment. Not only do the major turns in Clare's life seem dictated by others, but by Scene Seven, even Clare's fantasies are beyond his control. Mary and Darkie, expressionistically projected figures, turn on him with a vengeful and violent life of their own, at striking variance to both Clare's own memory and the ideal scenario he wishfully envisions for them.

Thus *The Fool* dramatizes the movement of history as it is lived by its characters – as belatedly grasped consequences of events initiated, and concluded, elsewhere. As scenes unfold, a pattern emerges that suggests the disruptive and threatening nature of the decisions being made, one that reinforces Clare's feeling of entrapment. Thus in Scene One, the villagers' festive occasion is appropriated by the Parson's lecture and Lord Milton's mood-puncturing comments in defense of the changes about to occur. In Scene Two, the urgency of Darkie's news (the fens are being drained) interrupts a discussion of marriage between Patty and Clare, the conversation that follows disrupted yet again by the appearance of Milton's newly hired game-keepers. These same game-keepers intrude upon the intimacy of Clare and Mary's rendezvous, forcing them into the bushes like the rutting animals to which they are compared. Lord Milton and his armed gentlemen interrupt and forcibly put down the peasants' uprising; and the Parson follows up with an unwelcome prison visit. While solemn, pessimistic comments may be a fitting prelude to Darkie's death sentence, they seem cruel and mean-spirited in the context of a family visit. In the opening scene of Part II, Clare's pleasant stroll in a London park is interrupted and punctuated by a brutal boxing match upstage. In Scene Six, Mrs. Emmerson, Lord Milton, the Parson, and finally Dr. Skrimshire himself descend upon Clare in his own backyard, physically separating him from his wife and home. Even the brief sanctuary Clare finds with the Irish workers in Scene Seven is quickly and forcefully dispersed by a vigilant game-keeper. The lack of freedom that characters directly and subjectively experience onstage is thus explained by the pattern of action through which it is recorded; the causes of suffering are located not in some immutable fate, but in the decisions and physical acts of the ruling class characters and their representatives.

Unlike Shakespeare in *Bingo*, also faced with the harsh consequences of historical change, Clare feels neither despair over the future nor much remorse about the past. Near the end of the play, Clare remembers giving away everything for Mary: "I had you once. Lived all my life off that. Always hev you in my head. [...] Good 'an bad. Never git tired. Never lose hope. Everything goo t'gither in you" (143). Without the accommodating nature that allows Patty to survive, nor the anger with which Darkie forces an issue, Clare simply gets silenced, reduced to the level of a kept animal. Although his condition provides adequate comment on the attitudes of his visitors at the end of the play, Bond bestows no dignity on the poet in the final scene. Rather Clare is represented as much a victim of his own "foolishness" as a man beaten by forces outside his control. Clare's obsession with Mary, an oft-cited symptom of John Clare's real mental breakdown, not only provides Clare with a life-sustaining illusion, but in Bond's play prevents the poet from attaining the class consciousness that Darkie and even Mary herself come to represent. Not only is Clare's vision limited, then, but it is limited in a particular way. Isolated from his origins by his poetic vocation, and from polite society by his origins, Clare's position as an outsider determines the very limits and possibilities of his art.[25]

Here Bond's continued fascination with Shakepeare provides an important, and related, gloss on the play's title. Bond takes up the figure of the Shakespearean fool, not as a romantic myth of the outcast, but as a way of historicizing the problem of the contemporary writer; and he reworks it in order to clarify the causes of Clare's limitations. As a poet, Clare shares the artistic function of Shakespeare's court-employed fools. Despite their biting wit, facility with language, and worldly wisdom, the criticism of clowns is emasculated by their economic dependence on patrons. Granted immunity from censure by virtue of their role, what fools say is unthreatening because, by social definition, untrue (foolish). Because the way in which society views the function of art invariably determines its effect (not to mention its worth), Bond avoids the use of Clare's own poetry in the play. In Clare's society, artistic activity is circumscribed by the tastes and attitudes of the paying public, and given such a situation, Clare's very role as a poet becomes a measure of his loss of freedom.

The precise nature of the relationship between patron and artist is brought out most clearly in Scene Five. Here Bond situates and comments upon Clare's poetic activity through the multiple contexts provided by Mrs. Emmerson's effusive support, Lord Radstock's impossible advice, Charles Lamb's drunken but perceptive comments ("in vino veritas"), Mary Lamb's madness, and the simultaneous presence of the boxing match upstage.[26] In retrospect, the differing perspectives of the characters provide more than irony. Through them, Bond visually dramatizes the objective relations between labor and capital (the fight), the contradictions of which are reproduced in the relation between artist and patron (Clare–Radstock), and the human consequences of which are presented in physical and mental suffering (the boxer's beaten body and Mary's deranged mind). Moreover, only the poet (Lamb) sees the truth in this scene, but the very language he uses prevents him from being understood (at least by Mrs. Emmerson), just as his poetic profession prevents him from being taken seriously. Lamb likes Clare's poetry because "Clare tells the truth. [. . .] truth isn't governed by the law of supply and demand" (121). The implicit comment is clear: in a society that *is* governed by those laws, the artist is lucky to be able to write at all. Lord Radstock is Clare's biggest backer, and as such, his relationship to Clare is sharply analogous to that between the boxers and the investors who financially back them. In both cases, the interests of the two parties are diametrically opposed, despite verbal assurances to the contrary. Lord Radstock likes poetry that reflects his own sentiments and refuses support for what might be construed as criticism of "polite society." Poems about the simple rural life, in the decades during which that life was disappearing, just as poems about unspoiled nature after a century of draining and reclaiming the land, find an enthusiastic audience.[27] Even Clare recognizes as much. When Patty earlier announces Clare's good luck to Darkie and the others, Miles asks: "What you write, boy? Write 'bout this place. What goo on." Clare answers, "Who'd read that?" (106). In view of what Clare might have written, the decision to cut the love poems to Mary has an almost comic logic, the political implications of which escape Clare himself. Radstock wants Clare to transplant Arcadia to Helpstone; but Clare can only write what he knows.

Acknowledging that the poet's creative vision is grounded in experience, Clare finds that his are not suitable for publication. "On't see no nymphs in our fields but I seen a workhouse" (126). Nor can he simply assume Lord Radstock's settled and conventional viewpoint. If Radstock's support must be purchased in this way, Clare's mental labor will in no way insure his physical survival. The same holds true for the physical labor of the boxers – the fourth backer extracts a profit from the defeated man he claims to be supporting, having bet on the other side. Clare is a fool for believing that his upper-class admirers have his best interests at heart, something he is forced to realize by the end of the next scene.

In the words of Lamb, only a wise man speaks the truth – "or another sort of fool" (121). Clare himself described this kind of fool in an essay "On Money Catching or Common Honesty":

if a man would live & be successful in life he is told not to be honest at all times or speak the truth at all times but he must act just as chances give him the oppertunity [*sic*] [. . .] but if ever he suffers his conscience or his honesty to stand in the way of his self-interest, he is considerd [*sic*] nothing but a fool & instead of merely praise will receive nothing but contempt for his pains.[28]

Clare's inability to cater prudently to his paying public (as opposed, perhaps, to his unwillingness to do so) leads finally to ruin. In Bond's play, such a notion of art is simply foreign to Clare's thinking. Fascinated with the images of his own future as they appear in the figure of the beaten boxer and Mary Lamb's madness, Clare's real situation provides the ground of his later identification with the fighter he falsely assumes got paid for his beating. While the scene itself traces the transformation of labor into commodities, Mary is voicing her neurotic dissatisfaction with the produce she has purchased: "They're going off before you can get them home. I complain to the shopkeepers – [. . .] The tomatoes were quite blue. You find dust everywhere" (122, 126). Mary has a houseful of food rotting on the floor, as if she were afraid of starving. The commodities provide no nourishment; as organized, her society can no more satisfy her hunger than it can Clare's. The actions of this scene not only demonstrate the socio-economic laws of Clare's world, but provide the concrete referents for Clare's madness in Scene Seven.

As the play progresses, Clare more closely resembles the court-banished fools of Shakespeare's plays. Such a fool invariably tells the truth, despite the metaphoric and elliptical language he speaks. At

one point, Patty accuses Clare of using language totally inappropriate to his situation, with the implication that if he thought
correctly he would speak differently:

On't talk so daft. Talk straight so a body can hev a proper conversation. If
you're on fire you goo up in smoke. [. . .] Limbs! Normal people hev arms
and legs. Chriss sake, talk like a man. On't comfortable with you in the
house. (132)

Patty's reaction shows how Clare's activity has isolated him from his
community, an isolation that may have prevented an accurate
depiction of that life in his verse. The community Clare represents
can neither read nor afford to buy his books; the public that
appreciates his artistic turns of phrase won't buy them. But the
language Clare speaks is also a measure of the developing self-
consciousness that allows him finally to understand and articulate
the problems he shares with the villagers. While the poetic images
that find their way into Clare's everyday speech confuse and irritate
Patty, those same images, arising as they do from Clare's actual
experiences, make literal and compelling sense to the audience.

In John Clare's own poetry, the description of natural scenes of
harvest and plenty gradually give way to darker poems, dotted with
images of famine, hunger, deprivation, and loss. Mary's absence
provides the theme and lament of most of his songs. In *The Fool* the
same holds true. Clare's obsession with Mary moves, for example,
from a real and sexually specific desire in Part I to the more general
and symbolic desire of Part II ("An' all those years my life was waste.
You on't there. On'y in my head," 143). By the end of the play, Clare
knows freedom, and with it health, happiness, and mental stability,
only through its absence, a perceived lack he fills with the image of a
lost love. While his search for Mary in Part I will separate him from
his friends and prevent the kind of class consciousness that Darkie
represents and the parson-stripping scene evokes, his search in Part II
will return him to that world as Mary and Darkie become conflated
in his mind. Images of hunger, starvation, physical suffering, and
loss provide the play's metaphoric force and concretely converge in
the expressionistically projected figure of Darkie in Scene Seven:

On't see too well. Tell the truth the boxin' give me a squint an' I goo blind.
Punch punch or summat – knock all the sight out my head. [. . .] Need all
my strength t'crack their heads. On't eat. No grub for years. Sit here an' try
t'forgit. But the cravin goo on. [. . .] I'm hungry an' I can't swallow. [. . .]

Summat in my neck. Summat goo crosst or thass a twist. Can't eat [...] It hurt. It hurt. (68, 69–70)

Despite the symbolic and thematic resonance, such images are grounded in the real hunger and physical pain faced by the characters. With the material conditions shaping Clare's consciousness so carefully detailed, the audience can read the play's political comment through the same images and distortions that illustrate Clare's insanity.

The essentially biographical and subjective structure described above coincides in *The Fool* with the objective presentation of an entire community whose individual members represent the increasingly contradictory interests of a society based on class – and their responses differ, even within the same economic group. Only in light of the failure, limited success, and alternate perspectives of others do the force and perimeters of Clare's own vision come clearly into view. Like Clare, most of the characters experience the stable, semi-feudal community of their youth as a natural and familial one, even when the changing economy forces class tensions into view. Yet only Darkie seems to understand the implications of Lord Milton's decision to enclose – as a theft of common land that had provided them for generations a minimal but independent living. Darkie's extreme poverty not only isolates him from the traditional institutions of his community, but allows him to see through the pretenses of the ruling class and to challenge them directly. In Scene One, his legitimate protest provokes a patronizing response from the Parson that highlights the unspoken alliance between the church, the landowners, and the state: "Our rulers guide our affairs in such a way that each of us reaps the best possible reward for his labours. Without their guidance – though you might not understand it – there'd be chaos" (88–89).

When the verbal confrontation of Scene One becomes the physical confrontation of Scene Three, Darkie and those with him discover the falseness of the Parson's position. Through their spontaneous uprising they not only voice discontent with worsening conditions, but learn a lesson in class consciousness when they uncover and touch the soft, "stolen flesh" of the Parson's shivering body. The carefully choreographed moment is emotionally compelling and potentially violent, but the "aggro-effect" is muted by the slowed tempo and reflective dialogue of the characters who briefly distinguish themselves from a mere rioting mob. Indeed, the Parson's humiliation takes place within the (less disturbing?) view of the wounded Lawrence, bleeding and whimpering throughout the scene. Appropriately, Darkie comes to understand the real economic relations of his community through a confrontation with its ideological representative. As Milton's symbolic substitute, the Parson remains impotent without the economic force provided by Lord Milton's position – something the workers discover when they overcome their religious awe. By the time Lord Milton arrives to quell the disturbance, he finds his mere presence no longer commands the same unquestioned obedience. Darkie openly defies the patriarchal authority who not only controls the community's livelihood, but would legislate its values as well:

You steal from us. Parson steal from us. What we doo t'parson? Make a mock. Took – what? Trinkets! When I steal from parson what you doo t'me? Law hang us. Thass the on'y difference 'tween you an' me: you on't think twice 'fore you use violence. (107)

In the face of such open rebellion, Lord Milton must back his fatherly disapproval with the gentlemen's guns; and in retrospect, the armed violence surrounding the arrests may provide a more disturbing image to the audience than the stripping of the Parson that precedes it.

In *Bingo*, the Son expresses the need for radical change by rejecting the play's father-figures, and against his activity Shakespeare's particular limitations take shape. In *The Fool*, Darkie plays a similar role; in his rejection of Lord Milton, the line between victim and enemy is most clearly drawn. And Clare's own attitude appears less sympathetic in view of Darkie's energetic responses in Part I. At this particular moment in history, remaining aloof from one's community can be read as lack of solidarity, even betrayal. Clare doesn't refuse to participate in the food riot: he is not sufficiently aware of what is going on to do so. In prison, Darkie encourages Clare's writing, offers him his coat, and asks him to take good care of his sister Patty. Clare, on the other hand, laughs at moments that seem entirely inappropriate and inquires about Mary. Their meeting ends uneasily, with a sense of misunderstanding between them (110–112). Darkie's trust may indeed be misplaced, and the audience's sympathy with Clare is in part measured by Clare's increasing identification with Darkie. But the understanding that allows Clare to say, in Scene Six, "Her dead brother Darkie know"

(138) comes too late. When Clare finally defies Lord Milton in his own incarceration scene, the verbal confrontation quickly turns physical: "*MILTON grabs at CLARE and finds himself pinioning him with his arms. There is a shocked silence. MILTON stops in surprise and lets CLARE go*"(140); and with "*sudden anger*" bids the Keeper to tie him up. The parallel to earlier arrests is difficult to overlook.

Throughout the play, material conditions seem to change faster than individual psychologies, which helps explain the confusion Lord Milton expresses both here and later in the play. As the patriarchal head of the feudal community (in the words of Bond's stage direction, "*a giant,*" 2), Milton's formidable presence alone is enough to make Patty "goo all hot" when she looks at him. As a willing father-figure, he treats the workers like children, kindly condescending until his patience is strained. At the end of the play he confides in Clare (thinking, perhaps, he cannot be heard) with nostalgia for a past very different from the one Clare might remember:

D'you remember us? Seeing you brings it back. The afternoon in your garden. So long ago. Another world. The estate went to church every Sunday. I sat in front in my high pew. The parson read the story of the centurion. The man with authority. [...] *You* had some books out too. Time to write here? No. It's changed. The village is there. But new houses. [...] I hate my son. A vicious bastard. I was cruel sometimes. Foolish. But did I hate? No. Never a hater. [...] It's changed. D'you know who I am? (151)

The industrial age Milton has helped usher in has already crushed Clare; and a society obeying the laws of production and money can look forward to a corrosion of personal relationships like that evidenced between Milton and his son. Like Patty, Lord Milton knows things have changed but does not see clearly his own role in it. As the public land became privately owned, Milton has been forced to arm himself against the very people he sought to protect, and he can no more escape the destructive consequences of that economic change than those he victimizes. The end result is a feeling of shame, guilt, and incomprehension – a sympathetic portrait which does nothing, however, to exempt him from responsibility.

Patty, on the other hand, functions as Lord Milton's maternal counterpart, and it is not by accident they appear together in the final scene. Although her interests and his are diametrically opposed, she continues to share the traditional values that once bound their familial community, despite the devastating changes she witnesses. Her optimistic counsel in the opening scene ("Sit yourself up, boy, an' look on the bright side. No crack heads yit," 89) proves typical of a sheer will to survive, and she does so by avoiding conflict and settling rows. But her common-sense outlook prevents her from adequately conceptualizing from her experience; like Brecht's *Mother Courage*, she survives, but her "children" do not. In fact, Bond tones down the sheer weight of Patty's oppressive circumstances by reducing the number of children mentioned in the play – perhaps the seven she and Clare had might have strained belief. More likely, the change insures that Patty's character be neither pitied nor perceived as the play's moral center. Like Clare, she too misses the rioting workers' action in Scene Three, along with its political lesson. Although her mistrust of Mrs. Emmerson provides one measure of her social awareness, she remains in thrall to the fear and respect that the lord of the manor has always inspired.

Patty cannot help but see Clare's actions in terms of an individuality at odds with the interests of the larger community – her complaint ("Tired a all this self," 132) the same that the upper-class characters would levy against him. Yet in *The Fool*, only the characters sufficiently isolated from the community can represent in broader terms the individual needs for which their community cannot provide. In this regard, Mary, the most unabashedly selfish character in the play, plays an important role. In actual fact, what prevented a relationship from developing between John Clare and the Mary he met at school was her father's disapproval and her own higher economic class. In *The Fool*, Mary is introduced as a servant of the manor, an energetic, sensual, and independent woman more than able to look out for her own interests and feeling little solidarity with her class, even after she loses her job. In the parson-stripping scene, she carts off the pickings without stopping with the others to discover the meaning of their actions. She scoffs at Patty's desire for respectable marriage, is sexually uninhibited, both able and willing to fend for herself with the gypsies. Undoubtedly suggested by Clare's autobiographical writings, Mary's connection to gypsies provides an illuminating transformation of her real-life status. Although perceived as outcasts and thieves by the larger community, gypsies held a continued fascination for Clare, embodying for him the qualities of independence and freedom from social constraints he felt so lacking in his own life. For both the audience and the other characters in the play, Mary is a marginal and unproductive element of society. But when Clare reads in her his own lost independence, and comes to see her loss as inseparable from Darkie's fate and his own, our viewpoint changes.

In Scene Seven, Clare identifies himself with Darkie – a blind, beaten boxer who is starving but cannot swallow, who cannot remember his past, and who goes off in the end with Mary. However "mad" Clare's dream, the viewers see in his vision the real experiences that are here transmuted into subjective terms:

I dreamt I saw bread spat on the ground, and her say: Waste, I risk my life! (Shakes his head) No. Bread on't waste. Thass on'y seed so you threw it on the ground. Birds hev it. Or that soak away. Bread goo from mouth t'mouth an' what it taste of: other mouths. Talkin' an' laughin'. Thinkin' people. I wandered round an' round. Where to? Here. An' a blind man git here before me. The blind goo in a straight line. We should hev come t'gither. She git the bread. He crack the heads when they come after us. An' I – I'ld hev teach him how to eat. I am a poet an' teach men how to eat. Then she on't goo in rags. He on't blind. An' I – on't goo mad in a madhouse. (73)

With the elliptical, colloquial, non-symbolic poetry of Clare's most "foolish" speech, we return to the problem of the modern artist, who, in order to "tell the truth" and speak for a rational society that does not yet exist, must resist the conventional artistic discourse of his own historical time. At this moment, perhaps, Clare comes closest to speaking for Bond than anywhere else in the play, articulating (however obliquely) the play's "truth." As isolated figures, these three characters – Mary, Darkie, and Clare – are incapable of effecting the changes required by their own society, but their very isolation impresses on the audience the need for change. Thus through the community's outcasts, Bond monitors the destructiveness of this society's economic organization – its inability to provide a fully human, nourishing existence for any of its members. By providing a structure that so fully illuminates the causes of these characters' suffering, a structure that allows us to "read" Clare's speech as more than the meaningless words of a fool, Bond transforms his history play into a vision for his own time – and a warning to those who would not measure "progress" in primarily human terms.

CHAPTER 4

Rewriting classics

Like *Bingo* and *The Fool, Lear* (1971) and *The Woman* (1978) explore the relationship of the individual to history, but do so within the context of a specific literary form – tragedy – and a general literary practice – adaptation. As adaptations, *Lear* and *The Woman* engage history in a recognizably "literary" fashion, self-consciously intervening in the formation of cultural myths. So many dramatists mine classical literature for material that distinctions between original plays and adaptations often seem absurd. But in the twentieth century, self-conscious use of the classics has engendered a strain of plays that might usefully be identified as "theatre of quotation." George Bernard Shaw, Friedrich Dürrenmatt, Eugène Ionesco, Tom Stoppard, Bertolt Brecht, and Heiner Müller have all written updated transformations of Shakespearean plots. Jean-Paul Sartre, Jean Giraudoux, Jean Cocteau, and Jean Anouilh are perhaps best known for their use of classical Greek material. But not one of them claims to write tragedy. With their modernized settings, interpolated scenes, new characters, modern psychological motivation, and/or altered philosophical perspective, contemporary adaptations either celebrate the "death of tragedy" or self-consciously acknowledge their reduced scope of vision. In most cases, both the humor of the plays and their intellectual force depend upon knowledge of the original, the adaptation sustaining its source text in symbiotic relationship through parody and allusion. Should *Hamlet* disappear from our cultural repertoire, the peculiar power of *Rosencrantz and Guildenstern Are Dead* would go with it. Likewise, the intellectual brilliance and polemical depth of Sartre's *The Flies* or Giraudoux's *The Trojan War Will Not Take Place* would be lost without knowledge of the classical material they re-work.

The principles of adaptation governing Bond's use of a classical counter-text are quite different. Both *Lear* and *The Woman* invite comparison with their sources, calling forth the contexts within which they are understood and judged; but Bond reverses our expectations with the ambitiousness of his "classical" projects. Unlike his contemporaries, Bond competes with Shakespeare and the Greeks on their own terms to write tragedies of comparable vision for his own century. While others are engaged in "theatre of quotation," usually in a tragi-comic mode, Bond seeks a more profound imitation of his tragic sources – and in doing so, elevates rather than diminishes the tragic stature of his plays. Not surprisingly, the unspoken charge of presumptuousness tempers both positive and negative responses to Bond's project, reinforced no doubt by Bond's own comments on the subject.[1] Such charges may indeed strike the mark, for Bond's argument is not with Shakespeare, and far less with Euripides, but rather with the agencies and institutions that determine (through classroom, performance, or publication) their cultural value. In both *Lear* and *The Woman*, Bond contests the "ownership" of a hallowed stage, the use to which our literary heritage is put, and most importantly, the right to speak for a position not generally associated with a classical education. In so doing, he reconstructs a genre, restoring to tragedy the power and resonance of its broadly humanistic questions, its communal voice, and its social function. Understanding the process through which Bond legitimizes his own class-informed perspective should help to explain the kind of resentment and misunderstanding these plays engender in particular audiences.

Given the nature of the project, Bond's *Lear* paves the way for the writing of *The Woman*, while the latter addresses and further clarifies issues introduced in the earlier text. In retrospect, it is easy to see that Lear more closely resembles Hecuba than any of the protagonists of Bond's earlier plays. And in *Lear*, Bond reworks certain tragic conventions to suggest a vision of history *The Woman* more forcefully elaborates. As tragedies, both share an interest in the nature of human justice and in the causes and consequences of intense human suffering; and both provide larger-than-life characters who gain some insight through the course of the play. Although *Lear* and *The Woman* share broad similarities in subject-matter, structure, and political implication, their adaptive strategies are not identical. Separated by seven years, the two plays come at different stages of Bond's career and development as an artist. In simplest terms, Bond sees *Lear* as a "problem play," and *The Woman* as "an answer play."[2]

But if both stand as formidable and significant works in their own right, it is due to the particular ways in which they use and transform their very different source material. Tracing Bond's adaptive practice through two plays that speak in such different voices for such similar ends should not only clarify their relationship to each other, but also contribute to a discussion of the adaptive and creative strategies of Bond's more recent work.

Lear

Bond's fascination with Shakespeare has been duly noted by critics and reviewers of his work, but the attraction is not simply idiosyncratic. Shakespeare fathers a literary tradition, dominates the British repertory, and is underwritten by richly funded theatres and a thriving tourist industry. As such, he is a figure Bond can neither dismiss nor wholeheartedly accept. To write a new *Lear* is to assert an important claim for contemporary playwrights over the center stages of their own culture. On the other hand, Shakespeare's cultural authority, socially constructed and historically bound, seems ripe for deconstruction. For this purpose, Shakespeare's texts cannot be entirely disengaged from the interpretive practices, theatrical or literary, that mediate and inform their reception. While Bond's *The Pope's Wedding* was getting scant notice at the Royal Court, Peter Brook was moving his "revolutionary" production of *King Lear* from Stratford to London amid rave reviews.[3] Leaning heavily on Jan Kott's existential interpretation of the play, Brook's production reclaimed Shakespeare's text for a post-Holocaust age by highlighting (often grotesquely) its bleakest, most Beckettian aspects.[4] Focusing on Shakespeare's anatomy of a cruel and indifferent universe and on inexplicable suffering at the hands of some inexorable "mechanism" beyond human control, Brook's production self-consciously disputed traditional approaches to the play, especially those finding evidence in *King Lear* of a poetic justice that exalts the Christian or Stoic virtues of humility, patience, love, and the acceptance of suffering.[5] For Bond's purposes, both modern and traditional camps treat Shakespeare's most pessimistic tragedy with enough reverence to discourage social criticism. The popularity of the Brook production also suggested a public ready to embrace its nihilistic worldview. While the "vision" of the two approaches may radically differ, Bond's comment in a program note to *Lear* applies to both:

Shakespeare's *Lear* is usually seen as an image of high, academic culture. The play is seen as a sublime action and the audience are expected to show the depth of their culture by the extent to which they penetrate its mysteries ... But the social moral of Shakespeare's *Lear* is this: endure till in time the world will be made right. That's a dangerous moral for us. We have less time than Shakespeare. Time is running out.[6]

Without denying the extremity of the play's suffering or its startling applicability to our own age, Bond suggests in his rewritten version of *King Lear* that more can be learned from history and literature than the lessons of survival. While potentially as pessimistic as Shakespeare's play, *Lear* prevents the audience from uncritically accepting its action as tragically inevitable, sublimely beautiful, or representative of an unalterable human condition.

Lear's close connection to its Shakespearean source does have certain consequences. *Lear* remains, for example, the most self-consciously metaphoric of Bond's plays to date, the most unrelentingly bleak in vision, and the most dependent (despite the extensive cast) upon a single central figure. But the areas of weaknesses for which the play has been faulted – the metaphoric language, violent imagery, unwieldy structure, and pessimistic mood – all directly relate to Bond's use and transformation of Shakespearean precedents. Although the meaning of *Lear* in no way depends on specific literary references, its allusive texture unavoidably invites comparison.[7] In fact, one could argue that Bond is most himself in this play when he is most like Shakespeare. Again, the problem lies in comparing Bond's version to Shakespeare's play, as opposed to the conceptions of tragedy which mediate it. The audience's attitude towards Bond's project will ultimately be affected by their knowledge of dramatic conventions, the depth of their familiarity with Shakespeare, and the cultural values they bring into the theatre. Bond's "adaptations" usually work on at least two levels: restoring a social function to the source text by a version that critically "rereads" it, and offering a new narrative with strictly contemporary relevance. Thus the Royal Shakespeare Company's decision to stage Bond's *Lear* concurrently with Shakespeare's *King Lear* for the 1982 season surely affected the audience's understanding of both.[8]

Because *Lear*'s aesthetic complexity involves the interdependence of these two levels, Bond's distinctive strategies can best be seen in the use he makes of Shakespearean incidents, language, character, and structure.

The reasons for which *King Lear* is now regarded as significantly relevant to the modern condition are the same that made it, until the turn of the century, one of Shakespeare's least-performed and most-criticized plays. But Bond's recontextualization of *King Lear*'s un-mitigating pessimism involves, in both incident and thoroughness, an equally appalling vision of the human potential for cruelty. On one level, *Lear*'s plot moves fairly methodically from one act of cruelty to another. Opening with the accidental death of a wall-worker, the first scene builds to Lear's summary execution of the man he finds responsible for such an act of "political sabotage." Lear's daughters use the incident as an excuse for defection, and by Scene Two open war has been declared. In the following scenes Bond traces, with grotesquely comic overtones, the perverted lusts and cruelty of Bodice and Fontanelle as they engage in their wartime machinations, including the brutal torture of Warrington. Act I ends with the disruption of Lear's pastoral refuge by marauding soldiers – the Gravedigger's Son is murdered, his pregnant wife raped, and the rapist in turn is shot by the Carpenter. Act II opens with the psychological torture of Lear's "mock trial" and ends with the physical torture of his blinding. Between these moments the daughters are captured and put to death by Cordelia's new regime, an unknown soldier dies in a field, and an onstage autopsy is coldly performed on the body of Fontanelle. Act III is less violent, but offstage the boy's ghost is gored to a second death by his own pigs, and the play ends with yet another rifle shot as Lear is killed at the wall. While new governments with new goals come to power, the forms of oppression appear to remain the same; and viewed by itself, this steady accumulation of incidents suggests a society trapped in a pattern of increasingly aggressive behavior.

Much has been written of Bond's use of violence, but the precise nature of Bond's debt to Shakespeare here is rarely acknowledged.[9] Whatever approach critics take to *King Lear*, the point of their arguments rests on the meaning assigned to Lear's suffering, the extremity of which is undeniable. We are familiar with *King Lear*'s moments of physical cruelty and psychological violence, but as Caroline Spurgeon has pointed out, Shakespeare presents Lear's suffering most forcefully through the language itself. In a study of Shakespearean imagery, she notes:

In the play we are conscious all through of the atmosphere of buffeting, strain and strife, and at moments, of bodily tensions to the point of agony [...] kept constantly before us chiefly by means of the verbs used, but also in metaphor, of a human body in anguished movement, tugged, wrenched, beaten, pierced, stung, scourged, dislocated, flayed, gashed, scalded, tortured, and finally broken on a rack.[10]

The violent incidents of *Lear* provide one example of Bond's tendency to literalize (or concretize) motifs suggested by Shakespeare's imagery. Thus the physical torment metaphorically indicated in *King Lear* is represented in Bond's version by the exaggerated physical brutality of much of the action. Shakespeare's cracks of thunder, for example, become rifle shots as the natural storm metaphor is recast onto the social plane of modern warfare; King Lear's complaint that his daughters have created an "engine beating at my head," wrenching and torturing the mind, becomes an actual instrument of torture that blinds its victim by wrenching out the eyes; King Lear's desire to "anatomize" the soul of Regan becomes an actual autopsy; the unseen "army of France" becomes Cordelia's successful guerrilla forces. What separates Bond from Shakespeare on the question of the representation of violence is this constant move from the metaphoric to the literal, from the verbal gesture to the concrete action, from symbolic to physical reality – a movement central to the materialist poetic of Bond's plays as well as to their didactic function.

Lear's violence is motivated not by a desire to "revitalize" the original, but a desire to change its effect – to reinterpret the meaning of Lear's suffering. In order to do so, the violent sections of the play are carefully choreographed to produce a complex sequence of impressions. In this particular play, Bond's "aggro-effects" are akin to terrorist tactics, depend upon a certain amount of shock, and play upon the audience's socially conditioned fears. Unlike the aim of Aristotelian "pity and fear," the ultimate effect of these violent moments is not cathartic, but deliberately unsettling. One of the clearest examples is the unnerving sound of rifle shot that accompanies the opening execution, the murder of the Gravedigger's Son, the wounded soldier's last words, the two daughters' deaths, and the play's final moments. During rehearsals of *Lear* for the Royal Court production, Bond accurately described the effect of the play's authentic firearms:

The anachronisms are for the horrible moments in a dream when you know it's a dream but can't help being afraid. The anachronisms must increase and not lessen the seriousness. They are like a debt to be paid [. . .] not careless or frivolous touches – they are like desperate facts.[11]

Avoiding the playwright's prerogative to present a purely symbolic, self-contained world of illusion, Bond creates a nightmarish quality by this naturalistic insistence on the reality of the onstage action. The crude, colloquial joking that accompanies the rape of Cordelia and the "scientific" instrument of torture that blinds Lear are anachronistic touches which produce similarly disturbing effects. Ultimately, such violent moments should initiate the audience's process of education by providing the shock to the sensibilities that under any other circumstances would dictate a radical change in behavior.

So successful at provoking a reaction from his audience, Bond has occasionally been accused of belaboring his violent scenes with loving detail. For modern audiences, accustomed to stylized stage violence, the torture of Warrington and the blinding of Lear may indeed seem protracted. In contrast to the daughters' particular brand of cruelty, the soldiers' destruction of the Gravedigger's Son's home is clipped and methodical, but similarly unhurried. In both cases, the effect depends not so much on surprise as on the deliberate nature of the representation as Bond calls upon his audience to "witness" and "suffer" the full force of the characters' actions. On one level, the point is quite simple: one must *feel* the urgently unacceptable nature of events before desiring to change them. Sickness is felt before seeking a cure; the experience of discomfort works like a catalyst. Thus the audience, like Lear himself, should begin to search for some understanding of events, some analysis, that would relieve the suffering that empathetic identification produces. The anachronistic quality of the play's violence functions most decisively to focus the direction of that analysis. An audience whose recent history includes the Holocaust, the arms race, third world military actions, and the building (and since, dismantling) of the Berlin Wall cannot easily avoid the allusive resonance of Bond's play. The anachronisms of Bond's most violent scenes provide the social and historical references by which a post-World War II audience recognizes the situations as their own.

Perhaps the most important difference between Shakespeare's *King Lear* and Bond's *Lear* lies not in the events of the play, but in the reworking of Shakespearean language and imagery. As Ruby Cohn has noted, Bond manages to retain a certain Shakespearean texture by incorporating Shakespeare's grand metaphors and recycling many recognizably tragic themes and patterns of imagery – blindness and insight, madness and sanity, suffering and negation most notable among them.[12] However, Shakespeare creates a symbolic world that involves a constant shift in our perceptions away from a material reality to a spiritual one, from the concrete to the cosmic, from a particular landscape to a universal one. Although it is tempting to see Bond's use of metaphor in similar terms, his poetic strategy is not the same. As noted above, Bond tends to concretize certain Shakespearean motifs, to flesh out Shakespeare's metaphors with the literal incidents they inspire (Fontanelle's autopsy, Lear's mock trial, the blinding), and with stark, visual stage images (the wall, the prison, the onstage murders, the ghost). Some parallels are clearer than others: for example, the replacement of King Lear's foolish division of his kingdom with Lear's equally foolish wall-building project – the wall itself a grim, physical reminder of the connections between irrational public policy and social injustice. But even King Lear's map becomes an important stage prop in *Lear*. The government aides need it in Scene One to reconfirm the obvious ('Isn't it a swamp on this map?" 16), Bodice directs her war from it ("the map's my straitjacket," 62), and the soldiers get lost with it ("Useless bloody map!" 63). More than a humorous touch, the use of the map concretizes an entire set of social conflicts, reinforcing the territorial nature of the war and joining a series of images that highlight the contrast between the land as a natural habitat, an open living space, and the land as a wasted, unfarmed battleground.[13]

Bond reclaims Shakespeare's animal imagery for similar purposes. In *King Lear*, the images of tigers, wolves, vultures, and serpents emphasize the unnatural evil of Goneril and Regan; and the line, "unaccommodated man is no more but such a poor, bare, forked animal as thou art" (*King Lear*, III, iv, 109–110), accompanies Lear's awareness of his own mortality. As many have recognized, Lear's development is likewise accompanied by a change and expansion of the animal imagery. In Scene One, he refers to his people as cattle and sheep; but after defeat he refers to himself as a caged and broken animal. Lear's discovery of culpability comes as

he witnesses his daughter's autopsy: "She sleeps inside like a lion and
a lamb and a child . . . Did I make this – and destroy it?" (73). In
Act III, references to "an owl on the hill" (96) and the cunning fox
illuminate changes in Lear's response to previous events. Through
the animal imagery, Bond sets up an entire biological register which
constantly refers us back to the body as the location of goodness,
beauty, health, and pre-lapsarian innocence – with a reverence that
displaces the Christian concept of soul and spirit housed in the fallen
flesh. In fact, Bond's poetic materialism extends beyond Lear's
language to include a whole range of feelings, states of consciousness,
and human gestures (of kindness or cruelty) that are physically
represented through visual stage imagery. We *see* the boy's offer of
bread to an old man, Lear's whitened and bloodied hair, the ghost's
shrivelled and disintegrating body, Cordelia and then Susan's
pregnant figures, the rebel soldier abandoned to die in a field; we
hear the sound of rifle shot and of muted crying. The human values of
Bond's play are thus firmly rooted in the consciousness of an
ecological order which is not naturally corrupt, but has been abused
and violated.

The associative resonances of Bond's imagery force us to consider
whether Bond's use of a biological register is a way of extricating
himself from concrete social analysis, of obscuring the fundamental
social issues of the play in a literarily familiar manner. To the contrary, the vocabulary of Bond's preface suggests that he mobilizes the
Shakespearean imagery to counter specific and prevalent theories
of society based on human biological nature. The 1963 London
symposium entitled "The Natural History of Aggression," followed
closely by Robert Ardrey's widely celebrated book *The Territorial
Imperative*[14] provides but one example of the popularization of
controversial theories concerning the relation between human and
animal behavior. The debated issue was not whether, but how, the
violence and aggressiveness of contemporary society could be
explained as a consequence of an evolutionary and instinctual
heritage. The implied premise would discredit socialist theories that
locate the causes of violence in the socio-economic structures of
capitalist society. Although never directly mentioned by Bond, such
a debate undoubtedly lies behind his argument against "innate
aggression" in the otherwise self-explanatory preface to the play;
and it may equally illuminate Bond's metaphoric strategy in *Lear*.
Thus Bond's use of metaphor does not universalize a problem nor

evade rational argument, but rather addresses a particular ideological stance he finds dangerous and increasingly widespread. Just
as Bond's metaphors of madness carry specific social connotations
since the popularization of R. D. Laing's work in psychology, so the
biological metaphors add political resonance to Lear's development.

As in many of Bond's plays, the most image-laden language of the
play is offered by a figure whose development is foregrounded by
changes in speech – the highly subjective moments of poetic revelation indicating the limits as well as the depth of a character's new
insight. But Lear provides a rare example of a Bondian character
who moves the full circle from oppressor to victim to militant hero, a
movement that accounts in part for the linguistic range of his
dialogue. As in Shakespeare, the shifts in Lear's language correspond
to his abrupt change of circumstances and mark the stages of his
mental development. Throughout the first two scenes, Lear wields a
language of power that his daughters learn well. Like King Lear in
the early scenes of Shakespeare's play, Lear is dogmatic, assertive,
inflexible, and uncompromising; he speaks most often in the imperative voice and his questions (to officers and family alike) are
rhetorical ones. In Bond's play, the lucid tones of command quickly
give way to the elliptical speech of madness. In the last few scenes of
Act I, Lear's self-consciously metaphoric language indicates the
mental confusion caused by his military defeat and reflects no more
than a weary state of unenlightened self-pity. As we might expect,
Lear's obsession with his daughters' cruelty here predominates,
erupting at different points in the scene:

No daughters! Where he lives the rain can't be wet or the wind cold, and
the holes cry out when you're going to tread in them [. . .] The mouse comes
out of its hole and stares. The giant wants to eat the dragon, but the dragon
has grabbed the carving knife. [. . .] My daughters turned a dog out of its
kennel because it got fond of its sack. (32–34)

However uncalculated, such riddles also conceal Lear's identity, and
since no one can understand what he says, Lear facilitates the very
offer of assistance that will imperil his benefactors. While the
audience may understand the death of Warrington, the murder of
the Gravedigger's Son, and the rape of Cordelia as the catastrophic
consequences of Lear's own actions, Lear does not. By the end of Act
I, Lear's tormented self-pity has been established as the flip-side of
his former arrogance: his expressed regrets seem superficial and

escapist, his suggestion that Cordelia leave insensitive, his unrecognized responsibility for the soldier's brutality ironically underscored by his own raving words, "You've murdered the husband, slaughtered the cattle, poisoned the well, raped the mother, killed the child – you must burn the house! [etc.]" (44–45).[15]

Much of Act II traces Lear's gradual movement from madness to sanity, with Bond's metaphor of a caged animal replacing Shakespeare's storm as the controlling image of Lear's mental landscape. Here Lear's speeches are the most emotional and elaborately metaphoric of the play – privileged moments of perception as painful as the physical torture he endures. Like Ismene, Clare, and Trench of later plays, Lear's insights are a function of his status as both prisoner and madman. Freed from the former constraints of his social position, relieved of his "duty," and isolated from the march of historical events, Lear is an outsider to the play's given social order. But as victim and witness of that order, he is granted a perspective which corrects the limited perspectives of other characters. Because he sees more clearly than they, he ultimately becomes a spokesman for change. By the end of Act II, Lear has perhaps learned the lessons of compassion, humility, and personal culpability. But such wisdom, and the resolve that accompanies it, is neither sufficient nor redemptive – nor does it lead automatically to moral action. In Bond's later plays, the characters' process of moral development more clearly involves the aquisition of a "class consciousness," one that results from careful social analysis and radically qualifies the metaphorical insights of such characters as Shakespeare in *Bingo* and Trench in *The Worlds*. While Lear's education is more limited, his knowledge does grow beyond the highly personal and metaphorical insights of Act II to demand active rather than passive, real rather than symbolic, action against the society he helped create.

In Act III, the circuitous path to Lear's final gesture is traced by a similar progression in Lear's language, from the slightly arrogant parables of an old man, to the temper-tantrums of a frustrated child, to quiet images of dignified emotion, to rational arguments for social change. With each speech pattern, the audience is referred back to earlier moments to better measure the distance Lear has come. The stark, stylized emotion of Lear's epitaph ("I see my life, a black tree by a pool. The branches are covered with tears [...]," 100) provides sharp contrast to the self-indulgent rhetoric of earlier scenes; the narrative folk parables (88–89) elaborate and develop the poetic revelations of the prison cell; the self-knowledge generating Lear's frustration appears more sympathetic than earlier moments of self-righteous anger; and the persuasive lucidity of Lear's final speeches with Cordelia carries an authority absent from the flawed reasoning of his opening remarks.

Bond's use of Shakespearean imagery is clearest in Lear's speeches, but to invite a comparison between *Lear*'s language and *King Lear*'s is inevitably to highlight differences, not only in the historical moment that separates them, but in the very conception of character that they reveal. Bond writes in the preface to *Lear* that the seventy speaking parts are designed to show "the character of society," and in this regard, Bond's social picture is at least as broad as Shakespeare's own. But charges of lopsided character development and "unbelievable" characters are related to the Shakespearean precedents Bond evokes most blatantly in his use of language. In contrast to the subtextual depth we expect to find in Shakespeare, the characters of *Lear* reveal their thoughts in a direct, startlingly blunt manner. What might be mistaken for lack of poetic talent, however, is more probably due to the differing definitions of the relationship between self and society that govern the two works. Whether comic, ironic, contradictory, or extreme, the speech of Bond's characters can never be adequately explained through subtextual nuance, but is in every case a response to the pressures of social situations literally depicted onstage. Thus Bond's dialogue constantly points outward toward social relationship and away from the murky depths of psychological interiority; even Lear's most reflective moments starkly present rather than psychologically create an inward-looking subjectivity.

Shakespeare himself offers little motivation for the cruelty of Regan, Goneril, and Edmund, whose actions seem to emanate from their unexplained "evil" natures. However, much of the action of *King Lear* involves characters refusing, overstepping, or ignoring their assigned role in the social order – daughters rule father, son plots against father, king abdicates responsibility – and as a result, even the "good" characters, Edgar and Kent, are forced into disguise in order to fulfill their proper functions. In Bond's *Lear*, on the other hand, the social roles themselves tend to dominate the characters' actions. This is most apparent in the case of minor characters, trapped in roles which deprive them of humanity and over which they have little control. The soldier who tortures

Warrington despises his superiors, and tells his victim, "Don't blame me, I've got a job t'do" (30); the Councillor who betrays Lear claims "I did my duty as a man of conscience – " (48); the soldier in Act II protests, "Give it another minute. Best t'stick t'orders as long as yer can" (65). The prison mortician is similarly concerned about his job:

A little autopsy. Not a big one. We know what she died of. But I handle this routine work methodically. Otherwise they think you can't be trusted with bigger things. My new papers will open up many new opportunities for me. (72–73)

Beyond the distancing humor they provide, such asides highlight the inescapably destructive effects of a competitive, unjustly ordered society. Even Bodice admits "I don't decide anything. My decisions are forced on me [. . .] I'm trapped [. . .] Now I have all the power . . . and I'm a slave" (62–63). The theme is epitomized by the Old Orderly, who has served a lifetime in prison for an unrecorded crime that he cannot recall.

Unlike these minor figures, the Carpenter, Cordelia, and the Gravedigger's Son are characters whose behavior and "psychology" seem to change as much as Lear's; but unlike Lear, their development is not a positive one. The fearful, sobbing wife of Act I becomes an effective rebel organizer in Act II and an idealistically motivated tyrant in Act III. The boy who offers bread to Lear in Act I suggests that he poison the well in Act III. The lover of Act I bears little resemblance to the leader of guerrilla warfare and high official of Cordelia's regime later in the play. Such changes imply neither schizophrenic personalities nor lack of realistic development; rather, each represents the real alternatives that Lear eventually rejects. Understandable in context without being unified in retrospect, they too become victims of the social roles they actively take up. Through them, Bond represents "the human" in contemporary terms as both socially constructed and capable of change, as possible shapers of a by no means inevitable socialism.

While Bond's materialist poetics are most apparent in the reworking of Shakespearean language and character, they operate more radically in the appropriation of tragic form. In order to discuss *Lear*'s tragic structure, however, one must first distinguish between the generic model of tragedy Bond uses and transforms, and the received notions of "tragic vision" against which Bond writes. As tragedy, *Lear* displays elements from both Aristotelian and Shake-spearean models: it traces the fall of a man from an eminent position (*peripeteia*), involves the hero's discovery or recognition of his error through suffering (*anagnorisis*), and involves the death or destruction of the protagonist (*catastrophe*). A number of typically tragic themes could be added to the list. Bond's exploration of the complex relationship between history and the individual, between the experience of necessity and the desire for freedom, has many dramatic precedents; and we find a particularly Shakespearean concern in the dilemma of reconciling the moral and political order of the play's world.

If tragedy is to be an appropriate and useful genre for Bond's socialist themes, however, it must resist delivering up a sense of time that is unrelated to the real movement of history. In other words, Bond must avoid either the psychological sense of time or the providential sense of time that alternately lies behind modern and traditional interpretations of Shakespeare's *King Lear*. In the latter, represented so clearly in the work of A. C. Bradley, an equation is struck between injury and retribution: in a justly ordered cosmos, man learns through suffering and evil confounds itself. If time, as a providential form of justice, appears to reconcile the moral and political orders that men's actions have put out of joint, then Bond is right to find in this vision a dangerous moral ("endure till in time the world will be made right. That's a dangerous moral for us").[16] But the alternative vision, arising from a suspicion that the world is ruled by chance and epitomized in Brook's 1962 production, is even more seductive for its connection to subjective reality as it is usually experienced. If time is not redemptive, but entropic, an anonymous force that eats away life and against which all characters are pitted, then we are left with an experience of mortality that has nothing to do with the movement of history. For Bond, however, time is history; and the characters' subjective experience of time depends on their particular relation to history – as motive forces (progressive or destructive), as victims, or as a dangerous combination of both.

Bond structures *Lear* to present these alternative perspectives. Act I offers the accelerated tempo of chronological time; Lear himself appears overwhelmed by events and as a result, the course of history seems caught in a destructive cycle of aggression and counter-aggression. Moving so quickly from Lear's initial conflict with his daughters, to his fall from power, to the catastrophe at the boy's home, the structure of Act I recalls the linear, teleological progression of many tragic plots. Act II, the longest of the play, isolates Lear from the march of armies and conflict as the focus of the narrative splits to delineate historical events outside Lear's prison cell and the repercussions of those events on Lear's mental life. Inside the cell, the experience of time slows to the tidal flow of psychic life, sporadically interrupted by jailors, as Lear confronts his past and takes responsibility for the present with the help of the boy's ghost. Act III joins these two perspectives as Lear attempts to reinsert himself into the movement of history in order to change its ultimate direction. Here the tempo most closely reflects the everyday experience of time and ordinary use of it.

Like Shakespeare's *King Lear*, Bond's play includes a number of recognition scenes rather than a single crisis which would alter Lear's thoughts and course of action throughout the play. Just as Lear's development is accompanied by a change in the language he speaks, so Lear's progress towards the play's final gesture is composed of partial perceptions, false starts, and inadequate responses. But unlike the pattern of action found in most tragedies, here the protagonist's most important decisions are made at the very end of the play. The determining question for *Lear*, and by extension the audience as well, is not how to survive the experiences of the play, but how to act – how to change the conditions that cause such suffering. Lear's final gesture at the wall thus propels us towards a future that is not connected to the hero's death but to those nameless characters who witness it as the curtain falls. With the naturalistic treatment of time in Act III, then, Bond delivers back to the audience the sense of control over events that makes Lear's gesture of defiance meaningful.

This understanding of Bond's use of time allows us to see how *Lear*'s tragic structure works against the notions of inevitability that the term "tragic vision" has come to imply. It is one thing to suggest that the action of tragedy is one-directional, that human actions have consequences, and that time cannot be turned back. It is another to suggest that the impact of all tragedy is dependent on an inevitable catastrophe. Such a view informs Northrup Frye's definition of the genre. In *Anatomy of Criticism* he states:

The basis of the tragic vision is being in time, the sense of the one-directional quality of life, where everything happens once and for all, where every act brings unavoidable and fateful consequences [. . .] The action of tragedy will not abide our questions. Whether the context is Greek or Christian or undefined, tragedy seems to lead up to an epiphany of law, of that which is and must be.[17]

Since Aristotle believed that tragedy was possible without a catastrophe, and since the "tragic effect" of a play may in fact be heightened by the sense that the action was avoidable, the universal applicability of Frye's definition is highly questionable.[18] Like Shakespeare's own tragedies, Bond's *Lear* does not deliver up a sense of tightly woven, inevitably unfolding form. Although cause and effect is always evident (the action is not absurd), we do not find the same sense of irreversibility that we have come to expect (perhaps wrongly) from tragedy. There are points in *Lear* where the actions appear arbitrary or startling (as in the exaggerated gestures of Bodice and Fontanelle, or the second death of the ghost), places where things could have happened differently, moments of reevaluation that seem to affect the developing action and outcome of the play. The entire first scene moves with the logic of bad timing: Lear appears at the wall at an inopportune moment, the daughters offer news of their impending marriages at the worst possible time, Fontanelle accuses Warrington of not acting promptly enough, and so on. With a man's life literally "at the stake" throughout, the audience is constantly made aware of alternatives not taken. The element of farce, muted by the tragic consequences of the action, produces an unsettling effect as the audience's traditional responses (comic distance or empathetic identification) are short-circuited from the very beginning of the play. Moreover, the plot's climaxes – Fontanelle's autopsy, Lear's blinding, the ghost's goring, Lear's death on the wall – are not unifying in the sense that they are the necessary end to which the narrative must lead; and likewise, the obligatory scenes – Lear's trial and the meeting between Lear and Cordelia – are somewhat anti-climactic.

At least two issues are involved here: Bond's interest in educating his central character, and his recognition that the audience's identification with that protagonist cannot alone accomplish his didactic goal. As in *The Woman* and *The Bundle* after it, Bond constructs a dialectical narrative movement that coincides with, but does not mirror, his protagonist's consciousness-raising. Thus the conflicts which impel the dramatic action constantly shift from the psychological (or mythic) level to the economic, social, and political level, the former often left unresolved as they are displaced to the latter. Act I most closely resembles the structure of conventional tragedy, since Lear's own mistakes set in motion an inexorable chain of events which result in his own undoing and involve the lives of innocent people. That action is tentatively understood as a conflict of wills between Lear and his daughters, a conflict resolved and redirected with their deaths in Act II. Acts II and III offer a more complex narrative: the continuous evolution of plot gives way to a shifting, consciously episodic structure that depends on a series of contrasting and parallel scenes. With the transfer of power from the daughters' to Cordelia's regime, Bond sets up a new center of potential dramatic conflict – the familial conflict displaced to a figure more clearly representative of rational, idealistically motivated political ideology. As in Shakespeare's play, the final meeting between Lear and Cordelia offers a measure of Lear's moral development with the important difference that no reconciliation occurs; even in terms of Bond's play, the obligatory scene between Lear and Cordelia ends unexpectedly with the Ghost's death, not Lear's own. Most importantly, the final resolution offers only a "beginning," for Lear's "answer" at the wall cannot possibly resolve all the issues that Bond's play has deliberately raised.

The Woman

A play about the Trojan War and its consequences, Bond's *The Woman* shares more similarities to *Lear*, written seven years earlier, than to his intervening plays. Both are ambitious in scope, and deliberately invite comparison to their precedents in Shakespeare and Euripides; both plays appropriate a tragic form while undermining a tragic vision. As noted earlier, *The Woman* seeks a more profound imitation of its tragic sources than found in most contemporary adaptations of Greek myth. Unlike Sartre, Giraudoux, or Anouilh, for example, Bond does not offer modern psychological motivation for actors in classical plots. In neither form nor content does *The Woman* self-consciously reflect upon or parody its sources; nor do anachronisms jolt the audience back to the present. A mix of history play, myth, and political allegory, *The Woman* demands a different kind of comparison with its sources, one that should not be confused with an interest in reviving classical Greek tragedy. Believing the classics have outlived their social usefulness, Bond competes with the Greeks on their own terms, rewriting mythic material to reflect the broadest issues of a different historical moment.

In both *Lear* and *The Woman*, Bond's choice of subject-matter reveals his interest in the theatre as a public forum that deals with large social issues, yet his use of the tragic genre carries its own polemical weight in light of the history of the genre. Both plays could be said to critically reread their source texts or to criticize contemporary productions on which their interpretations are based. Bond's recasting of the Hecuba story, for example, can be viewed as a response to the uncritical assumptions on which revivals of Greek tragedy are usually based: that such classics have universal qualities that transcend their historical moment. Bond's version would restore the historically grounded critical dimension of Euripides' original with analogous, but not identical, political relevance. In addition, the structure and pacing of both plays deliberately undercut the sense of tragic inevitability with which the genre itself has come to be identified. Finally, Bond's serious use of the tragic genre indicates a desire to reclaim the communal voice of older theatrical models for audiences not usually found attending the theatre. The issue of audience is even more problematic to *The Woman*, whose historical vision is more positive, than to *Lear*, whose apparent pessimism has much to do with its demythologizing thrust. On the one hand, Bond uses the Greek tradition with more relish and to less violently jarring effect than he uses Shakespeare in *Lear*; yet such differences are as easily attributable to the distance between Greek and Shakespearean tragedy as to differences in Bond's adaptive approach. On the other hand, the problem of writing on behalf of an audience who must question the very nature of traditional theatre institutions influences this play's internal dynamics as well as its public reception.

Not surprisingly, *The Woman* was selected as the first contemporary play to be performed on the National Theatre's Olivier stage, a space specifically designed for full-scale productions of classical theatre. Although not commissioned, the play's ambitious scope, literary subtext, and social relevance give it all the markings of a National Theatre piece – and more so than earlier plays, *The Woman* seems to have been written with such a space and its audience in mind. While many of his contemporaries saw the self-appointed and expressed goals of the National Theatre as intrinsically conservative, elitist, and in conflict with experimental theatre companies who competed with it for Arts Council funding, Bond felt that the National's resources of "space, time, skill and technology" could assist a new and politically committed theatre. As he put it, "We must not merely occupy the fringe but the center."[19] Yet the National Theatre audience Bond knows is not the same audience in behalf of whom he writes. One of the most interesting aspects of *The Woman* is the way in which Bond manages this contradiction, creating a socialist vision of history that has the power and resonance of classical myth.

The Woman's connection to Greek tragedy is established by the heavily allusive texture of Part I. Here images, names, and dramatic situations appear remotely inspired by a number of Greek sources in addition to Euripides' two Hecuba plays. For example, the naked ambition of Hecuba's Son recalls that of Eteokles in Euripides' *Phoenician Women*, a character who ignores the wise counsel of his mother and brings his whole house to ruin before compromising his power. Bond's Hecuba rashly stabs out one eye and deliberately covers the other in gestures directly reminiscent of Sophocles' Oedipus; the image of self-blinding carries similar symbolic weight in both plays. Bond's Ismene, like her namesake in *Antigone*, urges a wise compromise in Act I of *The Woman*, but the pure idealism of her cause and the death sentence it provokes more closely recall Antigone's tragic heroism than the pragmatic stance of Sophocles' Ismene. Bond's Ismene also provides a variation on the legendary Helen, deserting the Greeks for the Trojans for quite different reasons; and her rescue from the wall by scavenging soldiers gives an ironic twist to the Euripidean Helen, who was spirited away by a goddess leaving an image in her stead. Bond's Trojan War is not fought over a real woman either, but over a statue. The Goddess of Good Fortune, however, is but a thinly disguised pretext for a Greek war of economic expansion; in neither Euripides nor Bond do the characters entirely believe in the gods, nor does the war seem justified in terms of the lives and suffering caused. Bond transfers Helen's fabled beauty, as well as her original crime, to Ismene's husband Heros, who leads the war against Troy. As his name implies, Heros is a composite portrait of Greek leaders: implacable and cruel, he rationalizes his desire for fame and fortune with appeals to honor, duty, and the common good. Like the Heros of Greek myth, he is young, attractive, ambitious, and proud.

Despite Bond's use of classical material, the meaning of the play is rarely illuminated through allusion. For an educated audience, then, Bond's style can as easily frustrate as engage. Bond's Trojan War, for example, lasts for five, not ten, years, and other changes appear similarly arbitrary. In *The Woman*, Astyanax's mother is Cassandra, not Andromache, but her character is nothing like the legendary prophetess her name evokes. Rather, it is Ismene who goes mad and prophesies (although not in that order). Bond transmutes the images of wind and sea that dominate the metaphoric pattern of Euripides' *Hecabe* into Hecuba's fascination and eventual death at sea, but the central passage in which Bond's Hecuba describes her own suffering turns on the metaphor of a tree.[20] The scattered references to well-known adaptations of Greek myth offer other red herrings for a literate audience. The alternation of the Greek war council with the Trojan defense council recalls the pattern and demythologizing thrust of Shakespeare's *Troilus and Cressida*, but the various betrayals of Bond's play are quite different in nature. Likewise, Bond's Thersites is a trusted counselor, not the scurrilous railer his name would certainly evoke in an English audience. Many other images and dramatic situations could be vaguely ascribed to either a classical source *or* its modern adaptation. For the National Theatre audience for whom the play was first performed, Bond's style may have worked well as a diversionary tactic. But in broader terms, Bond's allusive technique allows him to recapture the texture and resonance of classical Greek theatre without needing to depend on precise parallels.

The figure of Hecuba herself provides the clearest link between Bond's play and his sources, and a case could be made that *The Woman* subtly reworks the imagery, episodic structure, and thematic impact of Euripides' *The Trojan Women* in Act I and *The Hecabe* in Act II. What Bond retains from classical tragedy in Act I is the broadest outline of theme, structure, and dramatic impact. As in Euripides, we witness the suffering of war victims and are forced to consider the logic of events which has caused it. The differences between Acts I and II of Bond's play are found not only in their differing relation to Greek sources, however, but in the different pacing and dramatic impact of the narrative. The tragic impact of Part I is in some sense related to its myth-bound action. Here the action moves quickly and all the characters appear at times over-whelmed by historical events. The successive cuts from Greek to

Trojan camps create a sense of increasing intensity and barely controlled chaos. The Greek soldiers, smelling victory, are as difficult to restrain by their leaders as the Trojan mob by theirs. Although Hecuba and Ismene share a moment of respite in their prison cell, the decisions that forced them there are made under the pressure of the moment. When Ismene, as Greek envoy, decides to remain in Troy, she does so without thought of the consequences and with a swiftness that surprises even Hecuba. ("ISMENE: Fetch Thersites now – so I can't change my mind. HECUBA: What will your husband do? ISMENE: I shall see," 33.) Much of what follows is clearly improvised by the two women. But in the final days of a long war, any compromise or understanding that might alter the catastrophic end seems "hopeless," naive, or simply too late. Hecuba has already indicated the desperateness of her situation:

We both know the truth: your husband would take the statue and still burn and kill and loot . . . I can't shout any more. My son spends more and more time with the priests. When leaders do that it means you're lost. Shall I give you the statue – so at least some of you go and we can hope to hold out a little longer? Or face the worst now? No, you can take it from our dead hands. (33)

Any knowledge of the original narrative contributes to this sense of tragic inevitability: we know that Troy will burn and young Astyanax will be thrown from the wall despite the pleading of Trojan women. Hecuba's self-blinding only emphasizes the cruelty of such action.

On the other hand, Bond's focus on alternating war council scenes and on conversations in which the resulting policy is invoked, discussed, or actively resisted continually reminds the audience of human responsibility and alternatives. The play opens with news of Priam's death (from old age) and an official meeting of Greek leaders to discuss how best to take advantage of the unexpected opportunity. From the beginning of the play, we see a desire on all sides to end the war; and like Ismene, even the audience may be duped into believing some honorable compromise can be arranged. The courtroom scene works in similar fashion: while Ismene's inability to plea bargain leads directly to her death sentence, the discussion she provokes suggests more reasonable alternatives to "Greek justice." In the final scene of Part I, Heros justifies the killing of Astyanax only after the fact, as if the women's emotion had itself provoked the crime; his action and attitude brutally summarizes the

5 Ismene faces "Greek justice" in the tribunal scene of *The Woman*

consequences of Greek power and its human toll on victim and aggressor alike. As in many classical tragedies, the sense that the catastrophe might have been avoided tends to reinforce rather than mitigate the tragic impact.[21] In Part I, however, the structure and pacing of Bond's version of events is closer to Sophocles or to Shakespeare than to Euripides. Its compressed scenes, accelerated tempo, catastrophic consequences, and general sense of urgency recreate a tragic rhythm at the same time as they represent the irrational logic of nations at war.

As different in tone, texture and dramatic impact as Homer's *The Odyssey* is from *The Iliad*, the narrative of Part II makes a surprising but not impossible departure from Greek myth. Ismene has been saved by the greed of Greek soldiers for her jewels, but has lost her mind; Bond physically translates her innocent idealism into a childlike simplicity requiring Hecuba's maternal care. While Hecuba tries desperately to forget the past, Ismene spends much of Part II trying to remember. The storm that shipwrecked the two women is the same in which the Goddess of Good Fortune was lost, and the vain hope of recovering her lures Heros back to the island with his troops. Just as Hecuba's decision to cover her good eye causes her blindness, so Heros' decision to search for the goddess will cost him his life; Bond links both their actions to a dangerous desire to forget the past. In order to rid the island of the Greeks, Hecuba finally proposes a foot race between Heros and a crippled slave who has escaped from the Athenian silver mines. Like the manipulation of Pentheus by Dionysus in Euripides' *Bacchae*, the success of Hecuba's scheme depends both on knowing more than Heros and on Heros' own arrogant self-deception. Not realizing Hecuba is blind, Heros agrees to let her decide the race. So the miner wins, Heros is killed, and Hecuba's revenge is complete. Part II does not end with the resolution of the Greek–Trojan enmity, however, but on the promising but uncertain future of Ismene and the Dark Man. As Hecuba's body is unceremoniously burned on the beach, a villager reports the town council decisions to protect the refugee and abandon the island to avoid Greek retribution. Thus in Part II, Bond traces the consequences of the Trojan War from the victim's point of view, rewriting both Hecuba's revenge and Homer's island episodes to present the altered vision.

The issues raised in Part II remind us that Bond subtitled *The Woman* "Scenes of War and Freedom" rather than the expected "Scenes of War and Peace," suggesting that the latter dichotomy is not appropriate for understanding the connection between the play's two parts. Although Hecuba and Ismene, who provide the narrative link between Parts I and II, are clearly victims of Athens' war against the Trojans, so the villagers and the Dark Man are victims of Athenian peace. Before the arrival of the Greeks, the islanders enjoyed the freedom of a simple existence based on collective work which provided their basic needs; but the experience of Greek rule does not leave their society unchanged. When Heros returns twelve years after the war, still looking for the Goddess of Good Fortune, he speaks "Of the pax athenaea that covers the world. We have replaced fear with reason, violence with law, chaos with order, plunder with work –" (79); but his intrusion on the island creates the opposite: reason is replaced with fear, law with violence, order with chaos, work with plunder. Moreover, the cost of Heros' "New Athens" of "marble and silver" is visually represented in the crippled body of an escaped mineworker. Representative of the historical Greek's slave economy, the Dark Man also prefigures the urban proletariat of a later age: his eloquent description, quite late in the play, of the hellish existence of children in the silver mines provides a Blakean "Song of Experience" that turns Hecuba's revenge into an historically emblematic and politically justified act. Bond's stage direction that the Dark Man's part not be doubled highlights his importance to the play. Rather than focus on the pathos of individual suffering, the cruelty of fate, or the recurrent plight of the politically disenfranchised at the hands of those in power, Bond's narrative of the Hecuba story restores the edge of vigorous social protest to Euripides' version.[22] While not topical in the identical sense (this is not an anti-war polemic nor a plea for a more humane method of warfare), *The Woman* should be read against the shared historical moment of its own audience – one that includes the exploitation of third world countries in the form of both peaceful and openly militaristic interventions by Western powers. Wartime violence is here shown to be no more brutal than the peacetime policy to which it is vitally connected.

In *The Woman*, Bond facilitates his historical analysis by the potentially humorous addition of the Goddess of Good Fortune, a religious icon that ironically combines both the means and the end of Athenian society, like Marx's universal commodity.[23] Thus the same figure that reminds us of our historical distance from the Greeks also connects their society to our own. Unlike Helen, the goddess never speaks for herself, but through the men who worship her. In Act I, those men constantly summon "the wishes of the goddess" as they wield their authority, thereby indicating that no argument will be heard. For Heros and the priests, the goddess is safer than a woman – she is silent – and her presence is a measure of the women's powerlessness in the face of the men who rule in her name. The presence of the goddess in Part I is part of the problem. Captured, with the eastern mines, twenty-five years earlier, her recovery from Troy is the expressed end of the war and the cause uniting the Greek army. In the struggle for power, she thus plays a central ideological role, representing the same thing for both Greek and Trojan rulers – economic and military strength on which their survival depends. As such, the goddess reminds the audience that Greek and Trojan societies are structured in the same way, competing for the same things. Hecuba's response to Ismene's statement, "Athens is a republic" is both brief and telling: "Yes, they call you something else" (29). Both women become prisoners because their willingness to compromise threatens those societies in a fundamental way; and together, they expose the contradictions which the statue, as the

rallying cry for war, serves to mask. Although Heros blindly believes
in the goddess and the statue's efficacy, the Trojan priests and
Hecuba's Son are portrayed as blatantly hypocritical men who use
the goddess to serve their own ends. As the Son says, "That stone – is
only a stone. A goddess wouldn't let those sewer rats pester her!"
(46). But neither are the Trojan people easily deceived. To the Son's
call for support in the name of the goddess they respond with their
own request, chanting "Food! Water! Heal us! We're starving! Alms!
Bread! [...] Money! Help us!" (48). After assassinating the Son,
they simply hand over the goddess, symbol of the tyranny they have
endured, to the Greeks ("They deserve her!" 48). As in the world of
Lear, however, this potentially revolutionary action only succeeds in
passing power from one oppressive government to another.

In the male-dominated world of Part I, the presence of the goddess
is connected with power, ideological manipulation, enslavement by
brute force, and betrayal. Her absence in Part II is inseparable from
the women's freedom, reason, and truth. As Hecuba tells Heros,
"There are some things I thank you for. You got rid of the statue"
(86). Heros' refusal to accept this loss is one measure of his blindness
and the key to his downfall. Heros feels he cannot be free until he has
found the lost goddess; but the freedom Heros seeks in Part II is
freedom from responsibility for his actions, freedom from the past
and its consequences, freedom to assert his will without counting the
cost, and thus (like the freedom of the marketplace), a false and self-
deluding freedom that enslaves the people who help him. In Heros'
mind, as in the Greek democracy he represents, freedom and blind
will-to-power are hopelessly confused. Freedom means something
quite different to the women and the islanders. Thus while Nestor
sees in Heros only a boy with an obsession, Hecuba sees a man with
an ax (93–94). Blind to the contradictions of Greek society that the
Goddess of Good Fortune represents, Heros believes that his own
interests are universal ones, that the good fortune of Athens is the
good fortune of all. But when the goddess speaks through Hecuba at
the end of the play, she represents an entirely different perspective –
that of the victims of Athenian democracy: "Remember Troy!
(*General hesitation.*) The cost! I told him: Go! You told him! We
begged! Nothing could move him! [...] Is it a wonder he's dead?"
(106).

In *The Woman*, then, Bond replaces a psychological study of
human suffering with social analysis and an insight into the histori-

cal process. Because the individual's relation to history is central to the play, Part II deliberately moves from a symbolic and mythical world (the world of the play's sources) to an historical one. Here Bond rewrites the consequences of a myth-bound action as the island village moves from an isolated and ideal community into a Greek-dominated historical world. Whereas Heros, whose irrational inflexibility ultimately represents the Greek state, dominated Part I, Hecuba, whose wisdom comes to represent the possibility of change, dominates Part II. The shift in focus is accompanied by a change in both the pacing of events and the sense of time. The seasonal folk-dances which open Part II will be routed by Greek colonization, and so too will the cyclical time sense that dominates their lives and expresses itself through their myths. Yet the past is not idealized as it dissolves before our eyes; the changes are as painful and disruptive for the village as the future is uncertain. In Part II, Bond slows the pace of events to reflect the psychologically difficult decisions that characters must make. Scenes are separated by months, not days or hours; there is time to think, plan, remember, and carefully choose a course of action, affected but no longer overwhelmed by events. Thus the tempo itself, in contrast to that of Part I, reinforces Bond's thematic intent. Bond shows the movement of history as necessary in terms of broader class struggle, and yet entirely dependent upon the freely taken actions of individuals.

This dialectic of freedom and necessity is developed most clearly through the character of Hecuba herself, who assimilates the perspectives of others in the play. On the losing end of a ruling class, she understands Heros better than his wife and fully recognizes the implications of his power. Yet as a woman she identifies with Ismene's position, sympathizes with her idealism, and speaks her language. Later in the play, Hecuba comes to appreciate the communal freedom of the islanders without becoming one of them; but before she can become a force in history, she must also accept the Dark Man, whose instinctual hatred and class consciousness she directs into practical action. Through her Bond presents history as "a woman with a sword up her skirt,"[24] the optimistic nature of which is indicated by the success of her actions at the end of the play.

While Hecuba's suffering and slow process of education recalls that of Lear, her development is not marked by changes in speech. Just as the linguistic range of Bond's dialogue in *Lear* is connected to its Shakespearean source, so the language of *The Woman* more closely recalls the modern translations of its Greek precedents. But the differences are further related to changes in Bond's own style, the dialogue of *The Woman* more closely recalling that of *The Bundle* (1978) and *The Worlds* (1980) than any earlier work. In comparison, the dialogue of the latter may seem too straightforward, flattened out, or verbose. More is at issue than the change of set to ancient Greece. Indeed, the elliptical and witty dialect that highlights class difference in *Early Morning*, *The Sea*, and *The Fool* draws attention to issues of communication itself, much in the way the multi-focused stage, used to articulate social relationships, can accentuate the mere failure of relation. The depth of effect that comes from putting on stage several characters engrossed in their own worlds, speaking different languages, interacting on only the most superficial level, has become a modern theatrical convention – making it easy to mistake the plays' political issues for problems of communication alone. With the clear, discursive language of *The Woman*, Bond moves the audience from a world of relative values to one of truths and falsehoods. Here people who speak the same language and share the same basic experience of war may still disagree. As in classical Greek drama, the emphasis is often rhetorical, the relative merits of sharply contrasting opinion presented for judgment. Characters and audience alike must decide who is right. Concerned with the very relation between words and actions, *The Woman* directs attention away from issues of communication to those of political wisdom and trust.[25]

Like Lear, Hecuba's process of education is neither easy nor automatic; and while her suffering allows her access to a truth that other characters in the play never see, it is not the cause of her vision. Hecuba not only requires the means provided by the Dark Man, but the resolve provided by Ismene. While earlier in the play, Hecuba shamed Ismene into action by calling the good and pious wife a "whore, murdering children," in Part ii Ismene must taunt Hecuba ("Bitch!") and force up painful memories before Hecuba finally bends, "ready for all the old anger to sweep through me, like the fires of Troy" (82). In both scenes, anger is presented as a positive emotional force that prevents the characters from evading their moral obligations. Hecuba's decision to cover her good eye, whether in grief or defiance, has helped to shut out memory of the past – a past that makes too great a demand on her. She longs rather for peace and forgetfulness, to "die quietly here, in dignity" (72), listening to the sound of the sea. The Dark Man, too, seeks to free himself from his past, but he can no more escape the truth written on his crippled body than Hecuba can escape the truth written on hers.

As in Euripides, the characters' suffering is neither theraputic, enlightening, nor a universal human condition. But Bond goes a step further to suggest that history is cruel, meaningless, or repetitive only if, through ignorance or despair, we allow it to be so. Thus the meaning and dramatic impact of Hecuba's revenge must be altered. Euripides' Hecuba seems to overstep the bounds of justice. Her anger, however justified by past experience, turns her first into a raving madwoman and eventually, as Polydorous prophesies, into a dog (bitch). The murder of children and the blinding of their father seem terrifyingly vindictive, Hecuba's subsequent transfiguration into an animal an apt forfeiture of humanity. While the crime committed by Bond's Hecuba is as coldly calculated, the manner in which the execution takes place, the circumstances surrounding it, and the consequences it carries all weigh heavily in Hecuba's favor. Heros himself calls for justice, and given his actions in the play, his end seems all too appropriate. Hecuba's own death in the play is more ambiguous in import. In the final scene, a villager reports it as follows:

The waterspout picked her up from the beach and carried her into the fields. She was caught in a fence like a piece of sheep's wool. When the spout passed over her it ripped out her hair and her eyes. Her tits were sticking up like knives. Her face was screwed up and her tongue – a long thin tongue – was poking out. (108)

Although the speech lacks the eloquence found in most Greek messengers of death, the image is a powerful one in its concrete description of a physically ravished corpse. Evoking the defiant anger and suffering that destroyed Hecuba's life, we find in both Hecubas an awesomely undignified end. At the same time, the Hecuba "caught in a fence like a piece of sheep's wool" is one that reminds the audience of the sufferings of a real Hecuba, now fragmented and marginalized by her historical treatment. Bond's version reinvests the Hecuba story with a moral dimension without sacrificing her awe-inspiring stature. And as in Euripides, Bond's image of Hecuba's end undercuts any notion of a suffering that ennobles: the miner's twisted body, Ismene's madness, and Hecuba's ravished face are all manifestations of the dehumanizing effects of

Greek rule. The strength of Bond's characters appears *despite* their transfiguration, not because of it.

Whether the audience reads Hecuba's death in the storm as suicidal (self-inflicted punishment), accidental (meaningless and arbitrary), or the result of divine retribution (poetic justice) – there is support for each in the play – is a matter of pure speculation. The islanders don't bother, but get on with their business and burn the corpse on the beach. Bond's version of the story has at least made it difficult to judge Hecuba's actions in terms of ethical ideals universally applied. Retaining the ambiguity associated with great tragedy, Bond's ending leaves the audience with the problematic nature of justice and its relation to conventional morality. In terms of classical tragedy, *The Woman* returns to the tribal/matriarchal forms of justice (the contest and the vendetta) that the Hellenic legal system was intended to replace. But the ending also resonates with allegorical significance insofar as it anticipates a social formation in which the voluntarist actions of individuals and individual groups are themselves grasped as objective forces in history.[26] In the final analysis, Bond succeeds in demonstrating an historical imperative that influences the moral action of his characters. Thus Hecuba's actions are determined by her past (in a suffering that calls for revenge), consciously willed (in her decision to act), and historically prophetic (in her alliance with the Dark Man). Her manipulation of Heros not only fulfills a personal desire for revenge, but expresses the collective will of the islanders and prefigures the justice of a future age. As she says, "I've been blind for years and didn't know it. I thought I could choose" (84). Once she grasps the specific nature of her situation, freedom and necessity are dialectically united in her action.

As in most of his plays, Bond's approach in *The Woman* is a dialectical one: he keeps the terms, but stands the problem on its head. In other words, he embraces the tragic genre, but refuses the positions with which that genre has been historically identified. *The Woman* reminds us that the tragedy of the fifth century BC was informed by its own historical moment; that we idealize Hellenic culture at the risk of being, like Hecuba, either blind or forgetful of important historical facts. The implication of the play's structure is clear: those who do not learn from history are doomed to repeat it. On the other hand, the same narrative that de-mythologizes a "golden era" offers an exemplary re-mythologizing of a class-informed historical perspective. Like the Hecuba of Greek myth, Bond's "mobled Queen" witnesses, suffers, takes revenge, and eventually dies; but in the rewritten action of *The Woman*, she also aligns herself with a woman who speaks the truth, an escaped slave, and the fishing villagers, who together represent the needs and possibilities of the future.

In *The Political Unconscious*, Jameson reminds us that the dialogue of class struggle is an essentially antagonistic one in which "two opposing discourses fight it out within the general unity of a shared code."[27] In both *Lear* and *The Woman*, that code is tragedy. But the tragedy of *The Woman* is more self-consciously informed in both theme and structure by the irreconcilable demands of classes in struggle. Here Bond makes no attempt to resurrect older tragic conventions, such as the Greek chorus or Shakespearean soliloquy; dramatic conventions are not displayed at all, but resubmerged by a naturalistic technique more closely associated with the present. Because Bond never questions the appropriateness of the stage as a significant public forum or the adequacy of language to communicate his vision, *The Woman* assumes a tacit understanding between audience and playwright reminiscent of earlier drama. With its richly allusive texture, its broad social picture, its alternating rhythms of speech and action, and its apparent subject-matter, Bond successfully creates an "illusion" of classical theatre. But the myth he reconstructs, with its starkly represented class positions, may finally be unpalatable to a National Theatre audience with conservative investments in a unifying cultural heritage.

CHAPTER 5

Political parables

Like Brecht, Bond seeks to activate his audience and inspire social change. But Bond's post-war, post-68, postmodern generation not only lacks an identifiable proletariat but a strong political movement from which to write. The disturbing question that emerges is no longer "how" change will occur (a question of tactics), but who will do the changing? In an affluent society, how might a radical subject be produced? From *The Pope's Wedding* to *The War Plays*, Bond's central characters are thus engaged, more or less self-consciously and more or less successfully, in a quest for knowledge that would free them from oppressive conditions and the regressive patterns of behavior they engender. Not only do issues of education arise in every play, but Bond's polemical writing, and the early critical reception that provoked it, have given pedagogical issues a prominence they might not otherwise have assumed. As early as the 1966 "Author's Note to Saved," Bond called for "moral teaching" that would fully acknowledge the absence of a functioning religious system. In subsequent writing, Bond places his plays in direct opposition to the damaging effects of the religion he rejects and the education system he "escaped" – often appropriating the tone of moral rectitude that his earliest detractors assumed. In *Narrow Road to the Deep North* the "search for enlightenment" – enacted by the characters and mirrored in the audience – is both a serious theme and the subject of satire.

Narrow Road to the Deep North

Commissioned by the clergy for an international conference at Coventry Cathedral, *Narrow Road* proved to be Bond's first British success. Bond wrote the play in less than three days, angered by the critical response to *Early Morning* on which he had worked for over eighteen months; and *Narrow Road*, a comedy, did provide an effective antidote to the charges of obscenity, obscurity, and arbitrary violence his earlier plays had evoked.[1] In fact, the action of the play is as brutal as anything encountered in Bond previously. Opening with Basho's "innocent" murder of a baby, *Narrow Road* closes with two premeditated killings as the crucified and dismembered body of Shogo, who has slaughtered orphans and sent countless citizens to a watery grave, is paraded onstage, and Kiro, Basho's would-be disciple, commits hara-kiri. But the distancing effect of the humor and the setting ("Japan about the seventeenth, eighteenth or nineteenth century"[3]), as well as the contemplative stance represented (and parodied) in the figure of Basho encouraged a more rational approach to the play's violence. The immediate acceptance *Narrow Road* earned is attributable not simply to the play's comedy (*Early Morning* was as funny) or apparent simplicity (review summaries of Bond's "message" are remarkably varied), but rather to the form itself – recognized by reviewers as a political parable.[2]

Unlike other genres, the parable invites a particular interpretive stance from its audience – one attuned from the beginning to moral argument, and ready to make the quasi-allegorical series of substitutions that didactic literature often requires. Though less explicitly didactic than many of Bond's plays, the parable form helped audiences to "read" *Narrow Road* in a way that made the most disturbing stage images acceptable. As a descriptive term, "didactic" is weighted with a history of argument from Aristotle to the present over what constitutes "good" literature and the proper aims of art; hardly neutral, it is charged with the ambivalence with which contemporary Western audiences view any drama that openly aims to influence the viewer's attitudes and behavior. As the actor of Brecht's *Messingkauf Dialogues* complains, "there's nothing audiences loathe more than being sent back to school."[4] On the British stage, the trumpeting of a playwright's didactic intentions may keep audiences away from the theatre; ironically, perhaps, a play with *no* moral urgency may fare no better. By acknowledging the didactic impulse behind *Narrow Road*, critics managed to contain Bond's threat as an avant-garde (or experimental) artist and concede him credibility as a serious playwright with a single stroke. Since that time, critics have had difficulty separating the parable-like form of particular plays (e.g., *Narrow Road*, *Stone*, and *The Bundle*) from an inclination to see *all* Bond's plays as parables, moral lessons aimed at "educating" or persuading the audience to accept a particular point of view. With their epic narration, political stance and use of parable, Bond's "learning plays" do pay homage to Brecht, but as the reluctant reception of Brecht's own *Lehrstücke* illustrates, the charge of didacticism can easily short-circuit analysis of the plays.[5]

What attracted Bond to the parable form may well be what attracted Brecht: its history of instructional use, its connection with religious literature, and its tendency toward self-explication – the very elements that tend to put off literary critics. As an art form, the parable does not impart knowledge directly, but through narrative, privileging the story as a method of learning. But in Bond, as in Brecht, what the audiences learn is not identical to what the characters do; and summarizing statements of "meaning" inevitably distort the dialectical nature of the "truths" being explored. Whether deceptively simple or seemingly complex, Bond's parable plays appropriate a moral vocabulary to reexamine the basis of ethical action, always linking that action to the use or acquisition of knowledge. Unlike *Narrow Road*, however, Bond's later parable plays take more seriously the demands of the form by providing within their structure a guide to audience interpretation and use. Though Bond's parables vary over time, their dramatic strategies reveal a political aesthetic far more interesting and complex than is usually ascribed to overtly didactic literature.

Like all of Bond's parables, *Narrow Road* illustrates certain moral attitudes and their consequences, self-consciously inviting audience interpretation by making the search for knowledge itself an explicit theme. At the same time, *Narrow Road* seems to parody its own didactic intentions and make impossible any easy summary of its moral argument. The double-edged thrust of the play, as well as its "mixed" tone, is most clearly illustrated through the figure of Basho, who opens the play:

My name is Basho. I am, as you know, the great seventeenth-century Japanese poet, who brought the haiku verse form to perfection and gave it greater range and depth. For example:

> Silent old pool
> Frog jumps
> Kdang!

I've just left my home in the village here (*points offstage*) and I'm going on a journey along the narrow road to the deep north and when I reach there I shall become a hermit and get enlightenment. (173)

Bond's haiku translation is accurate, and Basho follows strict Noh convention by beginning his part with the announcement of who he is, where he has come from, and where he is going. But as one reviewer noted, "to deliver these lines at the start of a play without provoking laughter is impossible."[6] The only character to address the audience directly, Basho is a narrator figure who provides the view (and contemplative stance) from which the action of the play can be understood. But as the opening words demonstrate, it is impossible to distinguish between a pretentious and an ironic voice, to know just how seriously Basho takes himself, or how seriously we are to take him. As Kiro notes, Basho "looks intelligent," and by his own account he has "got enlightenment"; but how far can we trust a man who spent twenty-nine years and six months "facing a wall and staring into space" before deciding he had nothing to learn? Indeed, much of the play's comedy results from the self-parodic nature of Basho's comments – observant, quick-witted, ironic, and often quite cruel. When Kiro nearly suffocates with a sacred pot on his head, Basho responds in typical fashion:

Have you studied meditation? [...] Good. Think small [...] I can't help you, you still haven't learned anything. You live in darkness. [...] You would have to make the pot think big, and that's definitely beyond your powers. (187)

When Basho decides to bring the problem to Shogo, he does so for his own purposes, fully expecting the worst: "There's something *he* can do for us. (*To Argi*): You won't get it off till he's dead" (187). The moment is not surprising. Throughout the play, Basho's wit is inconsiderate and his wisdom self-serving. In the opening scene, he leaves an abandoned baby by the river, displacing his own responsibility onto "the irresistible will of heaven" (174). He comes to feel remorse for this action by the end of the play, but in an unexpected way: "O God forgive me! – If I had looked in its eyes I would have seen the devil," he says, and drowned it "with these poet's hands" (222). The final act recalls the conventional Noh "demon play" in which the demon or evil spirit, once revealed, is vanquished by a Buddhist priest. But Basho's final speech to the people appears as carefully crafted as his poetry to rationalize the play's most barbaric action, and through it Bond criticizes the violent uses to which most religions are eventually put.

Yet at times, Basho's artistic, intellectual, and individualistic form of enlightenment seems a reasonable alternative to the play's other religious representatives. Serving a wide variety of thematic targets, the play satirizes both the tendency of Eastern religions to ignore political reality and the use of Western religions to organize, control, and exploit it. The Japanese priests of *Narrow Road* are portrayed as essentially comic, benign, and totally useless, while Georgina's Christian morality is shown to be corrupt, dangerous, and frighteningly effective. With Georgina's divided character, the play links authoritarian control to a religious ideology that creates guilt over human sexuality.[7] At one point in the play, she states her methods directly:

So instead of atrocity I use morality. I persuade people – in their hearts – that they are sin, and that they have evil thoughts, and that they're greedy and violent and destructive, and – more than anything else – that their bodies must be hidden, and that sex is nasty and corrupting and must be secret. When they believe all that they do what they're told. (208)

The play implicitly questions whether such a method of maintaining "law and order" is more humane or "enlightened" than the barbaric practices it replaces. Whether Eastern or Western, however, religious fervor can only maintain what is won through more physical methods of warfare. Superior military force establishes rule over Shogo's city, despite the stupidity of the English Colonel who wields it. And the "enlightened" colonial enterprise being ridiculed owes its success to Basho's active support. Indeed, from the initial decision to ignore the cries of an abandoned baby to his involvement in the murder of Shogo, Basho's actions are morally self-implicating; and with them, the play condemns the conventional, "humanistic" wisdom that makes such acts possible.[8]

Basho's attitudes take shape, however, against the passive contemplation of Kiro, with whom the audience may identify, and the practical activity of Shogo, whose raw energy is brutally repressed at the play's end. Young, curious, and naive, Kiro takes up the search for enlightenment that Basho has abandoned by the play's second act. Like the father-figures of *Bingo* and *The Fool*, neither Basho nor Shogo provide acceptable models of behavior for their son-like counterpart; but in contrast to Basho's indifference to Kiro's fate, Shogo thoughtlessly saves Kiro's life when he breaks the "sacred pot." The friendship of these two characters provides an interesting development in the narrative, one that both accents and undermines the split figures of good and evil on which the traditional Noh drama relies. The symbolic resonance of their pairing in the play is inescapable: although both are orphans, Kiro is innocent, gentle, selfless, and reflective; Shogo is experienced, ruthless, selfish, and physical; Kiro seeks knowledge, Shogo power. Their obvious differences and unlikely friendship provide some of the play's humor, making their inseparability at the end of the play all the more striking: Kiro's suicide is clearly motivated by Shogo's death. Any judgment of Shogo as pure evil is complicated by his relationship to Kiro and preempted by the moral rhetoric with which Basho and the Colonel publicly justify the murder. Likewise, Kiro's simple goodness is undermined by his final despair, an attitude that prevents him from responding to calls for help from a drowning man nearby. The final image of a man saving himself from the river, self-resurrected from the graves of past citizens, comments on Kiro's mistaken notions of discipleship, juxtaposing an image of life, hope, and sanity to the mayhem, madness, and despair of the play's last scene.

In *Narrow Road*, Bond's desire to become more accessible to his audience without sacrificing the seriousness of his themes results in a fast-moving play that employs hilarious comic vignettes, bitter satire, and shocking visual images to create what can easily be read as a bleak picture of authoritarian structures and the men and women who make them. Like most of Bond's plays, *Narrow Road* refuses a single-character focus to direct attention to the broader community and its development. Thus the functioning of Shogo's city ultimately takes priority over Shogo himself, an obvious center of interest in the play. Shogo, a Shogun (Japanese military dictator) introduces the contradictions of his rule in conversation with Kiro:

My family were peasants, I had nothing, no one had to do what I told them – but they did. I am the city because I made it, but I made it in the image of other men. People wanted to follow me – so I had to lead them. I can't help shaping history – its my gift, like your piety [. . .] I *am* those people. (196)

Shogo both is and is not to blame for the effects of his rule, is and is not pushed by his people (he asserts both claims within a matter of minutes), is and is not to be pitied at the end of the play. As both villain and martyr, he can represent the belief that men both do and do not make their own history – are entirely responsible for their actions without being able to choose the conditions under which those actions are taken. When read dialectically, the contrasts of the play appear as contradictions, a pattern of action that resists resolution and undermines the stasis that its oppositional categories might otherwise imply.

The indirect technique, characteristic of Bond's early plays, thus makes certain interpretive demands on the audience; but there is little suggestion here of irresolvable enigma. As Kiro remarks, "Some problems have no solution, but it's hard to know which problems these are" (195). Kiro also tells of the "very religious" old priest, who has spent his life trying to put together pieces of a Chinese puzzle that are not designed to fit; sorting out questions that can be answered from those which cannot is one of the pedagogical tasks set by the play. Thus comic interrogations about the nature of God provide first Basho and then his soldiers with a method of identifying priests, but the transcendental project itself is made to look ridiculous. In *Narrow Road*, the nature of good and evil is grounded in the material world and involves issues of basic survival.

The episodic structure of *Narrow Road* accommodates the telling of a story with several narrative threads, while the analysis itself depends on the juxtaposition of stage images and incidents that must be actively "read" by the audience. By refusing the explicit moral, without depriving the audience of the expectation or desire of having one, the technique evokes a mood of thoughtful contemplation associated with both Noh drama and the haiku form. The final stage images, for example, connect narrative strands without resolving the parable or unifying its multiple focus. And yet here the parable seems visually, almost poetically, recapitulated in the action: Basho's poems are left scattered and abandoned as he ushers in the new government; Georgina is mad, her actions recalling both Ophelia and Lady MacBeth as she hallucinates in a manner befitting the victim/collaborator she has been; the city purges itself of Shogo in an act that reinscribes his legacy of violence; without a leader to follow or source of knowledge to guide him, Kiro commits suicide; and at the same moment, a new man, saved through his own practical action, clambers onto the stage.

Although the multi-focused stage technique developed in *Narrow Road* invites interpretation, the alternately startling and comic effects it produces can also obscure the political analysis. Thus praise of the play's extraordinary power, clarity, and simplicity were more than balanced by an admission of confusion by original reviewers,

6 Georgina mistakes Kiro's hara-kiri knife for a murder weapon in
Narrow Road to the Deep North

especially regarding the end, the point at which audiences generally
expect "enlightenment." While not perceived as difficult, the play
was described as "cryptic," "obscure," and "enigmatic."[9] Indeed,
the play works most effectively on the level of satire, not only in the
humorous treatment of its central figures, but in the potential
parody that underlies Bond's use of a didactic form. In this regard,
Narrow Road (1968) seems closer to the agit-prop theatre that found a
home on the British fringe in the late sixties and early seventies than
to the work of Brecht, whose name was invoked at the time to
describe it.[10]

The agit-prop style of Bond's earliest parables is thrown into
sharper relief by *Stone* (1976) and *The Bundle* (1978), plays that take
more seriously the parable form and pay conscious homage, in both
theme and technique, to Brecht's epic theatre. The shift from a
highly allusive, expressionistic interpretation of real events to a
narrative method that relies more systematically on its own internal
structure for meaning may have been governed by Bond's desire to
limit the kind of misunderstanding to which *Early Morning* fell prey,

as well as to prolong the usable life of works written for specific events.[11] Clearly audiences had been distracted from the parabolic nature of *Early Morning* by its use of historical figures. Similar difficulties might have faced *Black Mass*, had the Queen and Prime Minister been identified by name, and *Passion*, in which Christ has a significant role (played by Bond himself in the original production); but the sponsoring occasion for which they were performed insured a receptive audience for whom such biting satire was a show of solidarity and support.[12] The power and humor of *Black Mass* and *Passion* are strengthened by, though not dependent on, their clear and close relationship to the Campaign for Nuclear Disarmament and Anti-Apartheid causes, the rallies for which they were performed grounding the allusions of the play to insure an appropriate response. A similar effect is produced in *September* (1989), a short parable written for the World Wildlife Fund about the death of environmental activist Chico Mendes.[13] But Bond's political parables rarely depend on allegorical reference, covert or explicit, to specific events outside the play. With the use of direct audience address and simple statements of intention and motive, the characters supply all the information necessary for them to make sense on their own terms.

Thus while *Narrow Road* might play differently to an Asian audience, for the purposes of its original production the figure of Basho (and the time-period covered) was sufficiently obscure to allow the character to be defined exclusively in terms of the onstage action. However, Bond's indirect techniques did not produce a uniform interpretation of the play, and the basic issues seemed important enough to return to them nearly a decade later in *The Bundle or New Narrow Road to the Deep North*. Indeed, a fine line exists between techniques that obscure a play's meaning and those which complicate it, of a representation that is ambiguously open-ended or productively so. In addition to the audience's own experience, political views, and interpretive skill, the production context also affects a play's interpretation. The issue can be illustrated with *Stone*, the first published parable play to allude with equal force to both Brecht and the Bible. Written two years before *The Bundle*, *Stone*'s extended allegory combines a Bunyanesque journey through life and the biblical parable of the talents with an occasional reference to Brecht's short "ballet," *The Seven Deadly Sins of the Petite Bourgeoisie*. As an overtly political parable, it provides an interesting stylistic transition to the *Bundle*, a full length "learning play" that elaborates its pedagogic issues with even greater force and clarity.

Stone

Written for Gay Sweatshop, *Stone* provides a more specifically Marxist social analysis than is found in *Narrow Road*, but shares the comic vitality, brevity, and heavily allusive character of parables written by Bond for particular organizations and events. In this case, however, Bond was concerned that some audience members might misread the central metaphor – a small stone that grows into an oppressive weight that "Man" must carry – as a direct reference to homosexuality rather than an indictment of the relations of production under capitalism. Since the original production context could have lead to such a reading, Bond inserted the following "chorus" at the beginning of the play's first production:

> Do I carry a burden?
> All people in an unfree society carry a burden.
> Is homosexuality a burden?
> No. Why should it be? But you may be made to feel its a burden.
> So is it not a burden?
> No, all people in an unfree society carry the *same* burden.
> What is the burden?
>
> Stone ... Stone ...[14]

The catechism introduces the play's central metaphor, identifies questions that the parable should or could evoke, invites interpretation, and forestalls the inappropriate (but expected) response on the part of the audience. The precise meaning of the allegorical image, however, is left open – to be answered, presumably, by the play itself ("Stone ..."). A similar clarifying gesture was inserted, in production, near the end of the play. Having wasted his life carrying a stone for someone else, the Man feels justly, if somewhat belatedly, cheated of his life by the Mason's false hope of salvation/reward. The published text ends with the Man killing the Mason, looking for a moment at his body, and calmly calling to the money-laundering washer Woman, "I want to wash my hands."[15] In the first production, the Woman responds from offstage, "No. They're already clean," an addition made too late for the play's first published edition.[16] Clearly intended to underscore the Man's innocence and the essential justice of his act, the additional handwashing comment does not entirely reverse the original connotation of remorse, nor can it erase the complicating weight of biblical and Shakespearean allusion to actions of murderers and their accomplices. In this way the parable manages, almost in spite of itself, to keep open the question as to whether such an extreme response might be justified.

To activate the audience's own interpretive powers and accentuate the play's interrogative force, other elements of the narrative are left deliberately ambiguous. For example, in Scene Six, the Man is accused of murdering an Irish Tramp who swindled him earlier. A Beckettian figure who combines the wisdom of Brecht's Beggar King Peachum with the rhetorical expertise of Shaw's burglar in *Heartbreak House*, the Tramp threatens first murder, then suicide to earn six of the Man's seven coins; and although we witness a rather violent fight between them at the inn, the Tramp may have died of cold, as the Judge unwittingly suggests. A body is produced, but the burlesque trial scene fails to reveal the cause of death – not only because each character is implicated in the murder and equally responsible, but because the legal system Bond satirizes seems to work better in the dark.[17] Here the ambiguity forestalls any judgment of the characters and their actions outside their interconnected relationship. If the system is to blame, then the problem of the playwright is to show the actions of the characters as one of its effects.

In *Stone*, the characters' emblematic nature derives from their social functions. On the one hand, the parable shows how every social relationship (court to accused, men to women, rich to poor, worker to capitalist) is corrupted by the change of "use value" to "price" that the capitalist production system involves. On the other hand, the play points to the self-destructive consequences of attempting to survive in such a society and suggests that the characters themselves are responsible for changing it. By accepting the Mason's offer of employment, the Man unwittingly sells his soul; and he finally kills in order to reclaim it. As Bond's materialist poetics dictate, the "soul" is located in the body, its absence represented in the unnatural attitudes and pained gestures of the actors onstage. The rigidity of the Policeman, for example, expresses the cost of his "soulless" attitude in physical terms. Likewise, the Girl's "striptease" involves a spellbinding dance by which she shrouds her naked and innocent body, one sheet at a time, periodically punctuated by the ritual-like exchange of coins between herself and the Man. Playing upon the audience's voyeuristic expectations, the sequence of movements begins "wildly" and grinds slowly to a standstill, the Girl finally crying under her sheets, the Man asleep.[18]

Equally important, *Stone* shows how the language of morality itself is implicated by the system it serves, the means by which the Man gets seduced, swindled, or coerced by other characters into supporting the system that entraps him. Indeed, much of the play's humor is found in observing the methods by which the Man is alternately forced, then fooled, into behaving against his own self-interest. If the Man learns anything, he learns it through trial and error, often in spite of himself – and the difficulties increase as the play progresses. As in *The Bundle*, where the issue is treated in more depth, the relationship between knowledge and action is one of *Stone*'s central concerns. Outside the system, the Man has no knowledge on which to base his decisions; once inside, his freedom proves illusory. The longer he works and the more he invests in the bargain, the harder it is to see any way out. By the end of the play, the Man is chained to the stone and the stone drives him. An extreme wearing down process, the bent and aging body represents, in negative terms, the cost of the Man's ignorance, while the stone he carries expresses its cause. As in *The Bundle*, the lessons of class consciousness are learned at great physical and mental cost – the experience that educates being the same as that which jeopardizes the ability to change it.

Precisely what the Man learns in *Stone* never gets explicit statement. Rather, the play suggests, in dialectical fashion, that knowledge follows action, not vice versa. Likewise, the mysterious alchemical process whereby the coins (or talents) of the play (prudence, soberness, courage, justice, honesty, love, and hope) turn into their opposite (pride, greed, lust, envy, gluttony, anger, sloth) is not directly explained. Although produced as evidence against the Man in the trial scene, at the end of the play the Mason cannot see (or will not admit) any difference in the coins at all; and indeed, they change back and forth more than once with no apparent explanation. The "good servant" of the Bible traded with his gold to make more for his master when he was away; the bad servant lost all burying his in the earth, leaving them unchanged. Appropriately, then, the Man approaches the Mason's yard with the same number of coins, covered with "muck" and easily washed into their original state. But the physical weight and size of the stone has increased tremendously. So is the Man to be praised or censured, and what should we learn from his situation? Again, the ambiguity is a productive one, providing in the form of a question ("Why did the coins change?") the key to the Man's liberation. In this regard, Marx, rather than the Bible, provides the explanatory text. Being, literally speaking, a "good servant" keeps the main character from being, metaphorically speaking, a "good man." Just as money and morals are conflated in the coins, so the impossibly growing stone provides a simple and evocative image for Marx's concept of labor power and its connection to both surplus value and alienation. At the final destination, the Man (worker) finds the Mason (owner) squeezing blood out of stones – a "miracle" that grants him ultimate authority over the man's life: "Fool, arguing! I can get blood out of a stone – and you stand there questioning me?" (60). If the capitalist process of exchange itself changes the value of the coins, then the Mason cannot answer the Man's question any more than he can provide him with a fully human life. The Man is rewarded with a new kind of slavery ("I'll make you a servant in my house," 60), but even that offer is jeopardized by the man's need to know ("Why did the stone grow . . . Why did the coins change?" 60); and within the context of the play, the urge toward understanding and self-knowledge is precisely what defines his humanity.

While *Stone* self-consciously invites such explication (and the Brechtian song lyrics prod the analysis), the play refuses the lucidity of simple allegory. The meaning rests in part in the multivalent nature of its terms, and something is inevitably lost in the translation to ordinary prose – not least the reliance on humor. With its comic routines and verbal/visual puns (on everything from "accepting life's burdens" to laundering money), *Stone* reworks received wisdom from a number of literary and philosophic sources into a highly entertaining tale, complicating the surface of the fable without sacrificing its allusive force.[19] The very instability of language and metaphor opens up the play's argument and points to the pedagogical limits and opportunities offered by the form. Like the parables of the Bible, the play is not to be understood literally; nor are its "mysteries" always self-explanatory. On the other hand, Bond refuses to use the form ironically, in the manner of Beckett or Kafka, or to exploit the essential ambiguity of language itself. The play's "enigmas" are not irresolvable. To the contrary, *Stone* warns against ignorance, the "original sin" for which the Man pays with a hellish existence on earth. In the penultimate scene, he states the point directly: "I cry at the stupidity of my life. Wasted on dragging a stone to somewhere I don't know for a reason I don't understand" (58). Such meaninglessness has a cause – it results from accepting the Mason's logic in the opening scene; the "straight and narrow path" leads in a circle; and the only way out is practical, truly self-interested action.

As a critique of biblical morality, and the society that uses it to perpetuate its own sins, *Stone* ends on an act of revolutionary violence – a "moral" that implicitly asks whether pity, patience, and forgiveness are the virtues most appropriate to our own situation. But the "reality" of the violence is muted by the play's allegorical style, one that prevents too literal a reading. While Bond's parables often reverse the content of their biblical reference, the form itself invites a range of interpretation – from the most fundamental literalism (armed violence is necessary to revolutionary change) to the most liberal hedging (education and informed activism make violence unnecessary). If the play pushes the audience to a discussion of tactics, then the larger battle is already won. However, it is far more likely that the audience has more in common with the Man than they are willing to admit. In this sense, the play indeed works like a biblical parable, dividing the audience into those who "understand" and those who do not – serving as both an illustrative and a cautionary tale that directly addresses the beliefs and behavior of "those who would hear."[20]

In *Stone*, a radical human subject is literally created by the weight of his burden, the extremity of his situation, and the questions that no one inside the story can answer. While the songs are addressed to the audience and help elucidate the play's argument, experience alone teaches the Man what he must do. Unless the audience finds the Man's experiences analogous to their own (something the play's humor and allusive qualities work against), his actions will not be taken as exemplary. As in many of Bond's early plays, the lesson stands more or less at odds with the "learning" of the characters, works against close identification with the characters, and depends for its effect on the critical attitude that the actions and attitudes depicted onstage should arouse. With *The Bundle*, however, Bond moves beyond the critique of particular religious institutions to criticize the nature of all socialized morality. Satire, parody, and direct allusion – to history, literature, or religion – are discarded in favor of epic narration and a more direct appropriation of the parable, one that embodies in a positive form the lessons of class consciousness.

Behind Bond's project lies the Chinese parable plays of Brecht and the world of the *Lehrstücke* from which they developed.[21] Like Brecht, Bond deals with issues of moral choice, the difficulty of making rational decisions under emotional duress, and the dilemma of weighing individual and narrowly defined interests against communal and broadly defined ones. Should a boy be saved and the village lost? Should a mother be sacrificed to save the town? Is kindness possible in an evil society? What are the costs and consequences of ethical action? And how do we know? Such questions are raised by both Brecht and Bond. Unlike Bond's earlier plays, the "moral" of *The Bundle* gets explicit statement in Wang's closing words to the audience:

We live in a time of great change. It is easy to find monsters – and as easy to find heroes. To judge rightly what is good – to choose between good and evil – that is all that it is to be human.[22]

But the apparent simplicity of the advice belies the difficulty of the choice in a world where humane instincts can be suicidal. As Wang cautions Tiger in an earlier scene, "Here only the evil can afford to do good" (54). An audience familiar with Brecht will recognize the argument, as well as its counterpart – the emotional difficulty of carrying through a rationally chosen course of action. For the characters of *The Bundle*, *choosing* between good and evil – in Brecht the impossible or unnatural decision mandated by an inhuman social system – is far easier than *distinguishing* between the two.

Because *The Bundle* so clearly builds upon the analysis of Brecht's earlier parables, some discussion of the issues they raise may illuminate Bond's development of the form. In *The Good Person of Setzuan*, as in *The Seven Deadly Sins*, Brecht condemns a society in which material success, even simple survival, depends on the suppression of "natural" instincts towards virtuous behavior, and does so through the split figures of Shen-Te and Shui-Ta, Anna I and Anna II. Yet both parables rely for their effect on some consensus regarding the natural "goodness" of Shen-Te and Anna I – not least in order to distinguish their heartfelt actions from the expedient measures required by their ruthless counterparts. Most simply put, Shen-Te's generosity and Anna I's innocence are shown to be preferable to the self-serving pragmatism of Shui-Ta and Anna II;

but within the world of these plays, the former cannot survive without the latter. In this way, Brecht exposes the hypocrisy of the capitalist system, blind (or cynically complacent) to its own moral contradictions and oiled by a religious ideology with no relevance to the characters' lives. The various oppositions (in *Good Person* forced to conclusion by the "historical" urgency of impending birth) lead to contradictions that cannot possibly be resolved in the terms set by the play; and the problem gets thrown to the observing audience for solution.

In the case of *Good Person*, however, the clarity with which the moral oppositions are posed does not necessarily activate the audience's dialectical imagination, nor lead to the kind of understanding on which revolutionary change depends. In a letter to Eric Bentley, Brecht writes of the critical misinterpretation *Good Person* suffered in this way: "One should really explain sometime the difference between symbol and parable [*Gleichnis*]. A parable is a simple, realistic reflection of an historical situation, a situation that is ephemeral or rather should be made so."[23] The comment alludes to the fact that many viewers found the problems irresolvable, the divided character "natural," and the moral choices representative of a universal human condition. If the masks (through which Shen-Te's split self gets represented) are understood as a symbolic device as opposed to an alienation-effect, if the audience's mindset is not already a dialectical one, then the action may acquire a tragic dimension, unwittingly reinforced by the pattern of oppositions elaborated by the narrative. In the struggle to change the way people think, both Brecht and Bond seek to break down conceptual notions, but do so with the same language and similar literary conventions with which they have first been learned. For neither playwright can the questions posed be answered in universal terms. But the parable form, and the pattern of interpretation and moral vocabulary on which it depends, can work against the dialectical and history-bound process of thinking that the plays otherwise work to generate.[24]

With the historicizing frame of *The Caucasian Chalk Circle*, Brecht avoided the clear moral oppositions of earlier parables, only to find himself cautioning against too literal (and narrow) an interpretation. He complains the "prologue may create confusion [. . .] since it looks superficially as if the whole story is being told in order to clear up the argument about who owns the valley. On closer inspection, however, the story is seen to be a true narrative [...] which proves nothing but merely displays a particular kind of wisdom, a potentially model attitude for the argument in question. Parables need to be practical, applicable. This play is only parable-like."[25] Interestingly, Bond finds *The Caucasian Chalk Circle* unsatisfactory for the same reason Brecht suggests here: the limits to its practicality. In the introduction to *The Bundle* (xix–xx), Bond's argument is with the character of Azdak, who disappears after showing justice is possible rather than staying to show that it is practical as well.

Brecht's question of a "model attitude for the argument in question" remains an issue for both playwrights. Indeed, if knowledge is not passively absorbed, but actively acquired, tested, and reshaped by action, then the play that leads to it must provide some aesthetic equivalent to the real-life experience it, by definition, excludes from the stage. In the *Lehrstücke*, Brecht sometimes dealt with the problem by eliminating the spectator's position altogether, insisting in *The Measures Taken*, for example, on the importance of the actors physically taking up the different roles through which the situation is presented. If the learning process is grounded in the concrete, bodily experiences of social action and attitudes, then actors would learn by "imitating" them. But a play that eliminates audience altogether may so radically challenge the conventions of Western theatre that it turns into something else – an acting exercise or "rehearsal."

Leaving the conventional audience-stage-actor-text relationship intact, *The Bundle* retains the dialectical approach to understanding on which Brecht's experiments with the *Lehrstücke* depended and develops the issues they raise. Bond approaches the pedagogical problem in two ways: (1) by directly demonstrating the dialectical process of education whereby very different characters come to understand their experience in a way that enables them to change it, and (2) by epic strategies that encourage an analogous process to occur in the observing audience. Whereas Brecht breaks up the unity of the parable with interruptive devices for the purpose of commentary, Bond preserves the artistic unity of the parable form by "dramatizing the analysis" – in other words, by incorporating interpretation, both directly and indirectly, into the story. *The Bundle* works through the good/evil oppositions characteristic of a class-divided society to suggest some practical solution – the "hardness" of the landowner and the "wisdom" of Basho are matched and bettered by that of the peasants, who must learn a new system of values in order to break the pattern of exploitation that turns moral action into its opposite. The positive thrust of *The Bundle*, and the enabling frame of mind it works to produce, suggests a more complete appropriation of the parable form. Like the New Testament parables, its narrative structure and evocative images are aimed at a "redescription of human possibility" – a method whereby ordinary ways of envisioning relationships are overturned and previously accepted values questioned in ways that the audience, when faced with their own ethical choices, might find useful.[26]

The Bundle

The Bundle implicitly recognizes that stories help people learn – that the way the world is represented and understood affects the actions of those who believe them. Indeed, the successful revolution that is chronicled owes as much to the story-telling of Wang as to the gun-running of his father, the ideological battle with Basho as important to the narrative as the tactical warfare carried on against the landowner. The competing worldviews expressed in Basho's poems, Wang's parables, and Tiger's story provide a form of class struggle, at the level of language, over the means of self-production. In this sense, the *Bundle* is a parable about parables, about the practical function and appropriate uses of art, a play that, despite its extreme clarity, reflects upon itself and its own didactic methods.

Unlike most of Bond's plays, *The Bundle* grants its central character something close to exemplary status. As a revolutionary "hero," Wang combines the energy, anger, and class consciousness of Bond's "dark men" with the artistic imagination and enlightened reason of Bond's more intellectually sensitive characters. But as a model of action, Wang's use to the audience is limited; indeed, those reviewers who judged the play as a call to armed revolution, or a discussion of means vs. ends, were the same who found the argument unconvincing.[27] In his introduction to the play, Bond attempts to preempt such a reading by suggesting that "the play is not best understood as the story of the hero Wang but as a demonstration of how the words 'good' and 'bad', and moral concepts in general, work in a society and how they ought to work" (xviii). Even the "moral" of the play's end reiterates the question on which each scene is built: "how to judge rightly?'' The lesson, if any, is to show the practical and political use of moral judgments and their link to concrete, changing, historical situations. For both characters and audience, a similar relationship obtains between sensory experience, conceptualization, attitude, and action. In this, Bond and Brecht agree: experience alone may teach nothing.[28] The pedagogical problem for the playwright is mirrored in the specific difficulties faced by the characters. Bond addresses the problem in *The Bundle* with narrative that invites but does not rely on audience identification; with a gestic technique that "teaches" the audience how to read the narrative; with a tempo that paces the audience for its emotional demands; and with moments that seem to reward the effort.

Like *The Pope's Wedding* and *The Fool*, *The Bundle* is grounded in the portrait of a community, only gradually focusing on a central character. Though divided into two parts, the cause–effect logic of the earlier plays is here rechanneled into a problem–solution structure. Roughly speaking, Part One articulates the problems Wang faces by depicting the society in which he is born, the people and experiences from which he must learn, and the attitudes from which he must break free. Part Two takes up a revolutionary solution, tracing its difficulties, costs, and consequences. The structure is not contrived for optimistic purposes, but reflects the well-known Marxist premise on which the action is based: "People make their own history. But they do not make it just as they please; they do not make it under circumstances chosen by themselves, but under circumstances found, given and transmitted from the past."[29] Thus Wang's education begins with the Ferryman, whose situation is typical, whose attitudes are common, and whose actions are as humanly exemplary as such a social system allows. Through Basho, Wang comes into contact with what is transmitted from the past through art, philosophy, and education in alliance with the ruling class. Wang eventually "finds" Tiger, the degraded human consequence of an oppressive regime. All three possess the wisdom of their class and social situation, and Wang's development depends on his association with each. In fact, the two-part "problem–solution" division of the play may overshadow the underlying three-part structure that more accurately reflects Bond's dialectical method. In the first third of *The Bundle*, the audience observes (and Wang experiences) social and economic conditions that breed violence and despair, the causes of which are only dimly understood by the characters themselves. In this setting of extreme poverty, the struggle to survive makes parenthood a luxury that few can afford. In the second third of the play, Wang acts upon what he has learned, changing himself and others in the process. The consequences of Wang's action, not all of them "happy," are traced in the final three scenes.

Given the epic scope of the story and the formal demands of the parable form, much of the play's coherence depends on the choice, ordering, and focus of scenes. Much of the action occurs offstage. Fourteen formative years elapse between Scenes One and Two as Wang grows up in the Ferryman's family. Another nine years pass in the service of Basho, where Wang witnesses the rule of the landowner from a closer perspective, behind the judge's seat. Tiger's past exploits and the incidents that shaped him are narrated in story form; his capture and actual death occur offstage. So do the skirmishes of the revolution that lead to the fall of the landowner's government. Though never seen, the landowner's presence is felt in every scene. What gets narrated is not strictly action, but analysis; every event in the play is shown to have both material and human causes, physical and emotional costs, and specific consequences in the scenes that follow. The story itself is interesting; but the process of analysis, not the action itself, is what finally proves exemplary. The play urges the audience to observe as carefully as do its characters, and to take up the dialectical attitude with which problems are put forward.

With the opening scene, Bond models such an attitude as first Basho, then the Ferryman, deliberate over whether or not to pick up an abandoned baby. The choice itself engages the audience's interest, and the care with which the moral dilemma is articulated sets a tone for the play – each subsequent scene presenting a situation that both requires and complicates moral choice. Though not inhuman, Basho leaves the child for self-serving reasons: "If the child had been big it could have carried my bundle. Then heaven's purpose would have been clear" (2). Nearly seduced by the Ferryman's suggestion that "people will take pity on him if he has a child," Basho decides to treat the child as a temptation from his spiritual quest, elaborating a philosophy and poetic stance ("Learn to be patient ... Would the sky alter by one tear if I took you with me?" 3) that Wang must later question. The Ferryman, rather than Basho, plays out at length the traditional temptation scene of the parable, caught between the calls of duty and desire – or in this case, between conflicting moral obligations, economic considerations, and emotions difficult to suppress. Left alone onstage with the child, he speaks as if he were observing his own thoughts – calmly, directly, and unemotionally. The audience is encouraged to keep a clear-sighted distance from the moral problem elaborated, an attitude "tested" (in characters and audience alike) by the increasing emotional strain posed by later scenes. The Ferryman defends the baby's parents: he would have done the same; the wisdom of leaving it is clear, the consequences of keeping it severe. He reports his doubts and misgivings even as he picks up the child. He knows he is too poor to feed it and that his wife will go without: "I love her. Yet I betray her for love of you. I kill her. [. . .] Where is the wisdom in that? [. . .] I must hope you're dead" (4–5).

His decision has consequences; but events that occur later in the play are impossible to predict, and the wisdom of the Ferryman's action cannot be judged in terms of them. The grown child will face another child by the river – and throw it in. History moves, times change, situations that share surface similarities require different choices – the play does not impose a value on the judgments of its characters so much as show how they are made. During the monologue, the Ferryman poles his boat away from the child, stops, poles back, arranges the baby's clothes, poles away, returns, reversing direction at each shift in the argument (and at the sound of the curlew that indicates his emotional instinct to save the child). The decision-making process is dramatized in visual, concrete form; and the Ferryman's clear statement of facts, thoughts, and emotions makes any acting of subtextual psychology redundant. The action of each subsequent scene recalls, comments, and elaborates upon the problem of moral choice introduced in Scene One.

The opening scene also introduces a reflective pace of narration that encourages the audience to observe with care. As Brecht once noted about epic theatre, "mental processes demand quite a different tempo from emotional ones and cannot necessarily stand the same speeding up."[30] Because it is a mental rather than an emotional resource that ultimately permits the characters (and the audience) to control the direction of their lives, Bond gives his characters time to weigh their actions and the audience time to reflect upon them. In earlier plays, a slower tempo often followed a period of accelerated action; characters like Lear, Clare, and Hecuba subjectively reflect upon their past only after being overwhelmed by it, and even their moments of reflection are interrupted by an objective world that changes faster than do their subjective responses to it. In the action of these plays, effect follows effect, and the real causes of the action are often understood only in retrospect, even by the audience. *The Bundle* also provides a pleasurably varied pace that holds audience attention, but here the causes of events are not as difficult to see. Scene Two, for example, ends with a test of the premises articulated by the Ferryman earlier in the scene – had the boat not belonged to the landowner, it might have been sunk; had Basho been simply a poet rather than the landowner's judge, he might have been drowned; and if Wang hadn't lied about the fishing-rod, they would have been arrested. Even the Keepers must decide on an appropriate course of action, and their process of reasoning, conditioned by fear, is made clear: "Poachers don't talk like that [...] No harm in stepping careful [...] In the dark – we can't take risks" (10). Throughout the play, the timing of choices is important, often generating psychological tension and suspense, but the decision-making process itself takes up most of the stage time. The analytical pace permits a clearer register of the factors influencing choice, draws attention to the characters' mental and emotional states, and refuses to let the audience off the hook by allowing habitually accepted notions of ethical behavior to be taken for granted.

Indeed, if the concrete theatre experience is to work as does real-life experience, urging the audience to question and to think, it must address the emotions as well as the intellect. Developing the position Brecht defended late in his career, Bond rarely presents emotion and reason as polar categories, but treats them dialectically. The question is how to use emotional appeal without universalizing or naturalizing the distinctly social and political issues of the play. In this regard, Scene Four, in which history repeats itself and the moral dilemma of Scene One is replayed, proves pivotal. By now, the audience may empathize with Wang – he has proved himself "good" by saving his family from the flood, and the abandoned child poses a threat to his well-deserved freedom. Yet we also expect (and even desire) Wang to repeat the gesture of kindness by which his own father is known ("He shelters travellers at home when they're too poor for the inn. He lets the sick cross for nothing, even in famine. He saved me from the river," 23). Whereas Basho could be faulted for his indifferent attitude, the scene is played out with the child's

7 Wang pleads with a mother to take back her child, before the revolution
in *The Bundle*

desperate mother, utterly exhausted and resigned to her fate. The
mother could have been Wang's own, a fact that makes his decision
harder still. Thus Wang's initial anger is shown to be misplaced; we
cannot, as Basho might, blame her. But what of Wang's subsequent
anger towards the child? We cannot blame the child, and yet Wang
likewise refuses to pity it: "Nine years! I planned – no, schemed,
plotted, dreamt! And now you're drowning me in the river? No! No!
No! No! No! [. . .] If there was a gun in your hand you'd pull it!"
(28–29). With gestures and arguments that recall Scene One, Wang
refuses the compromise that his father made earlier. But to do so, he
must rhetorically muster all of his strength to fight against the social
attitudes that have shaped him; in order to change the world, he
must change himself. He kills the child.

This action, and the words that follow, invokes an entirely different
relationship between Wang and his sympathetic audience: "The
world is shivering – there. Who will speak?" (29). The question turns
the issue back upon the audience to expose their own contradictory
desires. The emotionally spellbinding sequence leaves us in suspense

until the last moment as to what choice Wang will make. But once made, the child thrown out, in the direction of the audience, to its death, does the audience speak? Must we wait to judge his "murder" until we know what he will become? Has the crime been adequately justified? At this moment, we share Wang's former position as the silent observer of Basho's court. Earlier, Wang spoke of marvelling at "murderers who laughed over corpses [. . .] Each told the truth in his way, even against himself. How strange their lives, the stories of the little things that shaped them. You can go for a walk, and come back another man" (25). Basho's court provided for Wang a stage on which the everyday actions of individuals appeared strange and unnatural enough to be questioned. The audience, on the other hand, watches Wang "go for a walk, and come back another man," and Bond's courtroom-like staging of the incident is estranging in an analogous way. The audience must feel, as Wang did moments earlier, that "there is no argument I can use" – yet the deliberate pacing through which the problem is presented brings us to the point of questioning our own emotions. In retrospect, the Ferryman's decision to pick up Wang is the easiest of the play, at least for the audience. Once involved in the character's story, the emotional stakes of the play are gradually raised: it is difficult to watch Wang murder a child, to see prisoners suffer with help so close by, and to watch the mental and physical torture of characters we have grown to like. But once established, the pattern of reflection helps guide the audience through the argument of the most emotionally powerful, and thus "morally" imperilling, scenes of the play.

Given the issues involved, *The Bundle* needs a technique that will serve the social analysis – provide the equivalent of comment – without ignoring the potential use of emotional appeal. The danger is action that seems too "real," creating an immediacy that suppresses contradictions and discourages analysis. Bond's answer is not to "balance" or alternate one against the other, but to structure scenes in an essentially "gestic" manner. Brecht writes, "the eye that looks for the gest in everything is the moral sense," noting also that expressions, incidents, sound effects, visual images, physical gestures and language can all be gestic.[31] By highlighting the comment that the action can only imply, the gest stays in the audience's memory, dispels ambiguity, and invites comparison, drawing attention to interconnected social relationships and contradictions that narrative alone might not illuminate. The flood scene provides a good

example. While the interest is focused on Wang's immediate family
and the characters with whom they share the stage, the offstage cries
of help remind the audience of the larger community of which they
are a part. The most traumatizing emotional effects are not seen, but
heard, in the sounds of a woman in labor:

The WOMAN *is heard in labour. Slowly during the scene, shouting, moaning, and
sobbing increase to a climax and then fade into the hum, whimpering and stray cries of a
desperate crowd.* (17)

A woman experiencing the pain of childbirth under such circumstances provides a more poignant comment on the disaster than had
men drowned before our eyes. By punctuating the entire rescue
attempt with the sound of human cries, the audience is reminded
that some are being saved at the expense of others. The very length
of Wang's deliberation can be counted in lives lost, and, despite the
building of dramatic suspense, we cannot feel entirely relieved by his
narrow escape. The fact that the rescue boat is the Ferryman's own,
appropriated by the landowner and now being used by his soldiers,
is not simply ironic, but reinforces the political contradictions
exposed by Wang's "lesson" on property and taxes in Scene Two.
Finally, as Wang considers the landowner's offer (nine years' slavery
in exchange for the life of his family), the characters wager on the
outcome of his decision.

Although the decision is agonizing, no one suggests that Wang
could reject the offer altogether, except for the Ferryman, who tells
Wang to swim for his life. The other characters, who quickly accept
the proffered odds, find nothing unnatural in the businessman's
instinct for "a piece of the action." Through the gesture of betting on
the strength of human emotion, Bond reveals the underlying "truth"
of the situation as an economic transaction. Indeed, subjective
factors limit Wang's choice as severely as the objective situation;
Wang's "goodness" (the morality he has learned from his father)
demands that he save his family yet allows the landowner to profit
from the disaster. The scene builds to a dramatic highpoint and ends
with Wang's stiff gesture of defiance as he capitulates with shouts of
"Buy me!" As Bond notes in the introduction, the choice of the word
is itself part of the analysis, a gesture that embodies the emotional
cost of the decision and its social significance.[32]

The naturalistically compelling situation works directly on the
emotions without sacrificing analytical depth. As pitiable flood

victims in a life-threatening situation, the characters themselves feel relatively helpless; but through his gestic technique, Bond turns the experience of "natural disaster" into a comment upon it – showing how the characters' own attitudes, however unwittingly, have determined their fate. As Brecht writes, "most people take the price of bread, the lack of work, the declaration of war as if they were phenomena of nature: earthquakes or floods ... It may look as if their own decisions no longer played a part. The simple fact is that decisions have become more difficult."[33] Bond takes the observation one step further to suggest that natural disasters themselves may have human causes, and are not immune to social analysis. Thus we learn that the "catastrophe" is a recurring one ("OLD MAN: It always goes after six days," 11) that could be solved ("WANG: If we lived here instead of letting the dead have it –" 13) were it not for the inhibiting effect of conventional attitudes ("OLD MAN: What respect is it when we can't house the dead – who need it most! No wonder the flood's lasted six days!" 13–14). Although experience is crucial to education, it does not necessarily teach; the older members of the community ridicule Wang's simple suggestion that they build their house on the highland of ancestors' graves, showing just how entrenched are the attitudes that must be changed.

The gestic nature of the action not only clarifies the meaning within scenes, but also allows the audience to more easily compare and differentiate between similar actions that occur across the play. Important differences can be grasped between Basho's abandonment of a baby in Scene One and Wang's murder in Scene Four, between the Ferryman's decision to save Wang in Scene One and again in Scene Nine; between Tiger's violence against a landlord and the soldier's violence against Tiger; between the childlike egotism of the thieves in Scene Five and the corrupt egotism of the businessman in Scene Nine. Likewise, important similarities exist between Kung-Tu's gesture of charity in Scene Seven and Basho's gesture of charity toward Wang in Scene Four; in the soldier's killing of Tiger and Basho's killing of the Ferryman; in Wang's decision to save his family in Scene Three and his decision to jeopardize them in Scene Six. Once the argument offered by Wang's own political practice is grasped, the complicating, self-referential comparisons provided by the play's structure and imagery resolve into the clarity of self-evident logic.

The lesson of *The Bundle* resides finally in the practical nature of class consciousness as a guide to moral action; but the play recognizes with equal force the difficulty of attaining it, imputing cause to the falsely "humanizing" ideology of a class-divided society. Thus Wang's aesthetic practice and the dialectical vision he promotes provide a stark contrast to that of Basho, an artist whose poetic vision the play rejects and against whom Bond defines his own aesthetic practice. While Basho occasionally presents a humorous figure, *The Bundle* offers a more serious analysis of his philosophical stance than that found in *Narrow Road*. Indeed, Basho is an interesting and articulate character with an epigrammatic turn of phrase that is truly seductive. As with Shakespeare in *Bingo*, Basho's limitations are not simply due to close association with a corrupt ruling class, but to an idealistic mode of thinking that interprets experience in absolute, symbolic, ahistorical terms. Like Shakespeare, he searches for enlightenment, but is left with his own face in the water, and no more knowledge than all life ends in death. When Wang asks what he has learned in Scene Two, Basho says, "Do not ask for enlightenment till you're ready to lose all. I look into the mirror of this river. If this mirror appeared in your boat – a little round hole in the bottom – you would block it out –" (9). Useless and impractical, the wisdom Basho dispenses would sink the boat. Although much depends on delivery, the dialogue itself, both here and elsewhere in the play, fully expresses the social dimension of Basho's character: truly "gestic," nothing need be read "into" it for comment on his attitude.

Throughout the play, Basho's carefully structured phrasing invites moral assent, even as the logic of its "content" repels. The slightly alienated language enables the audience to see the dangers of his reasoning, even at its most persuasive. The most dangerous "moral blackmail" of the play thus occurs in Scene Four with Basho's appeals to Wang to stay on. Basho's offer sounds almost heartfelt ("If I could care for anything in this world it would be you. Stay." 24); his ordinance against taking babies into the temple almost reasonable ("The priests take too many infants. The old suffer [...]" 25); and Wang's decision to leave almost wilfully self-destructive:

You forget that your eyes can ache with cold, the grit that comes in your mouth when you starve, the thin dirt on the rice bowl, filth decaying in corners, the smell of unwashed clothes. You can be too tired to clean and too hopeless to think. Such people are always lost, even at home. One day you may scream on the street and break your neighbor's bones. (24)

Basho's bleak view of human nature, his philosophy of survival, his "enlightened self-interest" reflect the experience that others in the play have shared; what he says may be true. To such appeals, Wang has no answer, at least none to be put in Basho's terms ("WANG: There's no argument I can use," 25). From his silent, subservient position behind the judge's chair, Wang is free neither to accuse, defend, nor pass judgment. Like the audience of the play, he must observe and remain silent, imprisoned by the spectacle of the courtroom with its mesmerizing images of the living dead: "Living women with fingers twisting like ghosts, old men staring like lost children [etc.]" (25). Until Wang emerges with a different aesthetic practice, Basho "owns" the language of the play, a power that affects what those around him see. Class position, not experience, divides their point of view. Precisely what constitutes self-interest is another way of putting the question of morality that the play addresses.

Throughout the play, Basho's poetry serves rhetorical purposes, his natural metaphors revealing a pessimistic vision of life that legitimates his own cruelty. The distance from Basho's vision is illustrated, for both Wang and the playwright, through a different aesthetic. As Bond notes in the introduction, "not even imagery works for us as it did in the past" (xv). In *The Bundle*, Bond's images are rooted to concrete situations, and change accordingly. Thus the bundle of the play's title appears as the child who is saved in Scene One, the child murdered in Scene Four, the flood victims' bundle of worldly possessions in Scene Three, the gang's bundle of loot in Scene Five, the Ferryman's tortured body in Scene Eight (recorded as "*the sound of a wet bundle being hit,*" 69) and the rifles of the play's second half. As opposed to the river, the image of a bundle – created, shaped, cared for, or destroyed by human hands – provides an appropriate title for the play's argument about human needs and the possibility of change. Because the bundle shifts in meaning according to its use, which in turn is determined by the needs of its owners, judging its value immediately involves the audience in the socially relevant issues of the play. That only rifles can change a society that abandons its children is not a truth for all time, but a visual connection that helps us analyze the meaning of Bond's play in terms that may challenge habitual patterns of thought.

In every instance, the meaning of the bundle is established in relation to the river, a concrete and enduring element of the characters' material life. Unlike the wall of *Lear*, the river is never seen, but is referred to and imagined on the stage so often it provides the play's controlling metaphor. But the image changes, and through it Bond compares and contrasts the attitude of the characters as it affects behavior. Basho sees in the river the "mirror of eternity," a symbol of transcendent truth, and an image for man's immutable being: "Does the river ask, what is the way? Men are a dark river [etc.]" (1). But for Wang, the river is a mute and neutral witness to the actions of men and workings of society:

The young set out from this river. The old return to die. Merchants cross day after day till their lives are as soiled and faceless as old money. Orders are sent to buy or sell or accuse. Thieves plot while they wait on this worn-out landing. Soldiers with blood down to their underclothes. Monks without the child's right to innocence, with faces like snakes or pampered old women. They all came here, waited, stepped into the boat and trusted their lives to the dark river that crosses their path even as they pass over on it. This time we wait with rifles. (65)

Wang sees in the river, not his own reflection, but the connection between his life and the history of his community. The river is neither opaque (a natural fact and real presence) nor transluscent (a window on eternity). Rather, its "meaning" is found in the set of social relations to which it points; thus it plays a precise economic role in the play. The literal source of the Ferryman's livelihood, the river and its fish are owned by the landowner on whom the villagers actually depend, the perennial floods providing a recurring economic crisis that some do not survive. As the Ferryman puts it, "The river kept me alive and it almost killed me" (48). As Wang comes to understand, only by reclaiming the land and damming the river can the villagers end their unnecessary suffering, control their own lives, and begin to build a fully human existence. But in order to do so, they must first understand how the landowner works. The villagers accept the river, its flooding, and the landowner's rights as "given"; like the problem posed by too many children, natural and social facts are easily conflated. Just as Wang teaches the gang to identify their problem accurately, so the play encourages the audience to make similar distinctions between the natural and the social, between what can be changed and what cannot. For this purpose the river is always represented onstage, already "written," a concrete image that is, literally, opened to interpretation.

With the help of a water bowl, and his audience's own experience, Wang teaches the gang to "read" the river differently, oppositionally. "Everyman must open his mouth and drink to live. He [the landowner/Basho] uses the means by which men live to fill them with ignorance. They live by being condemned to death" (39). Before understanding such a concept, Wang "acts out" the process in a short play-within-the-play, imitating Bond's own didactic methods; the "teaching" scene ends as the house lights go up and Wang reads a poem intended for the larger audience as well, one that works against the dark insights offered by Basho's own poems: "[. . .] What is enlightenment? / Understanding who is the thief / And what is the great light" (39). The preceding action enables the audience to accurately interpret the lines. A related lesson underlies Scene Seven, the only incident that breaks the chronological order of the story. Here Tiger learns the importance of patience, the danger of acting impulsively and too soon. To what could be titled "the parable of the water-sellers," Wang says simply: "Watch. Learn" (55), a directive appropriate to the audience of the play, who watch and learn a different lesson when Wang and Tiger leave the stage. In Scene Eight, the Ferryman's bowl of water, offered "too late" to help the tortured Tiger, not only foreshadows the river that will soon be reddened with the Ferryman's own blood, but provides the moment of enlightenment that "teaches" him what to do.

Through the images of the water bowl, the actions of the water-sellers, and the profound changes that surround their "use" of water, Bond links the spiritually regenerative properties that Basho might see in the river to the concrete changes in behavior that the play encourages. That change is represented most dramatically in the heightened pause that follows the freeing of prisoners in Scene Seven. Their liberators gone, the characters slowly realize that they are no longer caught "between two tigers," but facing an entirely new situation. The water-sellers find themselves giving their water away with the whispered awe and reverence of a secret sacrament, as if sudden movement would dash the barely articulate hope that their own gestures represent. Bond's stage directions are explicit:

They all stare at one another in amazement. They hardly believe what they're doing.
SECOND WATER SELLER (*observing himself in amazement, watching the running water as if it were the first time he had seen it, handling the water can as if it had just dropped from space*): . . . I pour the water . . .

8 Tiger, the "dark force" of *The Bundle*, threatens to eat Wang alive

FIRST WATER SELLER (*staring at his own hand as it moves; almost whispering*): I
take the cup and ... (59–60)

The classic alienation-effect is hereby incorporated into the story,
part of the characters' own awakening and a foretaste of the simple
pleasures that a changed human community will take for granted in
the final scene. But the concrete portrayal of the feeling of freedom
also rewards the audience with a vision of possibility that makes the
violent repercussions of Scene Eight, with its mental and physical
torture, somewhat easier to bear. The final scene opens on the
healthy laughter of a happier, post-revolutionary life; but the river
remains to claim the life of a worker, and the incident serves
as a reminder of those things that cannot be changed. The sadness that accompanies this accidental death is far different from
either the pessimism of Basho or the painful experiences of past
injustice.

    The most disruptive, energetic, and effective language of the play
belongs finally to neither Basho nor Wang, but to Tiger, a figure
who tests the audience's conventional responses more thoroughly

than any other. Before Wang arrives, Tiger and his band of thieves
live "in darkness," avariciously preying on the poor like a pack of
wolves. Tiger, a leader by virtue of strength alone, appears to revel
in the violence by which they survive: "Kill! Kill all day today!
Heeeee!" (32). Their animalistic behavior is underscored by mono-
syllabic language, punctuated with grunts, howls, and groans. Like
ignorant and unruly children, the group fights over stolen loot and
delights in stories of thieves and murderers greater than themselves;
they have also learned to respect and fear those in power: "Sir, we
don't rob rich – only poor [. . .] Emperor to look on us as helpers"
(36–37). Curious and energetic, their childlike characteristics make
them more interesting than repellent to the audience; and their
portrayal highlights the promise that no appearance in Basho's court
could disclose. By cleverly turning his own capture into a test and
teaching session, Wang displays the power of his own wisdom;
however, the relationship he establishes is not based on moral
blackmail, but on a lesson that appeals to the gang's self-interest
and shared experience. Indeed, the scene might seem patronizing
were it not for the real threat (and promise) represented by
Tiger, a character who lives up to the legendary attributes of his
name.

Under most circumstances, Tiger would be viewed as an entirely
unsavory character: a hardened criminal, murderer, and social
parasite who bullies everyone onstage. But the story on which his
reputation for violence is based provides Wang (and the audience)
with the appropriate context for judging his character; and the
manner of its telling demonstrates an aesthetic practice that effectively challenges that of other characters. With "Story: True,"
Tiger recapitulates the events that led to the loss of his hand in a
language stripped to the bare essentials, simple, concrete, literal,
and gestic. Since the gang has heard this story as many times as
Tiger has repeated it, their meal goes on undisturbed. But for the
audience, the language of Tiger's story has an oddly estranging
effect, while the story itself compels interest and literally changes
our view of the character. Perhaps the most verbally arresting
moments of the play, Tiger begins with a threat to "eat" Wang for
his next meal and ends with an even greater appetite than when he
began:

Haaa! Smell: Tiger. Next-time smell: You! Ha! (*He shows his stump.*) Story.
How Tiger lost hand. (*The others sigh quietly.*) Ha! True! (*He sits.*) Town. I

live there then. Streets. Houses. White walls. People have clean clothes.
Walk in street. Children – hola! (*Imitates children's arms.*) Aahh ... (*Sighs. All
the thieves eat.*) Man. Dark Eyes. In the corner shop [...] Man. Bought and
sold. Next – town his. Earth his. Everything goes dry. Cloth on window-sill:
dry. Fields: dry. No rain: heaven forget.
                              [...]
Men came. My house – sold! Walls, roof, garden, tree. Police pull me out on
street. Hm. [...] Then I was quiet – before the prey. Walk to corner shop.
Stand in doorway. Humble. Ask: job. Man smiles like little window high up
on side of house. Beckons. So – I enter. Kow-tow. Rise. Left hand shuts his
mouth. Right hand: on throat. Squeeze. Like a bag of beans. (*He holds stump
up.*) Dead. Then walk down street. Still hold. One hand: throat. Lift him
up. One hand. Show. Soldiers run. Neighbours. First son. Second son.
Number one wife. Number two wife. Third son. Pull. Push. Shout: Let go! I
hold him up. One hand. Show [...] Judge tells soldiers: "He let's go – or
chop!" Hold corpse up! High! Show! Chop! Corpse falls. Hand still on
throat. Judge saw. (*Smiles at* WANG.) Ho! Tiger! (*Chews.*) Yum. Ah. (35)

Not only do the actions reported here "speak" for Tiger, but the
unembellished, ordinary, indicative language itself makes a truth
claim – inviting the audience, like the judge of the story, to "see"
far more than the decapitated head of the enemy brought to
the marketplace. Tiger is proud of his deed, and shows no remorse;
the story neither excuses nor justifies, but rather demonstrates the
material causes and physical consequences of his action. In the
context of the scene, Tiger uses the story to introduce himself; the
telling affords a pleasurable repetition that both substitutes for his
loss, and allows him to create (or actively assert) a subject position
from which his behavior (and its consequences) make sense. In other
words, the story is a practical one, its "truth" tested through use.
Like Bond's claim for his own plays, the narrative is not necessarily a
true story (fiction based on something that actually occurred) but
rather "Story: True," a statement of equivalence through which the
told account (story) stands unqualified by any adjective and true
becomes a noun.

Tiger's story, in first a humorous and later a serious sense, is
legendary. Indeed, the soldiers who cut out Tiger's tongue discredit
the facts on which the story is based: "Tiger told a great story – how
he lost his hand. A lie, of course. Lost it for pick-pocketing. No more
stories" (62). But the soldiers' effect on the "truth value" of Tiger's
story is negligible, their actions evoking in the audience (and the
Ferryman who watches them) the same visceral response that led to

Tiger's original crime – the anger (and resulting strength) that arises from a sense of unjust violation. Most importantly, perhaps, through voice, gesture, physical presence, and accompanying action, Tiger's story connects art to the primary life processes through which the self is produced. Tiger and the gang eat throughout the scene with as much relish as the story is told; and for the audience, Tiger's very body turns out to be a narrative in which hunger, desire, justice, truth, pleasure, and story-telling are inseparable human drives. Tiger not only represents the strength and energy necessary for revolutionary change, but has the literal imagination that puts Basho's vision of the world to the test. Indeed, through the practical struggle that Wang's teaching has inspired, Tiger learns to tell his own story better – that is, to write a moral for himself:

God has ten hands. Each side. Good for miracles. But never escape. [...] Life good. Wise say: "give hand in friendship." Tiger raises stump. Great friend! (49, 50)

Once Tiger sees himself as an instrument for change, rather than a criminal, he does work miracles. And as the Ferryman's change of heart shows, Tiger's active example is as instructive and powerful as Wang's rational arguments. With Tiger's blood in the water bowl (as well as the sequence it follows), Bond incorporates an "aggro-effect" into the story, one that finally teaches the Ferryman the futility of compromise when humanity itself seems at stake.

The emblematic thrust of *The Bundle* is positive, suggesting that social change is difficult, but possible, that moral choices can and must be made, that "right" and "wrong" are relative but not unknowable. The parable form itself demands a simplification of issues that promotes conceptual thought, and lack of contemporary allusions or an historical frame works against a more specific application of its arguments. Because the narrative of *The Bundle* examines the role of ideology in a class-divided society and the relationship between knowledge and action, its message cannot be reduced to any of the lessons argued within it. To extrapolate a "moral," as the final moments of the play invite us to do, distorts the complexity of the theatre experience; we must judge Wang's actions on the basis of situations depicted on the stage, in experiences that are observed, not lived, by the audience. But by presenting the political arguments through extreme situations, Bond forces "the question" of choice and judgment on which the audience's own potential for change is based. As in all Bond's parables, the series of questions on which the play reflects simply set the terms of analysis, to be tested through use, on the audience's own experience outside the theatre.

CHAPTER 6

Social pleasures

As a playwright, Bond is better known for his seriousness than for his comic talent, more for his use of violence on the stage than for his humor. Such a reputation distorts reality: not only does Bond write comedy, but he can make audiences laugh. So central is humor to Bond's writing that not a single play is without it. In *Saved, Lear,* and *The Swing,* the combination of joking and violence may increase the nightmarish effect – humor deployed as an "aggro-effect" intensifying the sense of violation experienced by the audience. With Clare in *The Fool* and Mrs. Lewis in *Jackets II,* laughter itself produces startling effects; disturbing, uncontrollable, credible and contagious, their laughter contributes to a complex moment of social analysis Bond later describes as a "TE" (theatre event).[1] Few of Bond's plays are unmixed in tone, but the range of comic techniques employed suggests some interest in the form. *Saved,* which earned Bond's reputation for violence, is subtitled *An Oedipal Comedy,* and *The Pope's Wedding* is as rich in comic possibility as its title implies. More than half of Bond's subsequent plays could be billed as comedy, with several so subtitled. *The Sea, Restoration,* and *The Cat,* for example, rework the traditional comic forms they take up, altering the class perspective and social effect of a genre historically "class conscious" in its subject-matter and socially conservative in its effects. The savage farce of *Early Morning,* the burlesque antics of *A-A-America!,* and the boardroom manners of *The Worlds* and *In the Company of Men* likewise recognize the conventional comic modes they parody and enlarge.

Not everyone thinks Bond is funny; but the effect of Bond's humor can be as telling as its intent. For sense of humor, like aesthetic pleasure itself, is a thoroughly socialized pleasure sensitized in complicated ways by education, culture, gender, and experience. Despite the stylistic diversity of Bond's comedy, and the range of

response it has evoked, certain comic strategies do seem distinctively
Bondian. To distinguish between the laughter and joking of Bond's
characters and that of the playwright and audience will ultimately
involve questions of pleasure, an area of importance to any socialist
aesthetic practice.[2] Using the comic theories of Freud, Bakhtin, and
Brecht as a guide, the following analysis suggests that Bond's comedy
can have liberating as well as nightmarish effects on its audience, can
be as reconstructive and restorative as it is deconstructive and satiric
– and often within the same play. Indeed, humor and joking, as
opposed to explicit themes, provide one key to the psychic economy
of Bond's plays, to their potential for dividing, repositioning, re-
warding, and energizing the audience according to the political
perspective from which they view the plays.

Saved

Ending a lengthy attack on the original production of *Saved*, one
London reviewer noted that Bond had "an amusing line in low
patter . . . [but] a dirty joke has as much relevance."[3] The comment
is typical, not merely for its critical slant, but for the general
recognition, amid hostile reaction to the play, of Bond's humor. The
joking that in *Lear* surrounds the torture of Warrington or the rape of
Cordelia may be no less unsettling, but the tragic context of the play
lends an appropriateness to such "aggro-effects" that earlier plays
had to generate on their own. As Shakespeare's example illustrates,
the intrusion of the comic into the world of tragedy, especially with
the joking of lower-class characters, is an expected and acceptable
convention; far fewer precedents pertain to the opposite – the
intrusion of violence and death into an essentially comic world.
Neither *Saved* nor the *The Pope's Wedding* were mistaken for comedy,
despite the joking of characters within the play, the focus on
domestic relationships, and Bond's subsequent attempts to establish
the "optimism" of his work.[4] Indeed, the "almost irresponsible"
optimism of *Saved*, like its claim to being "An Oedipal Comedy" is
based on what does *not* happen in the play: Len does not abandon
Pam, does not sleep with her mother, does not murder her father,
and does not leave at the end. The sexual ambivalence that provides
a key to the actions of Len in *Saved* and Scopey in *The Pope's Wedding*
is in fact mirrored in the alternating patterns of the play's formal
construction, which moves with great control between closed and

open sets, ordinary and abrasive language, intimate and public interaction, active movement and static tableau, noise and quiet.⁵ Tragic action is balanced by comic persistence; irreparable loss with cyclical resilience; sadistic gazing with the urge to exhibit.

Such patterns of ambivalence are typical of modern tragi-comedy in both its naturalistic and absurdist modes, but to call *Saved* tragi-comic would be misleading. In *Saved*, the psychological and social damage on which we are made to reflect reveal problems too broad and serious to be addressed by the courts or the social services, yet too specific and urgent to be accepted as a statement about the human condition. In other words, *Saved* is a comedy that refuses to condone, through humor, the world it represents, or to mitigate, through jokes, its serious effect. Unlike black humor, the joking of *Saved* promotes participation in rather than detachment from the reality reproduced onstage – not least because the wit is the characters' own, produced for each other, not simply the play-wright's, produced for us. As such, it sheds light on the characters' behavior, the psychosexual dynamics of which are central to the play. The situations in which joking arises, the actions to which joking leads, and the resources to which joking points help illustrate the enormous amounts of energy and ingenuity needed to keep such a corrupt social fabric together: Len's questions may stir things up, but jokes reveal and manage the tensions that are already there.

Indeed, if Freud has taught us anything about jokes, it is their inherently relative, interactive, social quality – as communication in which the unconscious plays a central role. Freud's distinction between the comic and wit (*Witz*) may prove useful to an analysis of the humor in *Saved*. While the comical is found, first of all in people and by transference in objects and situations, wit is made; in the latter, one's own mental processes contain the sources for the production of pleasure.⁶ Yet wit cannot be enjoyed alone, nor can it be separated from the impulse to impart it. While comedy requires only two "positions" – the one who finds the comical, and the one in whom it is found – wit requires three: the wit-maker, the object of the hostile or sexual tendency, and a listener who completes the circuit of pleasure. As Steve Neale has described it, comedy is a structure of observation, while wit is a structure of address.⁷ Within this context, Freud's breakdown of wit according to "tendency" proves helpful. Noting that some wit may be harmless and playful, Freud finds that the most successful wit (that which evokes the most explosive laughter) is "hostile wit serving as an aggression, satire or defense, or [. . .] obscene wit, serving as a sexual exhibition," the two tendencies that give a joke its power of "ruffling people who do not wish to hear it."[8]

As noted earlier, in *Saved*'s problems with the censor, as well as with original audiences, sexuality and violence were hard to disentangle, language and action being equally "offensive." The psychosexual dynamics of the play are established from the opening moments, primarily through the joking behavior of the characters, the obscene and aggressive tendencies of which are fairly evident. In Scene One, for example, an exchange of "dirty" jokes substitutes for the sexual act between Len and Pam that Harry's offstage presence has delayed:

LEN: Why did the woman with three tits shoot 'erself?
PAM: Eh?
LEN: She only 'ad two nipples.
They laugh.
PAM: I don't get it. (*She laughs.*) What did the midwife say to the nun?
LEN: Don' know.
She whispers in his ear. They laugh. (26–27)

Given that Bond built the scene "on the young man's sexual insecurity – he either invents interruptions himself or is interrupted by the old man" (310), the jokes provide Len with a less direct form of sexual intimacy and Pam with a social lubricant to get things moving. Such jokes are not created by the characters, but like those retold later, are part of the social currency, spent and circulated as needed within the group. In Scene Ten, for example, the exchange of jokes between gang members helps reestablish friendly connections after Fred's release from prison. The joking ends with Pete's remark, "Didn't know they let yer 'ave jokes inside" (108); and Pete's wit makes explicit the connection between jokes, sex, and weapons suggested by the action of earlier scenes. Once the joke-telling starts, the inhibitions relax, making social interaction easier. In Scene One, the verbal foreplay of the joke exchange gives Len enough self-confidence to become witty himself and begin to joke at Harry's expense. Like later scenes with harsher consequences, the situation gradually escalates from quiet, relatively ordinary conversation to the noisy energy of a "staged" event, the attack on Harry fuelled by the infectious energy of Len's sexual punning:

LEN: Let's 'ave a choose. (*Loudly*) 'Ow's that for size?
PAM: What yer shoutin?

LEN *he puts a sweet in her mouth*: Go easy! Yer wanna make it last! [. . .] Oo,
  yer got a lovely little soft centre. (*Aside to Pam.*) First time I seen choclit
  round it!
He jumps on the sofa.
PAM (*shrill*): Yer awful!
LEN: That still 'ard? [. . .] Come on. There's plenty more where that come
  from.
He puts a sweet in her mouth.
PAM (*splutters*): Can't take no more!
LEN: Yeh – open it. Yer can do a bit more!
PAM: Ow!
LEN: Oorr lovely!
He tickles her. She chokes. (27–28)

Len pushes his joke to the limit; were it not for Pam's complicit
laughter and cautionary advice ("Lay off, or 'e'll stay in out a spite,"
28), the aggressive tendency of Len's wit might be even more
apparent. In addition to the titillating function the joke serves for
the characters, the audience may take pleasure in Len's wit,
suddenly relieved of the self-consciousness of its own voyeuristic
position when Harry's presence prevents (on more than one level)
the unfolding of a more sexually explicit scene.

The joking in Scene One may seem relatively harmless; but the
frustrated desires, coping strategies, insecurity, and ingenuity it
reveals can be recognized in much that follows. At the end of Scene
Two, the *double entendres* of Fred's wit are as successful with Pam as
Len's seductive tactics in Scene One, with Len now the amused, but
helpless, onlooker. In Scene Nine, the sexual innuendo of Len's
comments, encouraged by Mary, leads to an encounter fraught with
Oedipal significance, which Harry's sudden entrance, like the return
of the repressed, again interrupts ("LEN: I 'ad a feelin' 'e'd come in,"
103). However unintentional, Len's expressions of sexual interest in
both Pam and Mary have violent consequences; and the wit with
which those relationships are marked provides one of the connections between Len and the rest of the gang, between what happens in
the park and what happens at home.

Herself the object of obscene or hostile joking, Pam uses ready
repartee to defend herself from Len's troubling questions, to parry
criticism, and to reestablish control of her situation. When Len asks,
"Ow many blokes yer 'ad this week?" Pam responds, "We ain't
finished Monday yet!" (26); to Len's suggestion that they go to bed
early, Pam rejoins, "If yer go t'bed much earlier it won't be worth
gettin' up" (33); to Fred's loaded comment, "I wouldn't mind a bit

a grind for you," she jokes "Yer'll 'ave t'join the union" (37). As the
play progresses, Pam's witticisms become increasingly pointed and
pathetic. As the family waits for Pam to tend her crying baby, Pam
comments that Len is "Too lazy t'get up an' fetch it. [...] 'Is last
servant died a over-work" (47); to Mary's prodding about the
baby's crying, she says, "I thought the cat was stuck up the
chimney" (48). Given Mary's fussing over Len, their obvious
indifference to the baby, and their readiness to blame Pam for the
irritation, her comments hit home: indeed, the relation of others to
the child is as murderous as Pam's own. As Pam's world collapses
around her, the witty edge of her conversation gets replaced by
pathetic pleading and direct insults, usually aimed at Len. The
repartee with which Len defends himself in turn reveals the passive–
aggressive nature of his decision to stay on. As Pam suggests, Len
seems to "Live on trouble" (92), and he changes his mind about
leaving with the words, "I'd like t'tell 'er t'jump off once more"
(130). Although the domestic quarrel is a staple of dramatic comedy,
in *Saved* the deadly insistence of the endless rows offers little pleasure
for the audience. More "civilized" perhaps than the battering in the
park, the interactions of the family reproduce the conditions of
violence and do so with the same strategies (silence, insult, irony,
and wit) that enable the characters to survive its effects. Len's mere
presence as a "third party" allows for the verbal expression of family
tensions that would otherwise be repressed and recycled; but the
restorative, reintegrative effects expected from traditional comedy
are muted by the perception of an already damaged social structure
– one that cannot be "fixed" by defensive maneuvers alone.

　　The joking of Pam and Len pales beside the energetic and far
more powerful banter of the gang's dialogue. Not only is most of the
group's stage time spent "havin' a laugh," their joke technique is
more complicated and potentially more interesting for the audience,
although wit functions similarly for both. On the one hand, the
joking behavior of the gang reveals complex codes of communication that permit social self-definition within a context of group
solidarity. Gang members frequently pick up each other's train of
thought and carry it forward – whether competitively, with out-
doing wit and repartee; cooperatively, with a shared rendition of an
old joke or limerick; or individually, with a spontaneously witty
remark. On the other hand, the content expressed through wit,
especially in its cynicism toward legal, religious, and social institu-

tions, points to the group's general level of alienation. In Scene Three, for example, Pete complains of being late for the funeral of a child in whose death he is implicated, irritated at having to go at all, then recounts the incident for the amusement of his friends as if he had orchestrated the entire event. In the following playful exchange, the group enlarges upon Pete's claims, verbally mastering and manipulating a system over which, in reality, they have little control:

BARRY: 'It 'im before yer knew 'e was comin'.
PETE (*lighting his pipe*): Think I can't drive?
COLIN: What a giggle, though.
MIKE: Accidents is legal.
COLIN: Can't touch yer.
PETE: This coroner-twit says 'e's sorry for troublin' me.
MIKE: The law thanks 'im for 'is elp.
PETE: They paid me for comin'.
MIKE: An' the nip's mother reckons 'e ain' got a blame 'issell. (38)

Such an introduction makes apparent the sadistic tendency of the gang, and in the irrepressible nature of the sexual and aggressive joking that follows, an energy is located that prepares the audience for the action of Scene Six.

In general, the gang's joking expresses their cynicism towards legal and social institutions, and despite the ritual teasing, some tolerance of difference within their own social ranks. Thus Len's response to Colin's question, "What yer doin now?" ("LEN: Waitin'," 77) sets off a spate of ironic wit, based on the gang's feigned disbelief:

COLIN: It was in the park, yer 'onour!
MIKE: This girl come up t'me.
COLIN: An' drags me in the bushes.
BARRY: Yer 'onour.
He laughs.
COLIN: I knew she was thirteen.
MIKE: But she twisted me arm.
COLIN: An' 'er ol' dad'd bin bashin' it off for years.
BARRY: Yer 'onour. (41)

Not only does "waiting" more than aptly describe Len's position in the play, but Len *is* seduced by Pam, not the other way around, takes pleasure in "getting his arm twisted," views her father as a sexual rival, is implicated in Pam's pregnancy, and will land in court looking far more innocent than he is. Likewise, Pam's promiscuity has the usual consequences, and the gang's mistaking of the mother for the fiancée paves the way for Len's later encounter with Mary ("BARRY: Bit past it, ain' she? PETE: She's still got the regulation 'oles [etc.]," 42). Here the playwright shows his hand in the making of wit with dialogue economically "overdetermined" in both theme and function.

The gang's pleasure in jokes seems self-consciously subversive, like their interest in picking up girls in church; but the joking also illustrates the extent to which the group participates in their own oppression. Whether deliberate or unconscious, their jesting attitudes mimic or parody the thought and philosophy of those who would keep them down: through jokes, spontaneous repartee, and recycled clichés, the characters present themselves by turns as animalistic, over-sexed, sexually perverse, slow-witted, and untrustworthy, as both hardened criminals and pathetic victims. Colin remarks that Len has probably been spending his time in reform school (41), Pete suggests that he sleeps with his own mother (41), Fred notes that the baby's brains would save money on bait (73), and relates with relish how he "slashed" in the chaplain's tea (110). Their conversation is punctuated with cliché-ridden common sense, often turned sarcastically upon themselves ("Takes all kinds," "Live and learn," "Trust the Unions!").[9] More disturbing, however, is the related line of reasoning, first suggested by Len in Scene Five, that crying is "Good for [the baby's] lungs," an attitude that takes hold with brutal consequences in Scene Six:

COLIN: [...] Ugh! Mind yer don't 'urt it.
MIKE: Yer can't.
BARRY: Not at that age.
MIKE: Course yer can't, no feelin's.
PETE: Like animals.
[...]
MIKE: What a giggle!
PETE: Cloutin's good for 'em. I read it.
BARRY (*to* FRED): Why don't you clout it?
FRED: It ain' mine.
PETE: Sherker. Yer got a do yer duty.
FRED: Ain' my worry. Serves 'er right.
[...]
MIKE: Reckon it'll grow up an idiot.

PETE: Or deformed.

BARRY: Look where it come from. (77, 78)

Likewise, when Fred is apprehended for the murder, he presents himself as a battered victim, displacing his own responsibility in an almost ludicrous manner: "Bloody 'eathens. Thumpin' and kickin' the van [. . .] Bloody housewives! [. . .] Ought a be stood up an' shot! [. . .] 'Alf murdered with a lot a 'and bags!" (83, 84). Yet his suggestion, "If I was ten years older I'd get a medal" (84), is not far off the mark. Through such wit, Bond manages to suggest the larger ideological determinants of the character's own behavior.

The joking context makes possible, but not less painful, the viewing of the murder, not least because of the relentless logic by which the scene unfolds, a logic akin to that of wit itself. Just as the production of wit involves the contribution of the unconscious to the comic, so the action of the scene seems to happen in spite of itself, for reasons unknown to the perpetrators, before the audience they provide for each other: "PETE (*quietly*): Yer can do what yer like. BARRY: Might as well enjoy ourselves" (79). The actions of Scene Six express, in concrete and therefore intensely disturbing form, the very tendencies that propel the joking exchanges both before and after the murder. Thus in one sense, nothing changes – the killing is not accidental, as Fred suggests, but symptomatic, as the audience must surely understand by the end of the play. Moreover, an uncanny sense of reality is produced by language that reproduces so accurately the dialogue, and thus the psychic reality, of the play's working-class characters. Indeed, the humor embedded in *Saved* makes a lasting impression that is not entirely negative in its effects; for the irrepressible nature of the joking exchanges displays the driving energy necessary for social change (again, wit is made, not found).

By depicting the action from the point of view of displaced energy and wasted human potential, the play implicitly recognizes that change is possible and locates its source in the characters themselves. The result is an unpatronizing view from "below" that helps verify the "truth" of the actions depicted. The audience is not invited to pity the characters – for they clearly make their own reality – nor condemn them – for they seem equally determined by the social reality to which their dialogue constantly refers. Laughing *at* the characters seems out of the question: the situations presented are not comic, the actions are not harmless, the threat of violence is never entirely defused. To derive pleasure from a feeling of superiority would involve a stronger initial identification than most audiences can share; and any superiority felt from the beginning does not allow for the sudden shifts of perception that might lead to laughter.[10] Yet to laugh *with* the characters is a possibility held out by the playwright, a possibility that perhaps more than anything else antagonized reviewers of the play.

In this regard, Freud's analysis of jokes offers further illumination. In a section entitled, "The Motives of Wit and Wit as a Social Process," Freud qualifies his discussion of wit technique with the observation that the pleasure of wit depends not only on similar states of mind, or a predisposition to be amused, but on the psychic compatibility of those involved. That such a shared point of view may be strictly inhibited by differences in social class is suggested by two of Freud's own examples:

In an assemblage of divines and pastors no one would dare to refer to Heine's comparison of Catholic and Protestant priests as retail dealers and employees of a wholesale business. In the presence of my opponent's friends the wittiest invectives with which I might assail him would not be considered witticisms but invectives, and in the minds of my hearers it would create not pleasure, but indignation [...] Whoever is focused on smutty jokes will not be able to derive pleasure from clever exhibitionist wit. Mr. N's and Mr. Wendell Phillip's aggressions will not be understood by uncultured people who are wont to give free rein to pleasure gained by insulting others. Every witticism thus demands its own public, and to laugh over the same witticisms is proof of absolute psychic agreement.[11]

Freud's comments clearly privilege the sublimated versions of wit in which he himself found pleasure, and yet his analysis points to both the social functions of wit as exhibited by Bond's working-class characters, and the difficulty such wit may present to an audience of a different social class. In *Saved*, the joking between gang members is alternately obscene and aggressive, cynical and defensive, aimed not only at each other, but at the hypocrisy of a society that censures (and censors) them. In other words, Bond's use of humor in *Saved* is essentially naturalistic: through it he presents a social class from its own point of view and in some sense lets the situation "speak for itself." Not surprisingly, then, Bond was accused of the excesses audience members perceived in the language and behavior of the characters: the play was labelled "sick," "bestial," "vulgar," and "sadistic," the apparent amorality of the action inspiring one particularly honest critic to mutter "Right – keep the bastards down."[12] The play divided, rather than unified, its audience, and the angry consensus that first emerged suggests that the playwright and his original audience were far from being in "psychic agreement." Bond's sense of humor proved to be rooted in an experience of working-class life that served the interests of others to deny.

Early Morning

Such issues clearly inform Bond's next comedy, *Early Morning* (1968), a dense, richly textured play that incorporates the working-class wit of *Saved*, develops the connection between humor and "aggro-effects," and evoked the same unfavorably mixed reception that has characterized Bond's boldest works. The negative response to *Early Morning*, however, could not have surprised the playwright. With its savage surrealism, its *Monty Python*-like caricatures, and its grotesque images, *Early Morning* was the last play to be banned in its entirety by the Lord Chamberlain; and even Methuen balked at its publication, fearing libel suits stemming from (among other things) Bond's prefatory comment that "the events of this play are true."[13] In it, Bond offers all the subjects of the Grand Guignol – torture, murder, rape, ghostly apparitions, suicide, and cannibalism, yet does so in the style and tempo of music hall burlesque. The characters and situations provide ample occasion for exhibitionist wit, "clever" or "smutty" depending on your point of view. Queen Victoria has a lesbian affair with Florence Nightingale, who is engaged to her son George. George is accidentally shot and miraculously revived by Victoria, then commits suicide (twice). His death proves inconvenient for his Siamese twin Arthur, who carries the corpse through most of the play. Lord Mennings has a shoe fetish that costs him his life, Disraeli is a closet transvestite, Gladstone a sado-masochistic thug, the Queen's chamberlain gay. Through half of the play, Florence Nightingale disguises her sex with a kilt and a bad Scottish accent. Later, she nurses the soldiers with sex and offers Arthur's decapitated (yet talking) head safe refuge under her skirt. Despite the act of mass genocide he orchestrates, Arthur gradually emerges as the play's moral center. *Early Morning* ends with Arthur's ghostly body resurrected over the play's last supper, a heavenly feast upon realistically portrayed human flesh. Given Bond's previous encounters with the Lord Chamberlain's office, the play seems written as both a deliberate affront and memorable farewell to the censor. Not only is the dream-like logic of the play apparent, but as Freud remarks of the dream process itself, "no connection was too loose and no witticism too objectionable to serve as a bridge from one thought to another."[14] For many viewers, the result was predictably nightmarish.

The disconcerting effect of *Early Morning* is produced, in part, by patterns of imagery that seem deliberately provocative in their use of the human body to represent a corrupt political system. Moreover, the exuberant sexual perversity displayed by characters is balanced by corresponding threats of severe bodily harm, as if the very processes of distortion through which dream thoughts normally evade the punishing censor had been exposed. Images of death and dismemberment, and their analogues in castration, dislocation, evisceration, and devouring are given particular prominence, perhaps tapping unconscious sources of anxiety in an audience sensitive to the tendentious nature of Bond's jokes. The castration anxiety flaunted and flouted by Bond's constant verbal/visual play upon the motif serves as one example. In Scene Four, Joyce reports the disappearance of a leg under suspicious circumstances, an image that returns with irrepressible force in Len's own castrated corpse, in the missing leg of George's decomposing body (a body Arthur refuses, more than once, to "cut off"), in the wound suffered by a soldier on the front, in the legs stolen from Albert in heaven and eaten by the masses, in the sleeping-leg alibi used to disguise Arthur's head between Florence's legs, and in the play's final punch-line: "Pass us that leg." Since war is the great castrator, Florence restores men through sexual activity that as frequently means their death: Ned, Disraeli, and Gladstone all die in her bed. In heaven, Arthur reminds Florence, "When they cut off a man's leg, he still feels it. I'm like that. They've cut off my body – but I'm alive. I could make love to you" (215). A sense prevails that as long as the castrating Queen survives, phallic appurtenances will regenerate for her pleasure – that a civilization based on violent repression is doomed to repeat itself like a Freudian nightmare in which pleasure is represented by pain, and pain self-inflicted for pleasure, interminably.

Phallic images of a wounded but aggressively regenerating patriarchy are complemented by equally resonant oral images to represent capitalism. On earth, an equation is struck between murder, cannibalism, consumption, and conflagration. George has recurring nightmares about dying of thirst in a desert. But heaven, too, is a dog-eat-dog world in which the mob is striking for "decent grub," a world whose culture Arthur literally refuses "to swallow," the consequences of which involve losing his head. The picture of a consumer society with no life-sustaining properties is reinforced by references to poison and purges, "noshing" and gorging, stomach aches, retching, chewing up and spitting out. Such image patterns gain further support from allusions to *Hamlet*. Although the parody is broad and intermittent, *Early Morning* shares with Shakespeare's play its metaphors of a diseased, rotten, and corrupt state, a morbid queen, a murdered father, and a central figure roused to action by a ghost.

As such examples suggest, the grotesque images of *Early Morning* are accompanied throughout by a sense of ribald farce and infantile fun; and we are never far from the feeling that Bond is pulling our leg. Jane Howell, who played in the 1968 production, suggests that the play may only work if "done like high-class Whitehall farce" – very fast and very funny.[15] The mad logic of the play's world is elaborated not only through the escalating improbability of the action, but through the relentless play of Bond's inspired verbal/ visual wit. However unpalatable critics found the play, the farcical thrust was readily acknowledged. Beside *Early Morning*'s flamboyant style, exaggerated expressionism, and broad satire, *Saved* seems restrained and remarkably understated. Despite their obvious differences, *Early Morning* takes from the earlier play a self-conscious interest in Freudian themes as well as the techniques, tendencies, and volatile effects of its jokes. But in *Early Morning* any urge toward psychological interpretation gets preempted by a high comic style that makes Freudian configurations and psychoanalytic themes an integral part of the play's wit-work. Whereas *Saved* makes it all but impossible for its audience to adopt the viewpoint from which it can laugh, in *Early Morning* laughter is the pay-off for those who can share Bond's pleasure in turning the obscene and hostile tendencies of working-class wit upon the sacred imagos of a society he wishes to change. By broadening the social picture, as well as the forms of humor, *Early Morning* makes explicit the social and ideological critique that *Saved* can only imply.

In *Early Morning*, the working-class characters provide constant comment upon the plots and counterplots of the main action; yet the

Oedipal strife, sexual perversity, and violent intrigue of the royal family and its entourage are reflected in the criminal depravity of their subjects. The Len of *Early Morning* begins as a prisoner who would "murder his mother for five shillings, if he hadn't done it already for the experience" (147), a marketable skill for which he is sought as a political assassin. He and his 50-year-old girlfriend Joyce stand trial in Scene Four for killing – and eating – Joseph Hobson outside the State Cinema, Kilburn High Street. Their defense: the man cut in on the queue as they waited to see "Policeman in Black Nylons," and they were hungry. Victoria puts Len on oath, but won't let him touch the Bible ("King James would turn in his grave," 148). The class-inflected dialogue, domestic bickering, and deadpan seriousness with which Len and Joyce describe the scene of the crime make it one of the funniest in the play, not least because of the defensive wit through which the characters implicate themselves. Neither can remember who did the cutting, but Joyce complains that she broke her purse in the attack, that Len was too generous with the handouts, that someone stole a leg right off the pavement, and that the Police Commissioner had the pickings when they were gone. Given the broader context, Joyce's distrust of authorities is well-founded, but the appeals to fairness and common decency in her digressive dialogue are equally revealing: "– an I'd like t'know why chair accommodation ain' provided. They don't wan'a know yer in this country. Thass 'ow yer get yer trouble. Yer pays enough" (149). Indeed, in this play, justice is getting what you paid for and morality is doing what you're told: as Joyce remarks to Len, "don't I always' tell yer count the queue in front? That could 'ang yer" (149).

The crime may seem horrific, but Len and Joyce are concerned about getting a fair shake, feel the victim got what he deserved, and despite the odds against them, will not be taken without a fight. They are, in fact, as guilty, violent, and animalistic as they are presumed to be before the trial: Joyce identifies the blood on an exhibit by sniffing it, and Len describes in detail the army-trained stabbing technique that "with 'er [. . .] comes natural" (150). Later, Joyce enthusiastically participates in Len's beating, demands his castration, and has memories no less shocking than the action seen onstage.

I was out late for bingo one night an' I 'ad t' smother three a me nippers. I never 'ad time t'get 'em t'bed. They look juss like that when I come 'ome next week. [. . .] me ol' gran was 'avin a knees-up one night when I wanted a watch telly. I 'ad t' put drain-cleaner in 'er meths t'quieten 'er down. She rolled down the stairs juss like that. (173, 204)

The play's working-class characters not only embody the attitudes and mirror the actions of the ruling classes, they tend to one-better the instruction, reproducing through their enthusiastic participation the very system of beliefs that have determined them. The result is both laughable and disturbing. Far from being disillusioned by the process whereby he is nearly beaten to death and castrated, Len sees his chance to be "rollin' in clover – if me internal 'aemorrhagin' olds out" (175). In the mock trials of Scene Four and Scene Eight, the only difference between the criminals and their judges is one of superior forces ("GLADSTONE: Yer 'ave t' 'ave yer trial t'make it legal," 70). Within such a world, Arthur's simple, but persistent question, "Why did you kill him?" makes no sense, and Len rightly meets it with suspicion and exasperated disbelief: "No fancy questions! [. . .] I got the right to be guilty same as you!" (153). In *Early Morning*, no one is innocent – heaven itself is a prison to which only the guilty are admitted.

Despite differences in social class (and sexual orientation), the characters of *Early Morning* are trapped by the lived ideology that imbues their common sense, as much as by the institutions (of family and state) that represent and enforce the moral code. No one escapes "intact." The characters' prominent familial ties – as fathers, mothers, sons, brothers, husbands, wives, in-laws, and lovers – are as distorted, unnatural and psychologically binding as the play's more literal representations of human bondage in Siamese twins, handcuffed prisoners, tug-of-war teams, and the ghosts *"joined together like a row of paper cut-out men"* (195–196). The multiple associations triggered by comedy, the ordinary language ("force is going to be necessary, let's be realistic," 140–141), and the recognizable situations (trials, picnics, military actions, and family squabbles) provide further links to the world of the viewing audience. Despite the Victorian cast, comic anachronisms (from cinema queues to radio technology, Hitler's Holocaust, and the bomb) and parodic allusions to present-day literary, cultural, and religious institutions help produce the contemporary frame of reference. Indeed, *Early Morning* implicitly recognizes that in its role of constituting individual human beings as subjects, ideology has been an instrument of class rule, with real, and particularly destructive, consequences. The irrationality of the play's action is thus predicated on the nineteenth-

century belief, still prevalent, that human beings are naturally
aggressive, and that civilization itself rests on the effective channel-
ling, control, and deployment of man's most primitive instinctual
urges. Thus, like Oedipus, whose example served Freud, Arthur
answers the "riddle" about man, but can do so only by fully
participating in the world's insanity:

This riddle isn't hard. When my men go over the side what will hers do?
What can you trust them to do? What would you expect them to do?
What's the natural thing, the normal thing, the human thing to do? Run to
the edge and watch the others die. (194)

Such thinking nearly makes possible the success of Arthur's genocidal plot, the destruction of all human life. Arthur's plan, of course,
is undermined by the comic indestructibility of Victoria, who
governs her subjects in heaven as on earth, and whose ability to
survive seems inversely related to her intellect. Whether consciously
or not, the shared patterns of thought that inform the characters'
actions serve to reproduce the material conditions of life that gave
them shape in the first place. In this play, the entrepreneurial
aggression of the Victorian age makes possible, in an all-too-literal
sense, a consumer-oriented heaven where "law and order, consent
and co-operation" allow characters to eat themselves and each other
in peace. From such a cannibalistic nightmare, only the living can
awake.

Exploiting the similarity between dream technique and wit, *Early
Morning* adopts a strategy that self-consciously recognizes its own
basis in the confining Freudian constructs it seeks to displace. The
dream-like narrative not only seems appropriate for a dissection of
human subjectivity and its relation to history, but suggests the
technical means whereby an enormous amount of thought can be
physically represented onstage. Like dreams, *Early Morning* uses
words, visual images, human figures, and scenarios as sliding signi-
fiers to carry its thought, all linked by chains of association that are,
in the strictest sense of the word, overdetermined. According to
Bond, the play took longer than two years to write, and the finished
script not only seems "worked on" (or "overwrought," depending
on your assessment of the play), but authentically dream-like if acted
in the matter-of-fact style that the language invites and the humor
demands. Bond himself recognized the difficulty of getting "all I
know about life ... in one play," later suggesting that "a more

relaxed writer might have got three plays out of *Early Morning*."[16] If nothing else, the play presents a remarkable work of condensation.

On the simplest level, the humor of *Early Morning* rests on broadly accepted notions about the nature of capitalism, the behavior of public figures, and the similarity of past historical periods to our own. As Arthur says in Scene Two, "The trouble with the world is it's run by politicians" (141). At another level, the action and imagery are derived from specific ideological constellations that give an underlying shape to the surreal surface: the authoritarian family, law and order, duty, and the spirit of Victorian empire-building to which the play explicitly refers are related to the repression of sexuality, the rise of fascism, the traffic in pornography, and the new science of psychoanalysis implied in Bond's own transformations of the material. By posing a dialectical, mutually determining link between objective history (events) and subjective psychology (human agency), social constructs and ideological formations, the play can be "true" without being factual. *Early Morning* gives body to the unseen but powerful distortions of ideology inherited from the past; by materializing misrecognitions, Bond can treat them as such, and begin to divest them of their insidious power.

Early Morning subverts from within by objectifying those very processes through which the contradictions of capitalism and its resulting history of violence are normally sutured up and covered over in the individual subject. When Arthur accepts the logic that informs Victoria's world, he does so simply and directly, bringing out with exaggerated force the kind of thought that will inevitably lead to a "final solution." If "justice depends on law and order," if "the mob [is] sadistic, violent, vicious, cruel, anarchic, dangerous, murderous, treacherous, cunning, crude, disloyal, dirty, destructive ... and unwashed," if people have no pity, then it is not by accident that live is "evil" spelled backwards and an anagram of "vile," and the problem of the world becomes enormously clear: "its inhabited" (189). Bond's argument confronts the irrational rationality of capitalism with its own "bad dream" – exposing the powerful unconscious wish that its ideological rhetoric takes such pains to deny. From the point of view of false consciousness, *Early Morning is* nothing but a bad dream – George, the conforming, unquestioning, and obedient son, has nightmares at the beginning of the play, stomach pains at the end, and would rather die than change his point of view, especially regarding the Queen. (If the reviews are accurate, the same could be said of the original audience.) *Early Morning* may disturb, because of its basis in a reality we know, *and* amuse, because of the playfulness with which that reality is recreated onstage. Using the techniques and contents of unconscious thought to "make light" of any discourse that would rationalize the irrational and impede social change, *Early Morning* represents, without recourse to "explanation," the liberating potential inherent in even the most deterministic conceptions of self and society. Human action, and the freedom it implies, remains possible even in a world where the self is nothing but an effect of language.

The play's subversive potential finds testimony in the Lord Chamberlain's denial of any redeeming value in the play, the highly mixed reaction in 1968 affected in turn by the censorship issues *Early Morning* so directly confronts. While dream technique was used to justify a certain amount of incomprehension, most critics treated such artistic license unfavorably, describing the play as "infantile" and "self-indulgent" (such nonsense being best ignored) or "obscene" and "barbaric," a morally reprehensible act rightly prosecuted by the Lord Chamberlain. Those who praised the play, on the other hand, admitted to sharing Bond's sense of humor, or, beyond the joking tendencies of the script, his point of view.[17] The split reaction brings us back to Freud's suggestion that socio-economic factors (education and class attitudes, for example) inhibit or enable the pleasure found in jokes – wit as a social process. Despite a similarity in technique, dreams are perfectly asocial products, deliberately constructed to confound and confuse, and of little interest to anyone but the dreamer. Wit, on the other hand, demands intelligibility, depending for success on direct, almost automatic, communication with an audience. Punch-lines like Victoria's "Call me Victor" meet Freud's first requirement of wit, that it be "funny without thinking."[18] Indeed, most of the play's humor is based on simple reversals, sight gags, burlesque turns, and obvious punning. Far from making the play more acceptable, the dream-like quality contributed to a nightmarish experience for those unamused by Bond's wit.

The disturbing and potentially liberating effects of the play's humor can be attributed not only to its "hostile" and "obscene" tendencies, but to the structure of the punning mechanism that so frequently carries them. Usually labelled the lowest form of humor, the pun places two or more distinct meanings within a single frame of reference. Whereas metaphor creates a new unity irreducible to a sum of its parts, the pun retains its simultaneous but separate meanings, providing a figure whereby conflict and contradiction are preserved at the level of the word. Other figures of speech may offer the "false" resolution of a "compromise formation" (as Freud calls the images of dreams), and take time to fully absorb; the pun strives for instant recognition of its contested meaning, and attacks with "vulgar" speed. When Gladstone asks Len to plead his case, for example, Griss remarks "E'll *plead* all right," the sadistic tendency of which is acknowledged and hypocritically suppressed by Gladstone's response to the pun: "It's a good joke – don't spoil it by over indulgin'. Yer get too worked up" (171). As a soldier, Griss puts his lower-class sensibility to work, in the most literal sense, for the ruling classes, resulting in a "sick" sense of humor that does not invite laughter. But Gladstone's patronizing reaction to it does, and the ambivalent structure of the pun on "plead" permits the language of courtroom justice to turn evidence against itself. Victoria, on the other hand, remains unaware of the comic contexts Bond provides for her dialogue, oblivious to the humor of her own lines, "not amused" throughout. Puns like, "I'm a constitutional monarch so far as medicine's concerned" (178) promote laughter at her expense.

The farcical energy of the play – its remorseless punning, snow-balling irreverence, and proliferating improbability – depends on the "obviousness" of its humor. But more is involved than satirizing specific public figures or a sweeping condemnation of the age. The references are too broad to be topical, too "crude" to seem clever, too general to play upon historical accounts or even widely known incidents of the period.[19] Victoria seems already once removed from reality when she appears on the stage, a figure from agit-prop revue evoking instant recognition, a send-up of a send-up, whose near miraculous escapes take on a cartoon-like quality. Although the play offers itself for elucidation, its "use value" for the audience is not limited to the decoding exercise of intellectual analysis it invites. As Terry Lovell points out, "It is impossible to produce a truly revolutionary text in a discourse in which only the dominant have any facility."[20] And indeed, audiences of *Early Morning* need no knowledge of comic or literary theory, Freudian psychology, Victor-ian history, tragic conventions, or even Shakespeare to be affected by the play. The play's social effect depends simply on an experience of the "lived reality" of contemporary British life. The more a viewer's individual identity is invested in a conservative ideology, the more unnerving or irritating the play may appear. But for audiences capable (through imagination or habit) of laughing at the humor produced by Bond's own working-class wit, *Early Morning* operates differently.

In *Rabelais and His World*, Mikhail Bakhtin writes: "all the acts of the drama of world history were performed before a chorus of laughing people," and to a certain extent, it is from their carnival-esque perspective that *Early Morning* is written.[21] The energy of the play, its generation of associative thought, its corporeal humor, and its liberating laughter are related to language and situations in which the bodily, physical underside of authority is being constantly exposed. The grotesque realism of the imagery, with its emphasis on the material body and its regenerative properties, its "lowering of all that is high, spiritual, ideal, abstract" to its own sphere of reference, its fantastic combinations and irreverent jests, connects the technique of the play to an entire history of folk humor that Bakhtin rediscovers in Rabelais.[22] On the other hand, *Early Morning* implicitly recognizes that the very language of the banquet and the body through which, according to Bakhtin, the lower orders once expressed their freedom from authority have themselves been debased, commodified, and linked to the methods of social control in a later historical age. Indeed, the play directly confronts the possibility that the class of exploited humanity from which revolutionary activity must emerge has been bought off by the material inducements made possible by capitalist production, a possibility that would literally mean the end of history (change, development). In *Early Morning*, such a terrifying vision of incorporation is expressed in scenes where images of "copulation, pregnancy, birth, growth, old age, disintegration and dismemberment"[23] are reinscribed in petrified, distorted, and monstrous forms – as a cyclical nightmare where historical time is superseded by farcical repetition.

Bakhtin finds in the affirmative power of the grotesque an ability "to liberate from the prevailing point of view of the world, from conventions and established truths, from clichés, from all that is humdrum and universally accepted."[24] The liberating potential is not based in images, but in the feeling of strength conveyed by what Bakhtin might call the play's "laughing truth." What he writes about laughter and its relation to the grotesque has particular relevance for *Early Morning*: "Laughter liberates not only from external censorship but first of all from the great interior censor; it liberates from the fear that developed in man during thousands of years: fear of the sacred, of prohibitions, of the past, of power."²⁵ The principle of laughter and the carnival spirit on which the grotesque is based "frees human consciousness, thought, and imagination for new potentialities," and because such a freedom exposes the historical relativity and variable nature of necessity itself, even "the Id is uncrowned and transformed into a 'funny monster'."²⁶ While the mood of *Early Morning* may be more funereal than festive, the laughter it produces is not always or only aggressive and derisory. Rather, the social pleasure the play delivers is an affirmative one, offered to that class of individuals most obviously oppressed by the history that Bond, with the broadest strokes of humor, distorts. The viewer's desire to interpret the bizarre vision is thus urged along and rewarded by jokes that are funniest to those who need no explanation of their underlying sense, to those who may laugh without knowing why. In this regard, *Early Morning* is as much about working-class life as *Saved*, and as grounded in its perspective.²⁷

Like *Saved*, *Early Morning* offers a central character whose questions provide the audience with an entrance to the play, and whose role as a moral center is undermined by involvement in the violence he observes. Although the dream-like quality prevents the structure from appearing self-evident, *Early Morning* can be understood in terms of Arthur's own slow process of enlightenment: his initial observation of and resistance to the plots and counter-plots of an insane society; his initiation into its ranks with a Hitler-like final solution; and his eventual escape through ironic martyrdom. Beneath the manifest criticism of the play's wit-work, then, lies a latent social message, a positive content that makes sense of the play's improbable action and suggests both the need and the possibility of acting against one's own oppression in a world defined by violence, ruthless competition, and injustice. Nor is the point as difficult to grasp as any necessarily complicated plot summary might suggest. Arthur's message in heaven is simple and resonant: "don't eat." So is his reaction to being devoured: laughter, a response that throws the enemy into total confusion. Although determined and confined by his world, Arthur finally emerges as somehow different. Arthur's only power is the power of negation, but using it enables him to "rise above it all" – his resurrecting body forcefully reminding the audience that only those who resist can escape. The analysis

promoted by Arthur's example (in Marxist terms, how one becomes
the subject as well as the object of history) is the socialist option Bond
offers his potentially confused audience, the analysis that turns
phantasmagoria into fable – an existential nightmare into political
parable.

Derek

Despite the surface complexity, *Early Morning* looks forward to
simpler, more popular, comic fables like *Stone* (1976) and *Derek*
(1982).[28] In the latter, energetic physical comedy remains alongside
central characters who, like Arthur, attempt to live happily and "do
the right thing." In a class-structured society, however, such simple
desires pit the characters against each other in a struggle unfairly
weighted by material wealth. As the parables make clear, the
cleverest of the poor stand little chance against the pervasive
privileges of the rich and a system that turns their very minds to
account. In *Derek*, for example, the underprivileged central character lands a job as a janitor, but with unsuspected mathematical
aptitude, he easily cracks the computer-programed security system
of the company safe – and helps himself. Once caught, Derek's love
for Julie and desire for freedom cloud his judgment, and he sells his
brain to his Eton-educated, imbecilic boss. Were the transplant not
so successful, Derek would regret the decision sooner. Later we
realize that Derek's freedom was cut short by his own mother, whose
"sudden glory" in unexpected wealth betrays his theft to the police.
Relaying this information in a comic aside to the audience, the
Mother can hardly suppress her hilarity:

When I saw those sacks of money I don't know what came over me.
(*Smiles.*) I felt as excited as a little girl with a skippin rope. (*Suddenly begins to
laugh.*) If it 'd've bin one I'd've bin all right. It was the – (*Her laughter becomes
uncontrollable. She can't say the number.*) – five! I opened the window and threw
'andfuls of notes down t'the street an shouted – (*Her laughter increases.*) – I'm
rich! I'm rich![29]

The Mother's foolishness is indeed laughable, and she recounts
Bond's unplayed discovery scene as if remembering a scene from
farce. The painful irony of her situation is heightened by the belated
recognition of her own role in Derek's undoing, a recognition, like
Derek's own, that comes too late. Despite his clear advantage as a
comic protagonist, Derek proves no match for the combined forces of

business, law, government, and the army, here represented and grandly manipulated by Biff, whose success must ultimately be attributed to the use of Derek's brain.

As in *Early Morning*, Bond plays with the patterns typified by farce, and a good deal of humor is generated from the unexpected uses to which they are put. In *Derek* the robber is robbed, the fools outwitted, the hypocrites exposed, the butts humiliated, and the scheming successful – but the sense of justice that finally prevails is not in accordance with the audience's desires. From Derek's point of view, the play is a wish that goes awry, a fantasy turned nightmare, with the dream itself (unlimited material wealth) a corrupted version of freedom carrying with it the seeds of his own destruction. The connections to the farcical and fantastical reality of *Early Morning* are clear, and the matter-of-fact playing style that Bond recommends for *Derek* is the same that William Gaskill found necessary for *Early Morning*.[30] In neither are the broad strokes of satire aimed at human folly nor at individual foibles, but rather at a socio-economic system whose self-propelling lunacy is unwittingly fueled by its members, rich and poor alike. In *Derek*, for example, the doctor assures Biff that his mental deficiency will not hamper the exercise of his class privileges: "Don't lose a moment's sleep over it. It gives you the mental tunnel vision that gets you to the top. Between ourselves, I doubt if the mental ages of most cabinets would add up to the calendar years of one moderately elderly statesman" (8). With a mental age of ten, Biff finds the whole situation beyond him, and much of the humor depends on the audience's assumption of superiority to the two main characters, an assumption the swift and surprising turns in the narrative serve constantly to challenge. In *Derek*, the hint of rigid caricature repeatedly gives way to a more complicated version of human character that suggests the limits of ideological conditioning: Biff's new brain, for example, gives him the dialect and working-class mannerisms to win a seat in Parliament on the "law and order" ticket; his change of head leads to a change of heart, but one that serves upper-class interests even better than before. With Biff's brain, Derek shows a grovelling respect for figures of authority, joins the army, and loses (along with everything else) his sense of humor. But just as the point has been made, Derek begins to talk to the voice of his old self ("Come on, yer remember. We 'ad all the laughs," 16) and the schizophrenic division promises hope.

Understanding whether Derek's desertion from the army is heroic, suicidal, or simply stupid is complicated by the way in which the audience learns of it. At the end of the play, Biff returns Derek's remains to his mother, along with his own interpretation of Derek's "heroism." Given Biff's transplant, any "true" perspective on the undramatized event is impossible to ascertain; the meaning of Derek's final action (and the "use" made of it) is thus handed over to the audience of the play. By the time we "get the joke," however, it may be too late – the very social contradictions that generate the farcical humor being the same that lead to the nuclear holocaust of the play's "Last Song." The political message is helped along by the commentary of Brechtian song lyrics in the manner of Bond's earlier parable *Stone*. Yet the wit with which Bond plays upon issues of heredity and environment, education and experience, will and desire in the formation of character also provides a positive antidote to any easy moralizing that the satire of public figures might evoke or to the deterministic interpretations that the action itself could imply. Appreciating Bond's sense of humor facilitates understanding of, and agreement with, the play's social analysis.

As *Derek* illustrates, the connections between pleasure, human liberation, and knowledge so important to *Early Morning* remain in Bond's later comedy, more explicitly tied to issues of class consciousness. Such issues are not simple. Bond's political analysis assumes both the necessity and the difficulty of understanding one's position as a conditioned subject of a post-industrial society – radical subjectivity is a goal, not a given. Audience sympathy may be directed toward the under classes, or to those with the curiosity and fortitude to act against them. But fantasies of triumph, like revolutionary heroics, are usually avoided. Nowhere is this more apparent than in Bond's comedies, where such triumph is an expected element of the form. Indeed, from the nineteenth-century "comedy of tears" to contemporary farce, the happy ending of comedy (like the notion of "poetic justice") can be viewed as an excess, produced by the imagination of the playwright, for the pleasure of an audience with few illusions about its relevance to life outside the theatre. And with it, comedy makes strong alliances with the diversionary and wish-fulfilling aspects of art.

In Bond's comedy, however, the just are not spared nor the damage undone; and time itself is not on our side. In *The Cat* (1982), a beast fable that parodies operatic melodrama to highly comic effect, the naive and innocent Minnette and her worldly, would-be lover Tom make several near-escapes, declare unending love, and recover long-lost title and fortune before meeting an untimely end: Minnette drowned in a sack, Tom stabbed in the back. In *Restoration* (1981), Bob, entirely innocent of the crime with which he is charged, believes to the bitter end that Lord Are will save him from the gallows. Derek, though not so innocent, also dies, losing first his money, his brain, his girlfriend, and his sense of self by plea-bargaining for his freedom. Even *The Sea* (1973), Bond's most conventional comedy, begins with the death of Colin and is followed by scenes in which his body is hacked on the beach and his ashes desecrated in a brawl. In other words, Bond's comedy sets itself in a world dominated by images of death, shock, and loss, a world wherein characters must make choices and sometimes choose unwisely, a world where actions have consequences.[31] Such concessions to "the reality principle" are in fact central to the particular pleasure of Bond's comedy – to the therapeutic, practical, and political affirmation to which they aspire. If what is staged is always already an illusion, safely removed from the real, then violent incidents and occasional deaths may be far less significant to the form than the perspective from which they are viewed and the uses to which they are put.

Unlike *Derek*, which could work as effectively on the streets as on a stage, *Restoration* and *The Sea* take up residence in the mannered comedy of polite society, appropriating forms of theatre commonly associated with the interests of privileged play-goers. Like their tragic counterparts in *Lear* and *The Woman*, *The Sea* and *Restoration* undermine the class affiliations and critique the tendencies inherent in the comic genres they self-consciously rework, rechannelling their energies towards revolutionary political ends. Both plays are comedies in the fullest sense of the term: they display a comic structure, make use of comic techniques, and seek from their audience a comic response. More importantly, both produce what Susanne Langer identifies as most crucial to the form: the comic rhythm of "felt life" – of a continuity, vitality, and strength that belongs to community – and a sense of enjoyment directly related to the self-preservative, self-restorative, functional tendencies of the human organism.[32] Yet *The Sea* and *Restoration* work against an equally prevalent notion of comedy as inherently tolerant, compromising, conciliatory, and conservative.[33] To do so, both appropriate a predominantly British form of drawing-room comedy –

witty, urbane, self-assured, and complacent – one that, from the Restoration to the present day, has best served the interests of the class for which it is written. Despite their obvious differences, both plays suggest that any "rational accommodation" to the world they reflect (a world at odds, in the most fundamental sense, with human survival) is an irrational, dangerous, and essentially "comic" pursuit.

The Sea

Unlike many of Bond's plays, *The Sea* was immediately accepted in the spirit in which it was written: as an optimistic counterstatement to the weighted problems of *Lear*, a tribute to human strength and resilience, and a deliberate attempt to make its audience laugh.[34] Much in the manner of Shakespearean comedy, the play transports the audience from the disorienting chaos of the opening "tempest" to a small sea-side village in 1907, an "island" that works its regenerative effects primarily in an anti-pastoral key. The idea of "retreat" can be found in the town itself, cut off from the larger world movements afoot (in 1907, just on the horizon), comically "out of touch," trapped in the provincial outlook and inward-looking tendencies of its own culture. Extending the comedy of fashionable society to characters normally outside its purview (to Hatch, the shopkeeper, Evens, a hermit, and Hollarcut, a laborer), *The Sea* shows the consequences of class rule through keen observance of the economic pressures and social tensions that generate what might otherwise be viewed as merely eccentric behavior. Mrs. Rafi's theatricals and aggressive wit, Evens' drinking and ironic awareness, Hatch's paranoid fantasies, Hollarcut's feigned compliance, and Mrs. Tilehouse's fainting spells not only evoke laughter, but represent the strategies through which each character, more or less successfully, copes with the stresses of living in a rigidly class-structured society.

That comedy is itself such a strategy gets suggested by a plot that traces (in digressive fashion typical of the form) Willy's maturation and slow awakening from dazed grief to a future filled with promise. As a character who spends most of his stage time observing the actions of others, Willy's link to the audience is clear. The social importance of art, and its ideological function, is further highlighted in Mrs. Rafi's own grandly stage-managed productions, the Ladies

Auxiliary rehearsal of Scene Four and Colin's funeral in Scene Seven, not by accident the funniest of the play. With the play-within-the-play of Scene Four, Bond provides, through comic diversion, an explicit critique of the diversionary uses of art, and ties those uses to particular class interests. Ironically mirroring *The Sea*'s larger movement, Mrs. Rafi begins with a tragedy (the story of Orpheus and Eurydice) but produces high comedy in a sequence with pointed similarities to the mechanicals' rehearsal in Shakespeare's *A Midsummer Night's Dream*. As in Shakespeare's play, Bond produces individuals inseparable from their class function and forces us to consider the uses to which art is put, as well as its relationship to real life. Mrs. Rafi shares with Peter Quince a public-spirited, high-minded project that strains the resources available for the task. No more disinterested than the mechanicals' wedding performance, Mrs. Rafi's play is organized in charitable support of the Coastguard Fund, a fact unwittingly reinforced by her own promotion of "disinterested" values. When Mrs. Tilehouse protests her assignment to the most menial stage-managing task (to crawl behind the curtain and splash water about), Mrs. Rafi responds: "Don't you aspire to be an artist? Think of miners who spend their lives crawling through darkness so that you may have light. That also, in its way, is the task of art."[35] Such lines contribute to the on-going battle of wills between Louise and her friend, lending humor and subtextual depth to the characters. But they also point to the very contradictions that Mrs. Rafi aims, through her art, to conceal. The epigrammatic retort to Mrs. Tilehouse's line corrections – "You can say what you like, as long as you can carry it off" (128) – works in similar fashion, capturing the very spirit of drawing-room comedy that Mrs. Rafi herself undoubtedly disdains. Bred behind closed curtains, Mrs. Rafi's use of classical literature is pretentious, sentimental, and self-indulgent; her "artistic" sensibility leads to patronizing condescension; and the creative atmosphere she fosters falls apart at the sound of the battery guns. Whatever relevance Mrs. Rafi's play holds to the events experienced by Willy and Rose in the world outside proves coincidental, an effect produced by Willy's imagination onstage, and the audience's off. Through Mrs. Rafi, Bond provides a clarifying, comic portrait of the bourgeois high culture to which she aspires.

Although Mrs. Rafi, like Evens, has moments of self-consciousness that suggest an awareness of her own limitations, the play does not invite the audience to judge the characters as they judge themselves. Rather, we view the play through the eyes of Willy, the outsider, whose disrupting presence forces to the surface class tensions otherwise "covered over" to produce the appearance of a settled, sane, and essentially unchanging society. Such is the impression towards which Mrs. Rafi strives, but her efforts are continually interrupted (or intentionally subverted) to expose the hypocritical, absurd, and tenuous nature of her hold over the community, a hold in which economic position and force of personality are not finally separable. Indeed, Hollarcut ends up as a more serious and sympathetic figure than any found in Mrs. Rafi's drawing-room. More importantly, he reminds the audience that Hatch, for all his madness, understood and spoke for those, like Hollarcut, who "count in the end." The respect Hatch offers Hollarcut directly contrasts with Mrs. Rafi, for whom Hollarcut is forced to work without pay at the end of the play. The sense of justice conveyed through his exit line provides one of the most unaffectedly pleasurable moments of the play: "I'll tell you something you ought a know, boy. I dig for her – (*He lays the side of his index finger against the side of his nose and looks crafty*) – but will anything grow?" (165).

Just as the presence of Rose and Willy frames Mrs. Rafi's rehearsal to promote a more serious, critical stance, so the opening and closing scenes on the beach provide an important interpretive frame for the comically diverting plays-within-the-play that Mrs. Rafi orchestrates. What Mrs. Rafi does with organized spectacle, Evens does with drink, Hatch does with fantasy, and society does with art. By exposing comedy itself as a displacement activity, *The Sea* encourages the audience to read its own diversions symptomatically, thereby turning the energy unlocked by laughter to more serious use. Indeed, the very tensions that most comedy manages through humor involve the same contradictions which, understood from a different perspective, might lead to social change. If the cause of the character's behavior is understood as a result of universal, inevitable human folly, then the audience's laughter of recognition has a potentially conservative and integrative social effect. But *The Sea* posits a causal connection between global events and a self-assured island culture that manages its class tensions in particular ways. Hatch's actions, in particular, provide a shock that the play's comic strategies cannot entirely contain. Although literally disarmed, the danger he represents is neither fully observed nor sufficiently under-

9 Hatch holds a secret meeting in the back of his draper's shop in *The Sea*

stood by the town inhabitants, a point that Willy's quite different reaction to Hatch fully clarifies.[36] The play carefully articulates the connection between Hatch's madness and real economic pressures, but the power and use of the portrait depends on the audience's knowledge of history and their ability to extend the play's analysis outside its frame – to Hitler and the neo-Nazi movements still alive, to forms of racial bigotry and the popular fantasies on which they thrive, and to the disaffected working class to whom they appeal. Thus *The Sea* may return to an earlier historical moment, but does not feign ignorance about the move. To the contrary, it suggests that if comedy is to retain its powerful relation to social continuity, survival, regeneration, and life, it cannot sever its connection to history. Enjoying art that depends for its effects on historical amnesia is to participate, in the same ridiculous way, in the provincial thinking that finds inspiration in amateur theatricals.

The accidental death on which *The Sea* opens ultimately strengthens the hope of what follows. Both Willy and Rose eventually "let go" – of Colin, and more importantly, of the conventional life he comes to represent. Despite the frame-breaking gesture of stopping the play mid-sentence, *The Sea* ends on a decidedly happy note. What gets thrown to the viewer is the unwritten (virtually unthought about) future facing Rose and Willy, who must remain, to a certain extent, ciphers for the audience – their problems, desires, hopes, and possibilities. Critics of the original production faulted the play for this very characteristic – finding Rose and Willy "shadowy" and unsatisfactorily developed.[37] The temptation to elaborate their personalities may be strong; but something is to be said for leaving Rose and Willy "unfilled," so the transference provoked by the play's abrupt end might work.

Restoration

The social analysis *The Sea* encourages its audience to make is in *Restoration* more vigorously demanded. Although both plays pay tribute to human resilience and resolve, *Restoration* was written in response to the 1979 re-election of Margaret Thatcher, a victory over which Bond was deeply depressed; the servant Bob's maddening collaboration in his own undoing thus historicizes, in a fairly specific way, the workers' vote of confidence for a Tory government.[38] While the "storms" of *The Sea*, contained by comedy, give way to silence and reflective calm, *Restoration* pushes with melodramatic force to Bob's unhappy end, the impact of which is marked and managed by Rose's final song. The shift in race and gender accent is important to note, for, despite her position as a black, female servant (daughter of a slave, wife of a prisoner) Rose plays a less marginal role than her earlier namesake, Mrs. Rafi's niece. Indeed, Rose figures for the audience of *Restoration* as Willy did in *The Sea*. In order to change the world, Willy must let go of personally disabling grief; for Rose to do the same, she must hold on to her anger. *The Sea* ends on uncertainty because Willy has not yet lived; *Restoration* ends on Rose's determination to act on what she has learned, and to become the inspiration she projects through song. Whereas Willy's grief cannot change the world, Bond suggests that Rose's anger might. Through the songs, *Restoration* gives the lower-class characters what is denied them in earlier plays – historical hindsight, political understanding, self-knowledge, and some freedom from the oppression of their stage roles. If Lord Are's power rests on the consent, approval, and admiration of those around him, then theatre-goers must shift their allegiance – not simply to the servants, however sympathetically depicted they may be – but to the characters of the songs, who speak from a future consensus Bond invites his audience to share.

Such a shift in allegiance proved difficult for many, and the divided critical response suggests that *Restoration* does more to expose the false consensus of aesthetically unified audiences than to build consensus through conventional dramatic means. Not surprisingly, audiences enjoyed the play's first half, with its self-conscious parody of Restoration comedy, more thoroughly than the second, where conventions shift and take their toll. But a dividing line of critical reaction was produced by the songs – the innovative, Brechtian element by which the play was originally "saved" or "damned" in the least uncertain terms. Reviewing for the *New Statesman*, Benedict Nightingale found Bond's songs to be unnecessary interpolations that "italicise the already apparent"; for Jane Bryce, reviewing in *The Leveller*, they helped "celebrate the impulse to freedom." John Russell Taylor described the songs from the original Royal Court production as "a dead weight around the show's neck"; Katherine Worth found them "increasingly thrilling and powerful," the one clear channel for the play's emotions, and an "intoxicating release" from the experience of the characters' social entrapment. Those for whom the play was a tedious experience pointed to "sub-Brechtian" lyrics that hammered home a "crudely didactic" message; others disliked the songs for interrupting with comment the alternately humorous and mesmerizing spectacle of onstage action.[39] Indeed, the action is funny and suspenseful by turns; the songs are neither. Perceiving the songs to be intrusive pays tribute to Bond's skillful narrative and handling of comic conventions. But the songs make direct and personal confrontation with the play's politics unavoidable. Brechtian in spirit, Bond's songs appropriate more popular and melodramatic forms to historicize and critique the mannered comedy with which the play begins. Far more than commentary, then, the songs provide the terrain on which audience pleasure itself is contested.

In this regard, *Restoration* shares much in common with *Lear* and *The Woman*, with comedy instead of tragedy the designated field of action. Although more pastiche than adaptation, *Restoration* begins with cultural capital bequeathed from an earlier age and thoroughly reworks its source material into something entirely new. As with the earlier tragedies, the allusive quality appeals to an informed theatre-goer without limiting access to the play; and Bond's argument is with the contemporary uses of a genre as opposed to its earlier authors. Bond explains his interest in the following way:

I wanted to write a play set in Restoration themes. These are still received almost totally uncritically in the theatre. The opportunism of the characters is applauded. Humour is taken as a self-consciousness which disarms the wicked and also in a way justifies them in their exploitation of others. So their "silliness" makes them both socially harmless and entitles them to their positions as exploiters.[40]

Behind the urgency of Bond's project lie the attitudes that forge Conservative election victories, the dire financial situation faced by the arts as a result of Thatcher's economic policies, and the theatre production decisions that get made as a result.

More so than many of Bond's plays, *Restoration* appears to address the regular British theatre-goer (their ranks swelled with tourists) on whom the Royal Shakespeare Company and the Royal Court depend, audiences who have welcomed the revival of classics. Katherine Worth summarizes well the instant recognition on which the humor of the opening scene depends: "we know where we are" as soon as the languid, overdressed gentleman opens his mouth – not by historical markers, but through Bond's parody of a theatrical convention "known by common consent as Restoration comedy, though it extends far beyond the Restoration into the eighteenth century."[41] As in *Lear* and *The Woman*, the recognition of Bond's use and manipulation of literary form is an important source of audience pleasure. *Restoration* is simply funnier if the viewer has some acquaintance with the Restoration and eighteenth-century drama from which the basic themes, situations, and characters are derived. Opening with Lord Are's vain attempt to copy the pastoral pose of "a gentleman drap[ing] himself across his fields," Bond introduces a typical Restoration hero, pushed to "extravagant gesture" by economic necessity. The scene is set with remarkable efficiency ("debts to honour a duke, and broke. So: a rich bride") and familiar themes follow apace.[42] Are's country estate is an accident of birth, but living there is the punishment to be inflicted upon his social-climbing wife. Like Etherege's Harriet, both Are and Ann so love London they "can scarce endure the country in landscapes and hangings," and Ann meets her death trying to escape. Ann's decision to frighten her husband into reform by dressing as a ghost recalls a similar ploy by Farquhar's Angelica, whose overtures to her husband Sir Harry Wildair meet with slightly more success.[43] But most of the allusions are broader in scope: the vision of a couple constantly at strife, of servants abused by the whims of their masters, and of characters forced to their stratagems by economic circumstance have ample precedents in earlier comedy, as do the characteristics displayed by Lord Are, who dominates the play's first half.

Are's epigrammatic wit, obsession with fashion, and blatant opportunism combine in a consummate comic portrait of the fortune-hunting aristocratic class he represents. The obvious villain of the play, Are also provides the major source of humor. As a foppish figure, he satirizes the morals and manners of the class he represents; as a clever and cynical manipulator of his own destiny, he invites complicity and assent from the audience for which he performs. The comedy is, from the beginning, double-edged. We laugh at Are's excessive concern with appearance ("Hang my scarf over the twig. Delicately! – as if some discriminating wind had cast it there," 7) and at the offense to his sensibilities that the lower orders, like nature itself, seem constantly to evoke ("I hate the gross odours the country gives off. 'Tis always in a sweat!" 7). The ease with which epithets roll off his tongue is telling: Frank is a "scab" and "city vermin," the peasants are "beasts," and the "swain" who wanders in "o'er the landscape" is recognized at closer range as a "fool," an "oaf," or a "harmless lunatic" (7–10). The mixture of fear, disgust, and impatience with servants introduced in the opening scene remains evident later, when the physical consequences of Are's attitudes are more disturbingly present. Are's rage over a missing button, directed at Bob's mother on the day of her son's execution, produces a terrifying moment in which the hilarious irony of the situation turns horrifying – an effect that depends on the somewhat shocking recognition that Are's excessive behavior is entirely consistent with the character he presents from the beginning of the play.

Among characters on equal footing, the humor plays differently. Are's cynicism towards Mr. Hardache and his daughter seems richly deserved; and the wit with which it is elaborated invites audience complicity without losing the edge of social satire. For example, Are's refusal to honor his pre-marital promises provides occasion for a devastating, bitingly funny oration on the value of a gentleman's word, excerpted below:

Why ma'am if a gentleman kept his promises society would fall apart. I promised? Forsooth and is that not enough? Have ye not had the pleasure of the promise? Your feet tapped when I promised you the opera! Your mouth watered when I promised you diamonds! Your knees shivered when I promised you the prince! What happiness I gave you! I denied you nothing. [...] Why ma'am have ye not noticed that I promise all the time? I am a christian. I go about the world scattering promises on the suffering and destitute [...] I promised! Ungrateful gal, was that not enough but that now you must have the promises kept? [...] 'Tis plain folly in a gentleman to keep his word [...] Ma'am I wonder that ye can live in this world at all with a mind so unschooled in polite society. (23–24)

With this speech, Are outwits his wife, motivates her revenge, and forcefully displays the attitudes on which Bond's class analysis depends. Ann's untimely death, farcically treated, is hereby linked to a mind "unschooled in polite society," just as Bob's death, melo-dramatically spun out, will be. Indeed, Are's words ring in our ears with each promise he makes for the rest of the play. While the content of Are's speech contributes heavily to the play's political point, the striking cadences and exuberant excess of Are's language contribute to his success as a comic "hero." So much wittier than his victims, Are effortlessly produces and unquestioningly embraces the self-justifying rhetoric of his "superior" social class. But in doing so, he provides for the audience a powerful and engaging figure of "enlightened self-interest." Are's control of language is matched by his manipulation of events, but unlike the models on which he is based, Are's destiny is not the one with which the playwright is primarily concerned. Yet Are emerges triumphant, and his char-acter generates more laughter than anyone else in the play. Maurice Charney provides a useful description of the effect as it occurs in conventional comedy:

we cling to illusions even when we know they are wrong, not only cling to them but actively pursue them against our own better judgment. Truth and morality are suspended as we watch the fascinating spectacle of con men magnificently conning us. The justification is in the magnificence. All the memorable comic pretenders are great talkers: inventive, hyperbolic, grandly absurd [...] their nuttiness endears them to us.[44]

Through Are, *Restoration* recognizes and caters to the comic sensibility of its probable audience even as it offers an alternative view. Simon Callow, who played the role under Bond's direction, found the task difficult until he alighted on the idea that Lord Are acts "in the confidence of his friend's approval," without whom, he

would be nothing.⁴⁵ The "essentially sunny disposition" Callow
found in the character is formed in collusion with the audience. As
the play progresses, that connection is strained to the breaking-point
– but not before exploiting "to the hilt" the audience's fascination
with his character. In Scene Five, by far the funniest of the play,
Lord Are "accidentally" kills his wife by running her through with a
sword, and we are brazenly invited to sympathize with his position
as he speaks alone on the stage: "here's a fine how-d'ye do. My wife.
Stretched out on the floor. With a hole in her breast. Before
breakfast. How is a man to put a good face on that?" (44). Just how
Are does manage it, by maneuvering Bob into taking the blame, was
rightly recognized as the theatrical *tour de force* that Bond intended it
to be. As the farcical mainspring of the action, the scene is the only
one without a song; and the energetic laughter it evokes is central to
the play's formal critique. As *Restoration* demonstrates, Lord Are's
comic "excess" is Marx's surplus value personified: based on the
extravagance associated with his class, Are's comic invulnerability is
produced and maintained by others; his comic freedom and final
triumph bought at Bob's expense.

A typical comedy of manners resolves the tension, cures the excess,
ends in good feeling, and reaffirms the status quo. By allowing Lord
Are to get away with murder, however, Bond avoids a comic
catharsis that would "purge" or contain the energies aroused by the
class-inflected conflicts of the play. Without forgoing all the gratifi-
cations associated with the form, *Restoration* pushes its conflicts to a
forceful resolution that denies the audience its normal *use* of comedy.
On his way to the scaffold, Bob's last words "I on't believe this!"
expose the audience's own expectations (of rescue, reversal, or relief)
and with it, the self-destructive illusions on which the very pleasure
of the older comic forms, whether witty or sentimental, are based.
Such an ending reverses the Brechtian strategy of *The Threepenny
Opera* or *The Caucasian Chalk Circle*, but for similar ends. In Brecht,
the rescuing agent appears in so exaggerated, unreal, or ironic a
manner that the mechanisms required of the convention are made
apparent. At the end of *Threepenny Opera*, the Queen's pardon is
delivered on horseback by a royal messenger who reprieves the real
criminal of the play. In *Caucasian Chalk Circle* justice is served only
because, through a series of "coincidences," a complete scoundrel is
sitting in judgment of Grusha's case. In both plays, the happy end is
a surprise, and a good deal of fun is had turning the "real" world

upside down, exposing its vulnerability, and letting the contradictions speak for themselves.

The world depicted in *Restoration* is no different, but here aesthetic forms turn evidence against themselves. As the comedy of manners in Part One gives way to the comedy of tears in Part Two, the audience's complicit, self-conscious laughter makes way for equally complicit, self-conscious suspense. The promise of rescue, kept alive by the most sympathetic characters, drives the narrative of Part Two to its "unbelievable" (but realistic) end. The urgency of the melodramatic form – with its trials of distressed innocence and the ultimate disaster that looms ahead – is both exploited and exposed, for the final catastrophe is not averted by outside agents, least of all the playwright. Rose is smart enough to figure out what really happened to Are's wife, but is stymied in every attempt to save her husband. Hardache uses her information to blackmail Are for mining rights to his land. Hope for a pardon sends Rose to Are's mother, whose words of dismissal hit home to the audience: "Ye made an old lady merry with a farce and now ye mar it with a wailing play!" (82). Unbeknownst to Rose, her suit proves successful, and a pardon does arrive in the nick of time. But Lord Are intercepts, outwits, and buys off the Royal Messenger, promising (with the word of a gentleman) to deliver the commission himself. As if such reversals were not painful enough, Are hands the pardon to Bob's mother, unable to read, so that she may start a fire. More maddening still, we have known since Scene Eight that Bob's chains are "only for show," that he could save himself by walking out the door. How and by whom a rescue will be managed proves less interesting than the suspense created over whether or not Bob will understand his situation soon enough to avert the disaster himself. Brecht's sense of the "Not – But" is everywhere – we see what could have been done, should have been done, and will be done with an empowering clarity.[46] Bob's vulnerability, hence his innocence, is seen to be alterable. By the end of the play, however, the audience has been duped, like Bob, into looking for a rescue that never comes. The deliberate manner in which the disappointment is rendered robs the humorous mechanisms of their conventionally uplifting effects. We are left irritated at Bob for learning too late, irritated at ourselves for hoping he might, and irritated at Bond for suggesting that our aesthetic pleasures and the desires to which they cater may be analogous to Bob's own investment in, and dependence on, a system shaped by the alliance between Are and Hardache, by upper-class values and industrial wealth.[47]

Since Bob, Rose, Frank, and the Mother are presented as more sympathetic, more serious, and more fully human than those for whom they work, they are the only characters with songs – a distinction appropriate to Bond's use of more popular art forms. The interspersed songs and music of earlier melodrama heightened the excitement and intensified the pathos of the action, contributing to a world of romance and illusion that could soften the painful effects of the narrative. The songs of *Restoration* play a similarly compensating role, but the gratification is inseparable from the political and realistic stance they promote. In Scene One, for example, Bob's pastoral love song to Rose provides a sharp and inviting contrast to the cynical attitudes displayed by Lord Are's courtship of Ann, and marks a shift of interest from upper- to lower-class characters. Bob woos Rose in a simple, straightforward, and openly sexual manner, using the same "pesky flower" that Are earlier demanded be ripped from the path. Unlike Are, Bob knows its name: "Lady's Smock" (14). Bob's song "Roses" equates the pleasure of loving to the pleasures of nature in a simple, traditional way; the situation is not sentimental because Bob's connection to nature (and Rose) is real, not "pastoral." At the end of the play, the nature imagery returns in Rose's love song to Bob, but the merging of man, nature, and desire that structures the earlier song is replaced by a more experienced, if equally "romantic," vision of human possibility. In "Man Is What He Knows" (the very phrase Bob struggles to read in Scene Eight), Rose complements and extends the emotional authenticity of Bob's "Roses" by suggesting that knowledge, not feeling, is what separates man from nature – that thoughtful observation of the social world is the key to survival. As such it marks a shift from the values and concerns of early eighteenth-century literature to those of the late nineteenth century, a shift embodied in the play's action and character development.[48] Whereas Bob learns too little too late, Rose's hard-won knowledge arms her for a future. Using the emotional resources of music and poetry to articulate a clear political stance may finally prove more pleasurable than the traditional "happy end."

As the songs shift from simpler folk ballads to the more insistent and dissonant rhythms of contemporary rock, a further connection is established between the popular melodrama of the nineteenth century and the modern musical or contemporary rock-opera into which it has evolved. *Restoration* reclaims the radical politics implicit in this tradition in part by reclaiming its music – that element most associated with the narcotic, escapist, illusionary qualities Brecht so despised in "the general drug traffic conducted by bourgeois show business."[49] Production numbers in film or stage musicals stop time and open the moment to a broader range of reference, but they also break the illusion of reality constructed by narrative. Bond's songs, on the other hand, introduce a level of reality that is closer to the world of the viewing audience than that of the play. The show-stopping numbers of *Restoration* may still transport the audience, but not to a timeless, dream-like world of self-gratifying sensation. Rather, the music invites the audience to reflect upon the play, to make connections to political issues of a later historical moment, and to think "above the stream" of the action without entirely leaving it.[50] In the "Song of Learning," for example, Frank steps outside his physically oppressed condition to speak from a position that pre-figures Rose's own at the end of the play. The song not only provides the audience with a political context from which to better judge Frank's theft, but it also provides the character with a broader, more radical, perspective on his own oppressed condition than is possible within the play. In song, Frank steps outside the determining mindset of his historical moment, but not outside his class interests and the socially significant aspects of his character. Rather, the song connects Frank to a "fifty thousand year old" history that has shaped his knowledge, his desires, and his anger. With the shift in pronoun from "them" to "you," the final stanza turns defiantly on the audience: "I have known pain and bowed before beauty / Shared in joy and died in duty / Fifty thousand years I lived well / I learned how to blow up your hell" (20). Frank does not speak for the playwright, but for himself, just as Rose in "Dream" speaks beyond, but within, her character for a utopian future in which race, rather than class, is the revolutionary prompt. Bond calls such moments "public soliloquy," privileged insights by the characters into their own condition.[51] In other words, the songs are not simply analytical, but empowering, not only commentary, but an articulation of the moral imperatives to which the characters' situations give rise.

While songs function differently across the play, connections remain between the singing characters' emotions (happiness, rage, fear, or sadness), the kind of music sung, the level of self-understanding that the character has achieved within the play, and a political awareness that redirects (without necessarily explaining) the energies produced by the previous scene's social tensions. The emotional directness of the folk-songs sung by Bob and his mother, for example, seems appropriate for the two characters most emotionally and intellectually "bound" to their situations. Bob's "Drum Song" at the end of the play will intensify rather than mitigate the pathos of his situation, and the painful desperation figured in the beating of a drum that has no sound gives angry voice to the heart-pounding fear with which he faces the gallows. Unlike Brecht's Katrin, whose fateful drumming awakens a city to resistance, Bob will sacrifice himself for the wrong cause; but his song alerts the audience to the danger from which he can no longer save himself. The riveting parable of "Song of the Conjuror," sung by Rose and Bob, not only prefigures Bob's death and acknowledges his own responsibility for it, but implicates the audience who "laughed as [the conjuror] struggled in the air," believed in his comic invulnerability, screamed with horror as "they saw him sinking down / And stood on the bank to watch him drown" (79). The lurid fascination with escape artists provides a telling comment on the audience's own viewing relationship to the stage spectacle. In the play's next song, sung by Rose and Frank, witnesses fare better: on "the fair tree of liberty / The fruit weighs the branches to the ground / And look! The fruit are eyes" (83): eyes that repel all aggressors and insure the tree's survival and growth. Here the song not only celebrates the attitudes of the singers within the play, but the importance of the audience's own presence in the theatre. While some songs play upon a lyrical tradition, others are angry or deliberately militant, giving voice to issues and ideological stances more politically divisive than aesthetically unifying. In nearly every case, the songs of *Restoration* invite the audience to identify with an attitude, respond to rhetorical questions, take a position. As such, they constantly remind that more is at stake than what narrative alone can suggest.

As the play's ironic subtitle suggests, *Restoration: A Pastoral* works within and against a pastoral vision of the world as much as it does the comic. In this regard, the blind swineherd Gabriel, who lost his eyesight fighting in the war, plays a small but important role. Another of the play's "victims," Gabriel has not only accepted his fate, but is grateful (to Are) for it, and advises others to be the same:

People allus fuss over what they can't mend. The whole world tip up an' everyone slid off – thass jist a saucer of spilt milk. Tell yoo what: [...] this job's all Sundays, like sit listenin' to bacon in the pan. Wife, roof, dry sty, eat an' sleep like an old boar. [...] Sight's a curse laid on them who lead me, feed me, thatch the roof an' hang the door – life a sweat an' grind an' small pittance in the end [...] Yoo see before yoo a happy man. (62, 63)

As in true pastoral, Gabriel embraces the essentially aristocratic code of idle ease and languid leisure, and mirrors the fatalistic attitudes of the class on whom he depends.[52] Although Rose refuses to believe that Gabriel prefers blindness to sight (the image speaks for itself), the Mother shares his stance: keep quiet, accept what comes, don't meddle. Her recognition of Are's power is thoroughly practical and grounded in experience. From the Mother's point of view, Gabriel's war injury was a stroke of good luck: "Look at him: come back from France an' got took on's if he had twenty eyes. Could have cost his lordship no end of pig" (63). In London, she notes, Bob would have ended up dead in the workhouse; with Are, he may be "set up for life" (63). So stated, the irony is unmistakable, but hardly comic. As the songs of *Restoration* make clear, analogous attitudes hold true today, and not only in the working class. The play suggests that if people had more knowledge of themselves, their world, and the consequences of their own beliefs, things would change – Rose herself models such conviction. Being able to identify with the ideological stance provided by the singing characters is a major source of pleasure offered by the play.

According to Empson, pastoral is a utopian, idealizing mode "about," but not by or for the people, one in which the complex is expressed as the simple, one that depends on a "proper relationship between the rich and the poor," and one shaped by the pressures of an (aristocratic) system of patronage. Through its expression of universal and fundamental truths, pastoral has often been the vehicle of moral and social criticism, as well as a representation of wishful thinking.[53] *Restoration* fits such definitions of pastoral, if one could only sufficiently forget the models on which they are based. Though most of the action takes place in the country, the lives of the principal characters are shown to be anything but simple, independent, and free from care. Gabriel, the closest to a real shepherd that the play offers, best represents the thrust of the historical form as a deceptive reconstruction of past and present, as "propaganda for the victors."[54] Yet *Restoration* does turn back to an earlier period, reflects upon the distance, and seems to conclude (in the circular pattern of thinking pastoral usually promotes) that certain fundamental truths have not changed. The truths promoted, however, reflect the values and sentiments of a militant working class, a class that exists somewhere between (or beyond) the time frame of both the play and the present day. Any nostalgia for an earlier age is thus replaced in *Restoration* by an analogous longing for a future world, one restored by the simple truths made available through song to the characters. Self-consciously constructed, admittedly simplified, and cognizant of the cultural space it inhabits, *Restoration* nevertheless offers similar pastoral pleasures to its audience – as a literary diversion from present-day reality, but one that promises regeneration and renewal of the human resources necessary to carry out social change. Katherine Worth's description of the play's last moments, colored by her own ability to accept the play's values, suggests the power that such a communal vision can have on the audience:

The play ends with a great swell of sound; the band comes forward for the last time and Rose, the only free being among the characters, is cut free of the grim world she has had to inhabit. She mounts the scaffold [. . .] and sings a song that is not sad but triumphantly militant [. . .] a passionate and moving memorial, and a thrilling theatrical climax.[55]

By taking on the pastoral tradition, in addition to that of conventional comedy, *Restoration* suggests that even the most artificially escapist, backward-looking, and conservative literary genres can be made to serve progressive political ends.

CHAPTER 7

Reading the present

The starkly naturalistic thrust of *Saved* and *The Pope's Wedding* mitigated against political interpretation, but the historical and/or geographical distancing of the plays Bond has written since has specifically promoted it. When Bond returns to a contemporary setting in *The Worlds* and *Summer*, the difference from his two earliest plays could hardly seem greater. Although the later plays create an impression of contemporary reality as strong as that evoked in *The Pope's Wedding* or *Saved*, *The Worlds* (1979) and *Summer* (1982) enable, through their broader social picture and more polemical approach, a "reading" of the present that the earliest plays, with their focus on a single social class, could not hope to achieve. *The Worlds* and *Summer* combine a naturalistic emphasis on the immediacy of lived experience with the parable's emphasis on ethical action, formal structure, and interpretation. Although their subject-matter and strategies differ, both plays explore the intersection of public events and private lives, of history and subjectivity, to suggest that the personal and the political can never be disengaged – and they do so with direct reference to the popular and prevalent modes through which reality is mediated, and consensus woven, for contemporary Western audiences. The combination of familiar dramatic techniques and an unpopular political stance resulted in predictably mixed reviews for both plays. By making political analysis and aesthetic experience so inseparable, *The Worlds* and *Summer*, even more so than earlier plays, tend to "judge their audience" and to reward the political interest audiences bring to the theatre.[1]

The Worlds

In contrast to the retrospective, inward-looking focus of *Summer*, the contemporary setting of *The Worlds* reflects a society saturated by the drama of the news event. In 1979, the broadly allusive, generically "newsworthy" events of the play – a winter workers' strike, two terrorist kidnappings, and the corporate restructuring of a major firm – provided instantly recognizable situations for the British audience of a recently elected Conservative government. Indeed, the combination of a failing economy, disabling winter strikes, and growing terrorist activity at home and abroad have since been seen as key factors in Thatcher's rise to power. That the American hostage crisis in Iran ran concurrent with the play's premiere was perhaps unlucky, but, as the argument of the play makes clear, not altogether fortuitous.[2] Indeed, two days before the opening of *The Worlds* at the Royal Court's Theatre Upstairs, an article appeared in *The Times* on terrorism as a new field of study; and a psychologist is quoted on its effect: "Terrorism is great theatre," he writes. "It's great fun for the terrorists and the audience. It's sheer heroics. You can hardly wait to open the paper and see what's new on the hostages."[3] Such comments may cloud the issues at stake; but by creating violent confrontations, demanding immediate action, and polarizing the discourse, terrorist activity in the 1970s and 1980s did provide the media with a kind of melodrama that captured the interest of large audiences who might otherwise seem politically indifferent. Since acts of terrorism assert the importance of larger political goals over the well-being of any individual, they appear inimical to the liberal humanist values of Western democracies; but the rigid reactions to terrorist violence suggest that crucial connections are often ignored. This is one of the problems Bond addresses in *The Worlds* when he asks his audience two related and difficult questions: is there a rational use of "the irrational"? And who are the real terrorists?

The Worlds both exploits and deflates the inherent theatricality of "crisis politics" to involve the audience in a political analysis of contemporary society – its structure, methods of operation, and morality. Because the focus is on "history in the making," the play readily acknowledges the pervasive forms whereby present-day political reality is recorded, interpreted, generated, and reproduced by broadcast news, the press, television docu-drama, contemporary theatre, and film. Everything from the "inside story," "people in the news" focus, to the "jump cut," docu-drama strategies suggests Bond's familiarity with the popular dramatic conventions through which social reality is constructed for present-day audiences. The scene-by-scene action could in fact be summarized by newspaper-like headlines: "Beleaguered Executives Retire to Country for Private Talks," "Company President Seized by Terrorists: Minister Expresses Concern," "Terrorists Escape; Company Resumes Negotiations," and so on. The limitations imposed by media representation are noted by Terry, who, near the end of the play, is invited to respond to reporters' questions: "'Militants condemn terror.' So everyone's still got their right label. We can go home happy. What good's that?"[4] Bond's own labels divide and contextualize sections of the script, each referring to a social form of communication that carries its own implicit content: "An Advertisement," "A Menu," "An Invitation," "A Speech at an Unveiling," "A Negotiations Speech," "A Workman's Biography," "A Lecture," "An Examination," "A Confession," "A Fantasy," "Press Release."[5] All call attention to the play's central issue: in Anna's words, whether or not our "public means of explanation" (25) can accurately record or adequately interpret current events.

Reviewers who found a lack of naturalistic depth in the characters tended to read *The Worlds* as a parable, and to equate, a little too easily, Bond's own political stance with that of the terrorist, Anna.[6] But the surface verisimilitude and conscious stagecraft prevent the play from approximating a Brechtian *Lehrstück*. Nor does it, despite the two-act division, suggest the problem–solution format of *The Woman* and *The Bundle*, Bond's first so-called "answer plays." In the enacted history of *The Woman* and *The Bundle*, Hecuba and Wang provide a centering focus: both learn from the past and change the direction of history by their actions, and their stories end optimistically. In *The Worlds*, however, solutions are not to be found in the particular sequence of events. Terrorism generates the play's action, prompts the businessmen's takeover, and affects the workers' negotiations. But in political terms, the story charts more failures than accomplishments: no one is better off at the end of the play than the beginning, with the possible exception of the company itself. TCC does not fall, but flourishes. Despite the hope for social change held out by the terrorists' action and the workers' experience, the pattern of the plot reflects the cyclical, periodic "crises" through which capitalism adjusts to changes in the economy and threats from the outside.

Indeed, the structure of the play recalls the opening lines of Marx's analysis of a failed revolutionary movement in "The Eighteenth Brumaire." Amending Hegel's remark that "all facts and personages of great importance in world history occur, as it were, twice," Marx adds, "the first time as tragedy, the second as farce."[7] The comment seems particularly applicable to the terrorists' own revolutionary "mistakes." In Part One, Trench is kidnapped, but somehow escapes (tragedy); in Part Two, Kendall's chauffeur is kidnapped by mistake (farce). Bond amends the tendency, however, by ending the first sequence of events with an absurdly comic scene, whereas the second hostage scenario, in which the chauffeur gets killed, is played out on a more somber note. The structural repetition allows Bond to more fully elaborate the issues brought up in the play's first part, and to do so from different perspectives. Things happen, but nothing really changes; at the end of the play, the exact result of the strike action is left ambiguous. While the businessman–terrorist conflict gets resolved, the narrative closure does not point to a satisfactory resolution of the issues posed by the play. Rather, the repetition suggests that the crisis will return in similar fashion and to similar effect until the underlying causes of the problem are better understood.

More important than the two-act division is Bond's division of characters into three separate groups, each with its own central figure (Trench, Anna, Terry), its own sphere of action (the boardroom, the hideout, the picket line), its own set of goals and methods of pursuing them. The linear juxtaposition of sharply defined social worlds invites the audience to observe, compare, and contrast, in an essentially dialectical manner, the attitudes and actions of each. In addition to the opposition both implied and enacted between the three worlds, each is beset with its own internal conflicts – a fact that contributes to the play's driving energy, its contrapuntal plot, and its thematic richness. With two exceptions (Trench's extended contact with the terrorists and Terry's brief encounter with the businessmen), the groups are kept separate throughout the play. As a result, the audience receives more information and commentary than any single character. Through the separation, Bond also diagnoses the fundamental problem of the world he sets out to examine – a world divided by class, controlled by big business, disrupted and restored by violence. Anna, Terry, and Trench provide the most sympathetic and articulate access to each social world. Through their speeches, Bond periodically reaches beyond the resources of common conversation to present a sharp delineation of the characters' differing

attitudes and a clear thematic elaboration of issues addressed
elsewhere by the plot. Characters in each group "read" their
situation in ways that explain their actions; but the radical separation maintained between the three worlds suggests that current
models of "consensus politics" may be inappropriate for curing our
social ills. If nothing else, the intercutting between groups of
characters with such different values, modes of behavior, and sense
of being in the world reminds the audience that the world in which
they live *is* divided – and that any aesthetic that glosses over such
deep divides is a false and mystifying one.

As in earlier plays, Bond is concerned with the meaning and
movement of history and the individual's relationship to it, both
objectively (as members of a particular class) and subjectively (as
individuals faced with moral choices). But the play's dual commit-
ment, to quasi-naturalistic dramatic techniques and to an accurate
representation of political reality, has certain consequences. In other
words, the action must appear plausible, even though the forms
through which plausibility is constructed are suspect; events must be
shown, but in a context that does not preempt political understanding in the usual ways. The new strategy of exposition involves an
alternating sequence of scenes that adheres to a strict internal logic
without telling the story in a predictable manner. For example, the
businessmen's callous reaction to Trench's kidnapping (Scene Two)
is shown chronologically out of order, before the completed abduc-
tion scene (Scene Three) and the workers' reaction to it (Scene
Four). Trench returns unharmed in Scene Five, but whether by
rescue, release, or escape is a question left unanswered until the
play's second half.[8] In Part Two, curiosity aroused about the
terrorists will be satisfied by a privileged view of the bungled second
kidnapping and its result. Here, scenes with the terrorists outnumber
those with the businessmen, but an exact chronology of events, so
crucial to accurate historical interpretation, is not forthcoming. The
final scene of each act is narratively unnecessary, but visually
reformulates and verbally summarizes the action it follows. Trench's
disillusionment in Scene Six helps explain his actions in Part Two;
the workers' disillusionment in Scene Twelve moves outside the
frame of the play toward the experience of the viewing audience.

Although a deliberately plotted, formal pattern governs the
macrostructure of *The Worlds*, a sense of spontaneity and improvisation informs the unfolding dialogue, especially in scenes that propel

the action forward. Under the pressure of the moment, all the characters make moral choices that affect the lives of others as well as themselves; as the play unfolds, the burden of responsibility is distributed equally among them before shifting it to the audience watching the play. The resulting pattern of movement suggests not simply that the present is conditioned by the past, affected by class, and shaped by institutional protocol, but that the future is being determined, at every moment, by actions taken now. Because the characters' behavior so clearly depends on a combination of beliefs, facts, and an ideology that enables interpretation, the play urges closer scrutiny of the institutional sources of knowledge. *The Worlds* finally suggests that the means and methods of social change cannot be divorced from a broader social analysis – that any solution to social problems depends on how they are posed.

As agents presently in control of history (and the institutions that interpret, move, and mediate it), Trench and his business partners dominate the stage time of *The Worlds* and provide the focus for Part One. From the beginning, they represent the status quo – not as given or unchanging, but as a constant struggle – and it is against Bond's portrait that the others will be measured. Opening with a toast in a world with clear affinities to Shavian social comedy, the characters unwittingly, though not implausibly, articulate the self-justifying rhetoric that attracts capitalism's entrepreneurs, masks its contradictions, and disguises the inherent injustice of its methods and consequences. Harris, for example, speaks of "a few more old-fashioned virtues. Such as guts. Go out and get it. Self-help" (11). Trench compares himself to Columbus, discovering and making a new world; and goes on to discuss his business ethic in speeches rich in dramatic irony, given events to come:

What you invest in a man is what you get out of him. Yes, at times we do harsh things. But we do it cleanly. For the good of the customer. With no malice. No pleasure. We push a man overboard and we sail on. But we throw a lifebelt in the sea behind us. We're all brothers. Big brothers and little brothers. As in every family. At the end of the day we can all offer the next man our hand. Be he from the shop floor or the directors' suite. Couldn't do the job if I didn't believe that. (13)

The analysis rings more than a bit false when we learn, rather late in the scene, that the company is in the midst of a paralyzing strike. By delaying the information, Bond forces the audience to consider the substance of the men's previous conversation in a surprising (yet no less plausible) context. The leisurely after-dinner conversation and comfortable setting suddenly takes on a different meaning; and by introducing the discordant note as a compliment to the civility of their host, the play suggests it will take more than a labor dispute to disturb the lives and convictions of the affluent.

Throughout the opening scene, Bond humorously elaborates a social dynamic clearly at odds with Trench's own description. Trench, whose fatherly attitude is predicated by relations of power, insists on the friendly, cooperative nature of his aggressively competitive, financially successful corporation. The interaction between an aesthetically discriminating man who values the country life and men who appreciate only its price, between a company director who writes poetry and junior executives who don't, is likewise fraught with comic possibility, as is the sycophantic rivalry between the junior executives. The banality of the after-dinner conversation, the careful decorum characters struggle to observe, and the general air of self-congratulation finally prevent the audience from taking the characters as seriously as they take themselves. Yet the play demands that we hear them out, especially on the issues Trench proposes for his "think tank" – how do you judge a man and "what is character?" (12). The question resurfaces in Part Two as the terrorists, businessmen, and workers in turn must determine the value of a chauffeur's life.

In Scene One, the businessmen articulate the very values (trust, loyalty, friendship, respect for authority) they abandon in the following scene, and against which Trench and the audience judge them in Part One. But the self-reflective touches are also important – Trench has hired an artist to paint a company portrait who sketches throughout the scene. "Catch their character," Trench instructs him, "That'll prove if you're an artist" (16). If the scene veers close to caricature, it does so in its self-conscious imitation of mannered comedy. Subsequent scenes with the businessmen present a jarring contrast to the genteel surface painted in the first, but do so without losing reference to the comic note on which the play begins. Insofar as "caricature" implies simplified figures less fully human than the viewing audience, it inaccurately describes the characters of *The Worlds*; yet notions of sketching, authorial comment, and conceptualization do inform Bond's construction of character in the play. In all three worlds, characters explain, rationalize, defend, and discuss in ways that make class analysis for the audience easier. In contrast to the impulse of psychological theatre – to identify, through personal details of performance and idiosyncrasies of language and behavior, a "humanity" that ultimately transcends class lines and age barriers – *The Worlds* works to identify, through social interaction, gestic language, and the structure of relationships, the forces that prevent individuals from being fully human. The major focus of Bond's own rehearsals was on stripping away the naturalistic detail to reveal a deeper, socio-economic, source of human behavior.[9] Although the businessmen (like the workers and terrorists) are more than adequately differentiated, the dialogue moves constantly to expose the underlying ideological determinants of their behavior.

In 1979, Trench's business partners provided an early fictive example of a soulless new breed of financiers now associated with the fiscally conservative Thatcher–Reagan decade. As capital moves from family-owned private businesses to larger public corporations, power shifts to those of a different class background, a distinction made apparent in the contrast between Trench and the pragmatic, cigar-smoking, hatchet man who replaces him. Against Trench's own analysis of events, then, the actions taken by his partners reflect broader economic necessities, which in turn affect character. Setting up a parallel of central importance to the argument of the play (that the businessmen are the play's real terrorists), Bond introduces the issue of violence with a quick dissolve from the country manners of Scene One to the cut-throat business practices of the managing board of Scene Two. However callous the businessmen's reaction to Trench's kidnapping may appear, Hubbard's tough stand on negotiations *is* the line Trench would take "provided he was in a position to give an unbiased verdict" (18). Only Harris finds the hostage situation disconcerting, but his emotional responses are dismissed as signs of weak and reckless thinking. The same profit motive that guides Hubbard's decision to stand firm against the terrorists' demands underlies his decision to put the company on the stock exchange during Trench's absence, a move Trench has blocked for years. Lord Bigdyke's remark that "civilization is built on the finding of substitutes for violence in the conduct of human affairs" (19) is thus illustrated in an aggressive and unexpected manner by Hubbard's decision to "exploit the situation." For the businessmen, the crisis becomes "a godsend," and theirs is language appropriate to the dog-eat-dog world of corporate enterprise being ridiculed:

HUBBARD: Harris thinks you stop the dog biting your leg by giving it your
   arm. [. . .] Exploit the situation: that's what it's about. They'll let JT
   go just to get him off their tits. If we let this slip away we deserve our
   bloody dicks chopped off. I waited for it. I hope he's shit scared and I'd
   like the pleasure of smelling his shit [. . .] Shouldn't read bloody
   poetry. (20–21).

Using the terrorists to do their own dirty work, the businessmen's
tactics appear as crude and barbarous as cold-blooded murder.

   With terrorists (and their "unacceptable" means) intervening
on behalf of an "acceptable" worker–management confrontation,
Bond's plot introduces a new variation on an old social picture.
Indeed, the worker–owner struggle is such a social "given" that it
hardly gets mentioned before Scene Four. For Lord Bigdyke, the real
problem has little to do with the workers at all. "We are almost
hardened to terrorism [. . .] but this is new" (19), he states,
elaborating the issue in the familiar language of means vs. ends. A
better educated, more civilized figure than the businessmen, Bigdyke
nevertheless demonstrates the ideological collusion of business and
government, especially insofar as the "good of society" ends up
being identical to "the good of the company." As an emissary of the
Conservative government, Lord Bigdyke is accompanied throughout the play by the Chief of Police, and this dynamic duo (no less
important for the comic strokes by which they are painted) completes Bond's portrait of the businessmen's world – a world legiti-
mated and perpetuated by the "reason" of civilized men, but
ultimately empowered and maintained through force of arms. The
inherent contradiction is dramatized by a contrast in the two men's
characters similar to that found between Hubbard and Trench. The
Police Chief (always smiling) takes obvious pleasure in crisis situations which allow him greater autonomy in the exercise of his
powers. When push comes to shove, the police, not Bigdyke or the
businessmen, will determine the outcome of events – even (and
especially) in the most civilized democracies. Indeed, Bigdyke's last
words in the play – "I would not hide from you my belief that the
times are dark. The Tiber cannot be defended by noble minds and
beautiful phrases" (69) – summarize the kind of cynical, apocalyptic
thinking that ultimately justifies the use of force. At the end of the
play, Trench, not Anna, kills the hostage. Anna is shot by the police.

   While Bigdyke's pessimism is caused by terrorists who disturb the
mechanical efficiency of his administration, Trench's pessimism is

rooted in the fate he suffers at the hands of his business partners. Perhaps the most interesting and well-developed character in the play, Trench is the only one to change through the course of events, and his presence in seven of the play's twelve scenes provides an important structural link between the businessmen and the terrorists. As in earlier plays, Bond goes to some lengths to show how Trench's subjectivity is socially created. However haunting his presence, Trench is neither mystifying nor enigmatic, but a psychic embodiment of clearly visible social relations. As a disillusioned victim of the society he helped shape, Trench provides the audience with an important, but limited, perspective on the play's events.

In Part One, Bond short-circuits our interest in the actual hostage situation with Trench's sudden and surprising reappearance (Scene Five). As the man of the hour the press has undoubtedly made of him, Trench returns to his world unshaken by his experience, happy, invigorated, triumphant, and eager to resume an office the audience knows is no longer his. The situation is rich in dramatic irony, and considerable tension is generated by uncertainty as to how Trench will receive the news. Not one to give in easily, Trench moves through a series of reactions, from simple denial to grandiloquent outrage, humorously counterpointed (and provoked) by the deliberate composure of his partners, who desperately seek to keep the situation under control. Although Hubbard tries to keep the meeting short, Trench plays out the scene to a passionate breaking-point. From an objective point of view, Trench is as much a victim of economic necessity as betrayal by his friends; and given the essentially comic style with which this world is depicted, his "tragic destiny" shrinks to the more pathetic proportions of a man sacked from his job. With the complications of Scene Two apparently exhausted, Bond here prepares the audience for yet another turn of events as Trench (comically) returns to deliver a quiet, ominously-spoken dinner invitation.

The prototype for Trench and his development is undoubtedly Shakespeare's *Timon of Athens*; as in Shakespeare's play, Trench is allowed to "once more feed the rascals" (III.v.113) and, again like Shakespeare, to condemn the businessmen through a member of their own class and in a manner appropriate to it. Much of the humor of Scene Six is made possible by the addition of the businessmen's wives, who attempt at several points to reconcile the breach between the men by appealing to their sense of social decorum. But the particular form of Trench's revenge involves the unveiling of the company portrait promised in Scene One, one Trench believes more accurately depicts the subjects: "That's important after all. If we knew what we are the world would change very fast. The little voice of truth. Most of you would have to jump off a bridge" (44–45). After a suspenseful delay, the portrait is unveiled to reveal an outrageous caricature Bond describes in the following manner:

It is a seaside photographer's prop. It shows a tropical beach. A man flexes the biceps of one arm and holds a cigar in the hand. The other arm is round a girl. She is a blonde. Both wear bathing costume. Both have a hole on top of the neck. These are for the heads to be pushed through. An ape swings in a coconut tree. A starfish is stranded on the beach. A battle cruiser is moored in the bay. (47)

Images of the family and the loyal team here give way to a crude, mass-produced artifact with empty holes for heads. Any head will do, Trench implies, to complete the "false image" of the painted canvas; and the businessmen are suddenly faced with a tasteless image of their own redundancy. Kendall can imagine no greater insult, and cries, "Pop art." Indeed, the prop has a startling effect on the characters and audience alike, for its camp, working-class accent seems so foreign to Trench's character. The symbolism is at once both obvious and enigmatic, as much an image of Trench's madness as of the class and world it is intended to portray.

The audience is given little time to reflect on the meaning, however, as the mild comedy of manners quickly explodes into abrasive social farce. Indeed, the prop works like some strange chemical weapon on the onstage viewers. As if on cue from Trench ("Put your head in. Show us what you are [. . .] Will it show the truth? Afraid of party games?" 47), the guests proceed to physically enact, in Trench's words, their "moral bankruptcy." Harris cries and whimpers throughout the scene; Pru dances a rowdy striptease ("it's strip-strip-stripping time") and runs naked on the set. Sylvia gives up chasing Pru with her clothes, and throws a screaming, full-scale tantrum; Hubbard jumps angrily up and down on his cigar. Marion wanders around the set smiling vacantly and making reassuring gestures to the rest. And Trench continues to rail:

O god o god o god. That there's no justice! People like you – smash smash smash. You smile and read reports and smash! [. . .] O are you late for an appointment? Buying up poison? Cornering the market in bones? Paying your hit man? Fixing some little clerk with figures to sell? A secretary in industrial espionage? Selling your family grave for redevelopment? (49)

The resulting pandemonium is bizarre and theatrically unsettling. While Trench may be saner than the world he rejects, the point is made in an essentially irrational manner. Disillusioned by the actions of his "friends," Trench ultimately sees through the hypocrisies of the business world; but he remains a cultural representative of the class he rejects. Scene Six thus presents itself as a caricature of serious contemporary theatre as well as a comment on the characters; the techniques borrowed from the theatre of the absurd have limited practical use to the audience, yet seem thoroughly appropriate to the worldview being "mirrored."[10] Just as Trench's private unmasking has no effect on the real lives of his guests, who proceed with business as usual in the scenes to follow, so Bond's absurd depiction remains a theatrical aside upon the nature of the world he "caricatures."

With his moral outrage and powerful speech, Trench wins a guarded sympathy from the audience in Part One by unmasking the businessmen's hypocrisy, exposing their unethical behavior, and speaking for a principle of justice denied him. At the opening of Part Two, Trench is living like a hermit, "off his head," having bought the house in which he was once held prisoner. As a disinherited member of the ruling class, he remains intelligible and articulate, but his isolation results in an increasingly nihilistic vision, one that the audience is invited to understand rather than to share. As Anna sees it, Trench's existential despair links him to the world of the businessmen he purports to reject by providing them with "the illusion that they have a moral sense" (76). Yet the audience is more likely to see him, in Part Two, as a victim of that world than its symptom. Like Lear, Trench's madness is rooted in a personal experience of betrayal, and his increasingly metaphoric language recalls Bond's earlier figure with the important difference that Trench never learns. Rather, Trench universalizes his feelings of futility and loss into a vision of history and human possibility diametrically opposed to that of the terrorists.

For Trench, the terrorists provide but one more illustration of an age-old pattern of human violence, cyclical and meaningless: "Mankind through the ages. A clown with a gun. An idiot with a stick. Little men plotting in tiny corners [. . .] Homo mob" (76). No longer angry, Trench feels soiled by human contact and the human voice gives him pain. He longs for silence, death, "peace after the last shot" (77); he prophesies the end of the world as a nuclear holocaust, and wants to witness it. The increasing inhumanity of his position becomes apparent with his callous description of the terrified hostage – the silent, hooded, stage-dominating white bundle (quite literally a cipher for man) who struggles to free himself at the end of the play.

That white worm. Crawling along the floor. Food shoved up its hood. Let out to shit. Covered with a gun. What keeps it alive? A little thread of hope or cunning or hate or malice. It doesn't know the difference under the hood. Not that it matters. As long as it can dangle on it for a little time before it drops into the hole. If you took off its hood it would hang itself. That white corpse. That – (80)

The speech is interrupted by an approaching car, and in the ensuing panic of approaching police helicopters, Trench unties the hostage's legs, hides, pokes a revolver through the canvas of the picture, and shoots him.

The surprising turn of events threatens to dramatically over-whelm rather than visually illustrate Bond's carefully structured argument, evoking questions for the audience left narratively unre-solved. Why, exactly, does he do it? The murder Trench commits offers a disturbing, iconographic moment that must be "inter-preted" by the audience. Given the apocalyptic pattern of Trench's thought, his inability to listen to the terrorists, and his despairing view of human nature, it is difficult to see his killing of the hostage as a sudden desire to help the terrorists or join their fight. Trench does not, as one reviewer of the play suggested, "become" a terrorist.[11] Rather, his actions demonstrate that he already is one, that the views he holds are fundamentally cruel, destructive, inhumane. Nor does Trench act entirely as "himself." Pushing his revolver through the picture, he takes on the persona of his business partners to reenact his own murder by his friends. The visual link to the unveiling scene recalls the earlier moment of "madness" in which Trench unmasked the truth behind the hollow social pretensions of the business world. But Trench is also "mad," and his irrational act remains consistent to the vision of human nature (inherently evil and violent) and the vision of history (cyclical and regressive) he articulates in the play's second half. As a moving tableau, the action serves as Bond's disturbing portrait of an audience inclined to identify with Trench's point of view.

As president of TCC, Trench provides the terrorists with their target and the audience with access to their world. Trench's presence in every terrorist scene subliminally supports the play's argument that terrorism is engendered by the society Trench represents. While Anna presents her revolutionary struggle as an effort to make two worlds – one of money and one of morality – into one, the viewer may agree with Trench's response: "There *are* two worlds: your's and mine. We're in mine" (79). But Trench's exception to the play's strict separation of worlds is only apparent. Despite the opportunity Trench's contact with the terrorists provides for the audience, Trench himself proves incapable of learning from, or even listening to, his captors. As he says in Part Two, "I didn't listen. I've heard it before. Better said" (79), preempting the probable response to Anna's analysis. Rather, the interaction between Anna and Trench provides Bond with the opportunity to elaborate two distinct and incompatible ways of viewing the world that have specific consequences on the characters' actions.

Although Trench provides a plausible pretext for much of the dialogue, the terrorist scenes differ from those with the businessmen in style, tempo, language and effect. Whereas the businessmen are depicted in a style appropriate to social comedy, the scenes with the terrorists reflect the serious tone of newsworthy docu-drama. Here tension and suspense are not generated by dialogue, but by action – and by the life-threatening nature of the situation itself. Because the terrorists' success depends on the care and precision with which they handle their weapons, observe prearranged signals, guard the hideout and hostage, and carry out their plans, their interchanges involve the delegation and performance of duties in a language clipped and precise. In keeping with the realism of the dramatic situation, the audience is given no more information about the terrorists than is available to Trench. And the difficulty Trench will present for the terrorists (both here and later) mirrors Bond's own artistic problem of getting the audience to listen seriously to the terrorists when their demands are being articulated at gunpoint. Indeed, the audience first hears the ultimatum as read into the tape recorder by Trench. Labelled in the script as "A Confused Reading of an Ultimatum," the demands themselves are read clearly, but the reasons for them (the longer part of the message) are mispunctuated to produce a garbled and incomprehensible string of words, sounding vaguely like left-wing political rhetoric, without the sense. So it sounds to Trench, and perhaps to the audience were Anna to read the message first.

Throughout the play, Anna's speeches share the direct language of Bond's own polemical essays, but if the response of reviewers is typical, her analysis is rarely "heard." The issue is of central importance to the play's strategy and argument, as outlined in the following exchange:

TRENCH: [...] You must have reasons for what you do. Then explain them. Make us listen.
ANNA: We just explained it. You read it.
TRENCH: But those – words.
ANNA: Meant nothing to you. This society *can't* explain itself to itself. You understand nothing. Yet the public means of explanation – press, television, theatres, courts, schools, universities – almost everywhere ideas are formed or information collected is owned in one way or another by people like you. Even our language is owned by you. We have to learn a new language. Even our morals. We have to be different people. You think you can live half your life by the laws of banking and the other half by truth. No! Think! (25)

If Anna speaks directly for Bond anywhere in the play, she does so here, for the ideas she introduces will be elaborated in the play's second part and events that unfold in the interim will help to illustrate them. The offstage sound of an approaching motorbike threatens to drown out Anna's "Clear Reading of an Ultimatum" on which the scene ends, forcing a heightened level of attention from the audience; and while the tape-recorded message is not by itself persuasive, simply restoring its syntactic logic makes a pointed dramatic impact.

Throughout the play, Trench's passionate outrage and increasingly sonorous monologues counterpoint the calm, lucid reasoning of Anna's speech. Their difficulties of communication are due not only to differing interpretations of the world, however, but to the shared language they use to communicate. As Anna's speech about "the public means of explanation" makes clear, the issue for Bond is neither existential (as Trench might have it) nor linguistic, but social – for language is shaped, controlled, and often emptied of meaning by the very social institutions that use it as currency. With her "lecture" in Part Two, Anna directly responds to Trench's "story," an interesting parable that illustrates the futility of all political action. Her language is simple, direct, reasonable:

The earth can't hold two worlds anymore. It's too small. So we make the two worlds one. That's all revolution is: making the two worlds one. Making morality strong so that the real world will be changed. [. . .] It's a matter of weapons. Using them causes suffering. But when appearance and reality are one there'll be less suffering, Men will know themselves – and the world will last in peace and prosperity. (79)

The very clarity of Anna's speech makes her analysis seem too simple, especially in view of Trench's literate asides. Yet the problem is sharing language in a society where phrases like "peace and prosperity" seem nothing but empty clichés. While Anna is the only character of the play to envision a future neither apocalyptic nor essentially the same, her optimism is set against the admitted difficulty of her own decisions, Lisa's doubts, the betrayal of someone in their own organization, and the obvious failure of their immediate political goals. Moreover, Anna's speech about the "two worlds" must be read against the play's structural set-up, the three worlds that the audience, by Scene Eleven, has come to accept as "given," and against the habitual sense of lived reality (one world) experienced outside the theatre. Anna's "one world" is a post-revolutionary one, but one that makes possible the ordinary and everyday. As Lisa puts it, "I'd've liked to have been an ordinary woman. Lived in a simple world. Loved Michael. Worked at what I wanted. Talked to the neighbors and children. The world isn't like that" (80). Bond offers no personal information that could explain the terrorists' actions in any terms but their own.

Despite the failure to achieve anything like their intended objective (the plausibility of the action is important), the terrorists' motives are beyond suspicion, and Bond grants them instead a moral and political vocabulary capable of posing, but not answering, the questions of the play. The very separation of the "worlds" Bond constructs limits the terrorists' effectiveness – they cannot confront the businessmen directly, nor do they have contact with the workers they purportedly support. Given that Anna is shot by the police – that the society represented uses force to preserve itself – Bond refuses to rule out (on principle) the use of weapons to achieve social change. Without uncritically advocating the use of terrorist tactics, *The Worlds* demonstrates that the question of violence cannot be understood nor solved by a society that provokes and perpetuates it. Within that society, Anna's actions may be criminal; but as Lord Bigdyke points out in Scene Nine, "Terrorism must be seen to be a crime. If ever the public saw it as politics we'd be lost" (61). The play in fact invites the audience to see terrorist violence as another form of politics and to reexamine the premises on which discussions of terrorism usually take place.

The connections between Trench's viewpoint and Anna's are deeper than might first be assumed, for both use a polarizing discourse grounded in, and dependent on, the social consensus of their differing communities. Trench comes to acknowledge that the world is not what it seems, and is emotionally devastated as a result; a similar insight inspires Anna to action. For both, the turn of events proves heavily ironic. Spatially isolated from the other two worlds, the workers neither advance nor resolve the complications of the plot; yet their situation, perspective, and discussion of issues prove more helpful in interpreting the events of the play than Anna's direct commentary or Trench's metaphoric one. Indeed, the workers provide the middle ground between Trench's ironic pessimism and Anna's radical alternative. Although neither is caricatured, both Anna and Trench tend toward moral, social, psychological extremes of behavior based on opposing points of view. As characters, the striking workers are far more appealing – and their situation most problematic. While the businessmen blame the terrorists and the terrorists blame the businessmen for the violence that erupts in their direct confrontation, the workers are caught in the middle, unable to condone terrorist tactics, but reluctant to express their disapproval in a self-defeating gesture of solidarity with the owners.

Scene Four, the only view of the workers in Part One, is thus strategically placed in the middle of the ongoing action. Here we find their situation has been made no easier by the terrorists' intervention. Verbally harassed by an Old Age Pensioner ("Reds. Went through the war for the lot of you. Day's work'd kill yer. [...] Locking your boss up. Don't play the innocent with me," 28), the strikers must not only contend with the businessmen, but with unfavorable public opinion; and the oldest paid-up union member is ready to "chuck it in" as a result. His reasons, identical in substance to those offered by Hubbard when he meets with Terry in Part Two, are understandable and humane:

It's your common humanity. [...] When you don't fight for money while some poor bleeder's fightin for his life. Keep em in the boot and throw food at em like a dog. Tie gelignite round their chests. Human bloody firework.

[...] I'm not havin blood on my hands. Not even Trench's. Couldn't look the wife in the face across the table. (29, 30)

Ray's sentiments recall Trench's discussion of values in the opening scene, and not because Ray is a "company man." Terry tries to explain that while things appear to be different, in terms of their own struggle, nothing has changed. Beryl seems instinctively to understand:

Trench is pullin a fast one. He's sunnin it out in Monte Carlo. He could pay us with what he picks up in the casino. Took all his loot back the yacht'd sink. It's time somethin changed. (29)

Terry believes that the terrorists may kill Trench no matter what they do, that they should let the others fight it out. Isolated from the sources of power and information, and wisely distrustful of the press, neither Beryl's view nor Terry's proves factually correct, yet their interpretation is better attuned to the situation than anyone else's. What most disturbs Ray is the use of violence, of course, and his reservations help focus the audience's own questions – questions that provoke a parable-like thinking process that the audience is expected to share.

As the scene unfolds, Terry and John move out from the factory wall in order to enact the differing points of view held by the workers, the terrorists, the "copper" and Trench – and in so doing present the clearest thinking on the issues the audience sees in the play. Without changing the language they speak, the workers perform what Bond will call a "public soliloquy" to illustrate how society works to keep the ruling class in power despite the basic injustice of its organization.[12] John first voices the worker's point of view:

JOHN: Where am I? Here? No ... (*He walks as far away as he can. Stops.*) Here! [...] On strike. I wait quietly and say: I sweat my balls off for all the Trenchs and their rich bints, and their little sonnies in their posh schools, and their classy little slags of daughters while they go round screwing multinational-millionaires an havin their pox cured in private clinics on what I put in their pockets. And I'm saying I want my money crook. I work [...] Now if you lot over there are playing gunfights that's your pleasure. Bang away. I'm over here askin for what's mine. (31)

John's language is powerful and his point of view familiar. But Terry goes on (using the same "game" metaphors invoked by Bigdyke in

Scene Two) to show how rules and regulations in themselves have no moral value, but serve to keep things as they are with "*them* on top" (32). In a Wang-like manner, Terry demonstrates (with Beryl's purse) how Trench is a thief who "relies on force as much as any terrorist" (33); the terrorists' threat is hardly new, but rather an extension of the methods used by society to preserve, protect, and perpetuate itself.

Terry does not really say anything that the workers do not already know or believe from their own practical experience, but he articulates it in such a way that their experience (like that of the audience) becomes instructive, a guide to political action. The process of change through lawful methods seems excruciatingly slow to the workers, because those laws are inimical to social change. With the image that opens and ends the strikers' scene, Bond points to the basic paradox of relying on lawful means to engage in what is, in reality, class warfare. The length of the strike shift itself is measured by Trench's clock, a clock Ray can't see from "working in Trench's bloody transit shed":

RAY: Worse than bein in the bloody army. Ain this stint over? Phoo. (*He blows on his hands. Pause.*) Stood here bloody hours.
JOHN (*looks off*): Twenty past.
BERYL: Don't read Trench's clock. He'll take it off yer bleedin packet.
JOHN: And it's never bloody right.
RAY: Bugger puts it on for the start of the shift and turns it back for the end. Worked it out in the admin. Had a conference. (27)

With seemingly endless hours of wasted time, the strike dramatizes a particular kind of inaction, a waiting game with a predetermined end. The space of the picket line here represents the sense of time lived by the workers.[13] At the end of the play, the strike issues remain unsettled, and the problem of time is more forcefully articulated: "How long can we go on like this? – Yet we sit here as if we had all the time in the world. All of us: we sit" (84). By accepting responsibility for the terror which characterizes our entire society, Terry articulates Bond's call for change and shifts the responsibility to the passively watching audience.

The workers play an essentially choric function in *The Worlds*, mediating between the audience and the action, expressing feelings and thoughts Bond wants his audience to share. Present at the end, they have the final word. Whereas Greek choruses often express conventional morality or the commonplace sentiments of the surviving community, the workers' value as "ideal spectators" lies in a class consciousness that constantly questions the prevailing attitudes and assumptions of their society, a capacity registered in part by the language they speak. In contrast to Lord Bigdyke's polished phrases, Trench's self-conscious metaphors, Hubbard's crude and manipulative rhetoric and Anna's flat pronouncements, the workers' colloquial and idiomatic language is enriched by the rhythms and images of everyday life and proves most suitable for expressing the practical concepts that can lead to effective political action. Unlike the language of Bond's earliest working-class characters, whose very inarticulateness indicated the extent of their oppression, the workers' dialogue proves flexible enough to be persuasive. While moments of joking displacement still occur, they no longer prevent the characters from adequately conceptualizing their experience. Indeed, here the same codes of communication that permit the workers to vent their frustration, anger, and skepticism within a supportive group context also generate and enable a focused discussion of the play's thematic issues. Through the various responses of Beryl, Ray, John, and Terry, Bond clearly delineates the characteristics of the working class, suggests their strengths and limitations, the reasons for the decisions they make, and the points at which they (and the audience who accepts their point of view) might become a real political force.

Anna believes that only through action can the world be changed and men "tell the truth"; but as Terry points out and the problems of the workers illustrate, in order to act effectively, one must first understand the world and one's position in it. Given the kinds of ideological manipulation to which they are subject – directly through Hubbard's negotiations speech (63–65) and indirectly through the press and the public opinion it mediates (83) – the problem proves difficult but not insoluble. Like the terrorists, the effectiveness of the workers is hampered by their separation from the other worlds – from the forces of production and important sources of basic information. Even the strike negotiations are not entirely open or honest. The businessmen leave the room to be briefed privately on police developments, and their final decision to pay ransom (using the chauffeur's kidnapping for a promotional campaign) occurs behind locked doors. Had Terry known of it, events might have turned out differently. Only the audience knows that

Trench, not Anna, killed the chauffeur. The workers' problems are aggravated by the very structures through which they must act. The play does not offer a plan of action, but rather a process of social analysis – with class as a central term – that might be applied to experience outside the theatre. The learning process demonstrated in the workers' scenes, and urged by Terry, suggests the possibility of thinking dialectically – of making practical use of everyday experience to generate social change. The narrative of *The Worlds* does not end happily, for living under capitalism (as any look at contemporary British theatre amply illustrates) involves disillusionment, betrayal, violence, and compromise. As the stasis of the final scene suggests, the workers, like the audience, may not share Terry's views nor seek political alternatives. But insofar as the play rephrases the questions to be answered, its "reading" of the world offers hope.

Summer

Bond's later plays challenge a liberal humanist viewpoint that makes social alternatives difficult to envision and the violence of the present system difficult to see. The political problem is also, for Bond, an aesthetic and formal one: how to represent a recognizable (i.e., always already mediated) reality without reproducing its very terms? In *The Worlds*, Bond represents the objectively "productive" world in a way that renders visible, both formally and thematically, the self-reproducing ideology that informs discussion of current events and limits the possibility of change. In *Summer*, Bond turns from the public to the private, from the world of work to a more intimate sphere of interpersonal relationship, but the aesthetic and political issues are similar. Whose "reading" of the world is truer? And what are the consequences? Both plays address the problem of human violence and its connection to history by pointing out how easily the issues get confused, "covered over," distorted, and displaced – in *The Worlds* by the self-generating logic of a capitalist economy, in *Summer* by the quotidian reality of everyday life. Like *The Worlds*, *Summer* naturalistically fleshes out the parable form by turning its attention to a "reading" of the present – rendering history visible as a set of social relations with far-reaching consequences.

In the turn from public to private, *Summer* responds to the dominant cultural forms through which psychological reality is still

mediated and encoded for contemporary audiences by the legacy of
Chekhov. In 1966, Bond translated *Three Sisters* for the 1967 Royal
Court production, and keeping the Chekhovian influence in mind
may help clarify the strategies of *Summer*, Bond's most reflective and
lyrical play to date.[14] In Chekhov's plays, characters remember the
past, suffer in the present, and think about the future; the focus is on
the ordinary and the everyday; and little seems to happen. In
Summer, the action is likewise indirect, the stage given over to
conversation between characters who reminisce, philosophize, quarrel, and seek reconciliation, but remain essentially separate. As in
Chekhov, Bond chronicles a moment in historical transition, with
the socio-historical dimension rendered through the ordinary behavior of characters. At times, Bond's portraiture directly recalls the
class-inflected characters of Chekhov's own plays; but if Bond's
characters and concerns have descended from Chekhov, the future
they inhabit could not have been imagined a century earlier. The
shift in historical perspective demands a shift in social perspective;
for all their similarities, in *Summer*, Bond explicitly critiques the ethic
of *tout comprendre, c'est tout pardonné* so closely associated with the
naturalistic form he takes up.

Although *Summer* consists of only five characters in seven scenes
(the last an epilogue of seventeen lines), its retrospective focus and
broad historical concerns complicate the subject and make the
"action" difficult to describe. Like most of Chekhov's plays, *Summer*
opens on an arrival and ends with a departure, while the "visit" itself
takes an emotional toll on the characters involved. Set in Eastern
Europe, Xenia and her daughter Ann arrive from London, as they
do every year, to vacation in the coastal town once "owned" by
Xenia's family.[15] They stay with Marthe, at one time a servant on
the estate, but, since the war, caretaker of the holiday flats into
which it has been divided. Marthe, we soon discover, is living "a
second life" as the survivor of a Nazi prison camp and is now
terminally ill. As her doctor, David is as prepared for his mother's
death as it is possible for a son to be. Xenia and Marthe speak of the
past with little indication they have not done so before. But Marthe's
impending death emotionally charges the situation and allows them
to speak, to each other and to Ann, in a way they might otherwise
not. Strands of the action overlap and intersect: Xenia will visit the
island and come face to face with her own complicity in Nazi
atrocity in an encounter with a former German prison guard,

himself on holiday. Marthe and Xenia will passionately argue and refuse to be reconciled. David and Ann will cautiously resume an affair, reclaim the island with their love-making, and part at the end of the play. As in Chekhov, time passes, things change, the old die, the young begin new lives, and the audience is left to contemplate the meaning of it all. In Chekhov, however, social and historical references tend to illuminate and deepen the psychological reality of individual characters. In *Summer*, Bond reverses the equation to suggest that the ordinary illuminates the socio-historical. In so doing, the play implicitly suggests that Chekhov's "balanced" view of character and ironic stance toward historical change (so often envisioned as natural, inevitable) may no longer be conducive to our own survival. The sensitive and sympathetic figures of Chekhov's dying aristocracy seem sadly ineffectual, but their legacy in *Summer*, embodied in the figure and attitudes of Xenia, has proven positively dangerous.

As most reviewers were quick to note, the uncertainty provided by delayed exposition creates most of the play's early tension; yet the gradual reconstruction of the past, and the subtextual depth it lends to the characters, is hardly the play's only goal. Rather, the contrasting figures of Marthe and Xenia provide the audience with an argument about the meaning of the past, without which, Bond argues, the meaning of the present cannot be usefully understood. Marthe, Xenia, and even the German tourist who turns up in Scene Four, have survived the war, suffered losses, and witnessed atrocities. In the course of three rather ordinary days, the central characters relive, from a distance, that history, which proves to be "shared" in only the most superficial sense. Not only does their conversation focus on the past, but in relation to it, their present behavior (down to the simplest gestures) reflects different class perspectives, different attitudes, different lifestyles, different values. Unlike Chekhov's characters, for whom some basic, universal level of humanity is assumed, Bond's play suggests that humanity itself is still in the making, and may be earned or forfeited over time. Insofar as the onstage situation emblematically repeats the past, the audience watching the play is invited to confront their own history in the way each character does – in terms of its meaning and use for them in the present.

The past, not fully revealed until Scene Three, and the future, as it plays itself out at the end, retrospectively informs the play's first two scenes. From the beginning, Xenia displays the controlling, wilful personality that has enabled her to survive the loss of her family and former way of life. She is stressed and irritable, but understandably so – by the long delay at Heathrow, a wearying flight, not being met at the airport, the presence and proximity of a "hideous new hotel" on the estate, ice-cream cartons on the beach, and (the final straw) the loss of her luggage keys. The narrow range of concerns does not introduce a comedy of manners, however, but a compulsive character who proves all the more dangerous for being slightly "out of touch."[16] Hearing Xenia's voice in Scene One, Marthe feels "as if I'm back in the past" (2), for Xenia arouses in her the feeling of powerlessness associated with former servitude: "I can't stop her [. . .] I don't mind her [. . .] Let things go on as before" (3). Indeed, the old social relation between mistress and servant dominates Scene Two. Xenia, ignoring David's request to act normally, insists that Marthe's illness changes everything. Momentarily thrown by the news in Scene One, Xenia expresses a desire to "do anything" to help; but by Scene Two, her controlling personality reasserts itself as in her own panic she urges Marthe to get a second opinion, take a loan, leave the island, and "fight" her illness. In contrast, her daughter Ann immediately accepts the truth ("It's just that there's nothing we can do to help," 12), asks about Marthe's feelings ("What is it like to be told?" 12) and listens sympathetically to her response. However well-meaning, Xenia's gestures of kindness prove thoughtless and self-serving; and in the stubborn attempt to avoid the truth, to manage and manipulate a situation beyond her control, and to lessen her own pain, she effectively denies the experiential reality of Marthe's suffering. What Xenia does is not "wrong," but characteristically inappropriate.

In Scene Two, both the difficulty and the importance of facing objective reality, and basing one's actions upon it, is powerfully introduced by David, who preempts Xenia's hopeful ministrations with a long and excessively detailed description of the treatments and usual complications of Marthe's diagnosis, right up until the moment of death. Far more than foreshadowing the end of the play (which it does), David's speech forces the audience and characters alike to confront the full horror of death, without suggesting that doing so makes it any easier to accept. With its factual precision, disturbing details, and shocking effect on the listeners, David's speech prefigures the German tourist's bureaucratic nightmare of

Nazi prison camp operations in Scene Four. Marthe has faced death once before, as a prisoner on the island, and hearing of the difficulty Germans had in killing and disposing of the bodies may recall the haunting notion that ends David's speech: "The body has not yet evolved means of terminating its life efficiently on all occasions when it's desirable from the patient's point of view for it to do so" (15). Xenia has, in fact, saved Marthe before, and her pathetic "rescue attempt" in Scene Two contextualizes that event when the audience learns of it later in the play. Metaphorically speaking, David's long speech spits in Xenia's face, rejects her point of view, and momentarily disarms her. Marthe will die; there is nothing Xenia can do to prevent it; and resisting this truth has a damaging effect on all the characters.

Xenia emotionally recoils from the attack implied by David's long speech, changing the subject with a mechanical civility and studied indifference that come to typify the defensive posture of her class. Yet even Marthe finds her son's speech unnecessarily cruel, and her response (bitter, suicidal, pleading, and angry by turns) suggests that David may in fact be right, that Xenia's presence "undoes everything" by offering false hope. Indeed, the physical facts, like the historical ones of our century, do not become more acceptable simply from being seen from the victim's point of view. Which approach to them the audience might prefer is left open, though the argument of the play and the tendency of the characterization will favor David's (softened, somewhat, by the presence of Ann). Marked as a survivor of a camp as surely as she is marked now with a terminal disease, Marthe will question, in each of the scenes that follow, how one should live the last moments of life. In Scene Five, Xenia's insistent presence forces Marthe to make a clear connection between the two lives she has led, and to make a clean (nearly fatal) break from the former. Thus Xenia ends up having as little, and as much, to do with Marthe's death in Scene Six as she did formerly. Marthe dies a "natural" and peaceful death, but the presence of Xenia in many ways precipitates it.

In *Summer*, as in plays of retrospective analysis since *Oedipus Rex*, the character's identity is established in relationship to a particular history, and not until that history has been fully revealed is the onstage situation, or its meaning, entirely grasped by the viewers. Thus the movement of play, and the action of Scenes Three, Four, and Five, involves the gradual revelation of the past through the compelling and competing narratives of Xenia, Marthe, and the German tourist. The facts themselves are rarely at issue, though getting them, as Xenia's relationship to her daughter makes clear, is not always easy. In Scene Two, Xenia tells Marthe that Ann: "knows too much about the past. It would be a terrible wrong to a child to force it to fight its parents' battles [. . .] I've simply told her the truth. Children have a right to know the world they're in [. . .] She knows the history of every stone in this house" (11). The history Ann knows is authentic, but selective, and only partially "true" – where her grandfather was arrested, the traces that mark where pictures hung on the walls. Distanced by her age from these events, Ann's innocent and sympathetic presence provides a perfect stand-in for the audience as the "mind" and future over which the two women are willing to battle. The story that unfolds in Scene Three, beginning before the war and moving through it, is recounted *for* Ann; with her, the audience is invited to experience the past from enormously different perspectives.

As the audience gradually realizes, Xenia's "real life" ended long ago; for her, the war and its aftermath "ruined everything," and the memory of that leisured, comfortable life is beautifully envisioned:

When I was a girl we went to the islands almost every day in the summer [. . .] Mother and father would bring their friends for the day. There was always some young man who could play the mandolin. The women sat under silk sunshades and the men rolled up their trouser-legs and stood in the shallows to fish [. . .] At night we dived from the rocks and floated in the sea, and looked at the stars [. . .] On this terrace [. . .] I sat in my father's lap and listened to his heart and the racing of his watch. He bought his cigars in Paris [. . .] the farmers sang in the hills [. . .] In those days my happiness frightened me – it was so great I thought I would die of it. (22)

The simple images and child-like perspective of the scene, recounted in the relaxed atmosphere of vacationing adults, contribute to the sense of past happiness evoked by the entire monologue, much longer than quoted here. In contrast to the weave of detail with which she remembers an idyllic past, Xenia's remembrance of the occupation is relatively brief and abstract, its crimes reduced to a single sentence ("People hounded and tortured and shot," 23), its meaning etched in her mind in the image of physical damage suffered by the estate: "ugly little huts on the island. [. . .] And when the war was over they threw down the gods and goddesses from the terraces. Zeus, Hera and Aphrodite lay on the rocks with no arms or heads" (23). Xenia's memories are mixed with an unmistakable, and entirely plausible, nostalgia for a lost world, and some bitterness over how it all ended – the mandolin-playing young man and the cigars from Paris are telling details that connect Xenia's family portrait to the cultured, sensitive Russian aristocracy of Chekhov's plays. Like Madame Ranevskaya herself, Xenia has little control over the loss of her world, compulsively returns to the site of her unresolved grief, and has difficulty "seeing" the islands and the estate of her past as a set of unjust social relationships that itself caused suffering.[17]

Such memories upset Marthe, for they are not ones she shares. Thus Marthe takes up the narrative where Xenia leaves off, with her own incarceration in the camp and rescue from it. For a few moments, the two women "help" each other tell the story, but when Xenia says, "That's enough" (24), Marthe proceeds to describe a different "photograph" from the "family album" – that found in a German soldier's wallet, of naked women facing guns. Linking the authentic photographic traces of the Holocaust to her own first-hand experience, her testimonial carries a certain authority about the events that Xenia, watching it all from a distance, cannot. And while the experiences related are obviously fictional, Marthe will come to represent the perspective of the women who died in her place – not as the suffering victims of unimaginable horror, but as the angry revolutionaries they might have been. ("When I told them the name of the woman I worked for she said, 'If I could live to spit in her face' and spat in the dirt," 25).

The characters' emotions do not come fully into play until Scene Five. Here, in the presence of Ann, Marthe sticks to what she has seen; and the description, with its simple, graphic images, is as fully moving as Xenia's own – the blurred, wartime-quality picture of women who, facing a gun, "huddled together and turned away as if it had started to rain"; a soldier releasing Marthe with a "thumbs up sign as if I'd won a lottery," the angry old woman "so doubled over that if she died facing soldiers the bullets went in her back" (24–25). The details are themselves important, especially the images of two photographs with which Marthe's story begins. The metaphor reminds the audience of their own limited access to the past, mediated by the photographic documentation of the killers them-selves, "read" and "authenticated" by the victims who survived, as witness to what remains necessarily a reconstructed event. The images captured on film, like the facts themselves, do not necessarily tell the truth. Marthe "sees" the missing rifle in the second picture by recognizing the women's bodily posture in the first, interpreting a simple and seemingly irrelevant gesture in terms of the social and historical relationship it conceals: "There were no soldiers in this picture. Nothing to show the women were going to be shot. But I knew they were. Immediately. From the gesture of their head and shoulders" (25). The photographs not only provide the interpretive context for Marthe's own story and the link to a history of suffering the audience instantly recognizes, but through its example a close reading of images that the viewing audience is expected to emulate.

Xenia doesn't deny this painful history; she would prefer to forget it, to let it rest. From her point of view, everyone's interests were the same under foreign occupation; people did what they could, and have suffered more than enough. Xenia's own father, she reminds Ann yet again, was imprisoned on the island and died there after the war, an event Xenia sees as a brutal and ironic continuation of wartime atrocity – one more unnecessary death. Since Marthe gave evidence against Xenia's father, the groundwork is laid for a more direct and emotional confrontation later in the play, but here the dialogue is primarily evocative as the audience is asked to identify, in turn, with both of the speaking characters.

The central revelation of the scene is two-fold: during the war Xenia saved Marthe's life, and after the war Marthe testified against Xenia's father. Ironically, both characters see their own actions as the only appropriate response, under the circumstances. Xenia admits no "heroism" was involved; she saved Marthe unhesitatingly, without thinking: "What was there to tell? We all helped each other under the occupation" (23). Marthe's court testimony was offered with similar compunction: "I described how he lived. The parties and gambling. Many in the court had starved. It was dangerous to live in your father's world" (27). Marthe feels no more remorse over her testimony than Xenia feels responsible for those on the islands she could not save. Indeed, the play suggests that the meaning of their actions cannot be determined individually, even though those actions and events have determined who they are and how they feel. Yet the conversation between Marthe and Xenia provides information essential for a "reading" of character along political lines. Xenia, for example, is hardly naive: she knows that her father paid farmers to sing in the hills, and that the unripe fruit was stripped from their trees by the starving crowd who awaited her father's arrest. She remarks that the Germans "insisted on paying rent" for the islands, that the commandant who issued Marthe's release "probably thought that if his soldiers shot her it would make conversation awkward the next time he came to dinner," and that they "were used to shooting by then" (24). Although Xenia obviously despises the Germans, her own idealistic understanding of "how people should act," based as it is on a false notion of "how things should be," has failed to account for her own experience. Once the conflicting viewpoints have clearly emerged, Ann asks the women not to argue; and the conversation of Scene Three ends on the happiness of Marthe's "second life" (an evocative speech that directly parallels Xenia's paradisial vision of lost youth), and trails off, in a Chekhovian manner, on a train of associations prompted by offstage sounds.

In Scene Three, little direct connection is made (or can even be seen) between Xenia's past experience of complete happiness and Marthe's past experience of hell, though both have occurred in the same place. Rather, the family usurpation constantly threatened in Chekhov's plays has already occurred, Marthe and Xenia have for all practical purposes exchanged roles, and the matter of who is "right" (though not quite the issue) remains to be decided. The balanced, opposing points of view traced in Scene Three, however, will be dialectically "sublated" in the viewpoint of the German tourist in Scene Four. As Xenia later acknowledges, "Now our roles are reversed," but, despite her suffering, she is hardly the one we will pity. Rather, *Summer* puts the insights of *The Bundle* to work on the audience's own recent past to demonstrate that Xenia's "goodness," her gestures of kindness, and her readiness to forgive and forget are rooted in a way of life that causes the very ills she seeks to ameliorate. As Marthe puts it in Scene Five, "In your world the good did evil [. . .] Faced with that [factories, banks, governments] kindness is like blowing on a storm to make it go away" (43). The reality of the Holocaust is hardly at issue, but the underlying causes and consequences are. Nor can the problem be addressed in terms of personal blame: even the German was "a private soldier. Not officers. Not Gestapo. Not guilty" (31). In *Summer*, the struggle for characters and audience alike is not, finally, with historical fact, but with its interpretation and use (in a practical way and with real consequences). Although the judgment of Xenia is political, not personal, the recognition scenes of the play suggest that the two cannot finally be separated.

The play's turning-point and moment of "truth" occurs on the island, in Scene Four, where Xenia (alone) meets the ghost of her dead father in the figure of a former German prison guard, returned to the scene of his crimes. In the attempt to represent fascism as a fully human reality, without somehow accepting, condoning, or mitigating the impact of its crimes, Bond here pushes the introspective Chekhovian technique to its practical and ideological limits. Indeed, the problem of representing the Holocaust in a naturalistic idiom has to do with the impossibility of fully imagining it, or politically understanding it, from a liberal humanist perspective that focuses so intently on the individual. *Summer* fully exploits the dual perception that often results – Nazi atrocity as something wholly "other" (inexpressibly evil, foreign, catastrophic, and unnatural) and yet recognizably human (mundane, ordinary, the fact of the death camps and their bureaucratic administration). Thus the most horrifying aspects of the play's past events are narrated by the most banal German tourist, a former prison guard, concerned above all else about missing his evening meal at the hotel.

Like the reminiscing of Marthe and Xenia earlier, the facts are gradually revealed and the texture of memory evoked through briefly narrated vignettes and oddly remembered details.[18] In addition to the testimonial stance on which much of the conversation is modelled, the German's narration of past events is tinged with a nostalgic note we recognize from Xenia's earlier speeches. Like Xenia, the German is on holiday, a survivor of the war, with beautiful memories of a girl in white standing as a beacon on the terrace. But he does not glamorize the war, and for a moment seems to share Xenia's own point of view: "Ah, that war. Terrible. Terrible. Terrible. So much killing" (30). Hardly villainous, the German has merely survived – he now sells refrigerators and takes packaged holiday tours with his two children. His manner is intrusive, but not unkind: "It is sad not to live in your own country" (31), he tells Xenia. Though Xenia is disgusted by his manners, irritated by his insinuations, and repulsed by his person, she feels compelled to listen and offers him food throughout the scene.

What the German most vividly recalls are his own deteriorating work conditions, "how hard things were" – commanding officers scrounging bullets, prisoners sitting in boats with no petrol, running out of ammunition, sinking prisoners in ships, running out of ships, and running out of room on the island to bury the dead. As his story unfolds, the narrative takes on a force of its own, creating a nightmarish vision of grotesque proportion that clearly misses its intended effect. By the end of the war, we are told, the island is bulging with bodies, "sealed up in caves and shoved down cracks." Then came the order to exhume, throw the bodies in the sea, erase the evidence:

Dig the bodies out of the rocks. It is an order. We stood guard while the prisoners dug and carried. Such stench. Can you imagine? For three days. The bodies were thrown into the sea. But there is no tide. The sea will not take them [...] They floated round the island. Only a few were skeletons. Sand had preserved the skin of the rest. They drifted on the surface or just below it. Some of them held hands – that's how they died [...] our boats towed the bodies behind us in our wakes as if they were swimming after us. (33)

The images of the unnaturally dead rejected by the sea itself, of corpses with fingers pointing up out of the waves at their murderers, may be horrifying to the audience, but the German offers the story as a chronicle of his own suffering, fully expecting his point of view to be understood. When he notes the effect on Xenia, he becomes apologetic – not from personal remorse, but for fear of appearing to exaggerate, or worse, to complain. He assures Xenia otherwise, going on to compare his own "good posting" by the sea to that of other guards, in places where "so much fat hung in the air you covered your coffee with your hand and drank from beneath it," jobs where you ended up "smelling like someone else" (34). Again, the facts of the story (the camps themselves, the dead, the history of war, occupation, and liberation) are not at issue – but rather the relationship of the speakers to it, as well as the attitudes that made it possible. From the German's point of view, it was the soldiers, not the prisoners, who were robbed of their identity. However callous and insensitive he may be, his language has a terrifying logic, and in terms of Bond's own argument, a certain amount of truth. In view of the grotesque situation described, the German's refrain, "It had to be," seems as laughable as his call for understanding seems danger- ously prophetic and close to home: "I risked my life. The sacrifice of young manhood should be respected. Our young people would have to do all we did should those times come again" (36–37). Here Marthe's analysis, offered to Ann in Scene Two, seems appropriate:

10 Xenia uncomfortably shares her lunch with a former Nazi prison guard on holiday in *Summer*

the "owners and the owned" obeyed the same laws, a certain necessity took over, and the result was madness: "Whole generations bleed for it," Marthe says earlier, "the kindness of one person to another can't change that" (20).

Though revolted by the German, Xenia remains civil until the end of the scene when, directly implicated by the German's story, she runs away. Indeed, throughout the long speeches she sits (very much like the audience) mesmerized, compelled to listen; and doing so presents the viewers with an older version of the girl in white who stared at the sea and embodied for the German soldiers stationed there a living symbol of the culture and lifestyle for which they fought. What Xenia refuses to believe, however, is that this German soldier, this petty-bourgeois tourist, can expect from her a sympathetic, understanding ear. Widening the perspective of the play to render judgment on Xenia and the attitudes she embodies, Bond exaggerates the irony of this quintessentially Chekhovian situation to the very edge of social farce.

Thus the "pleasure" of Scene Four – and much of it is funny – comes not from the horrifying account itself, but from the relationship between speaker, hearer, and playwright that it illuminates. A certain justice seems to be served by bringing Xenia into closer touch with the events on the island she watched earlier from such a distance. Like Len of *Saved*, Xenia does nothing but watch, and her single gesture of kindness (like Len's own attempts to help) can be used against her. Her complicity rests not on a single action, but on "who she is" and what she represents to the occupying forces – wilfully or not, her presence has been misunderstood, her silence misread, and her well-meaning behavior used to foster the very crimes she abhors. Xenia's position and its consequences can here be "read" in her manners – her cold but civil demeanor, her offers of food, and her supercilious response to this uninvited guest, gestures that emblematically repeat the earlier attitude of her family toward the occupying forces. Indeed, Xenia's ambivalent response to the German's cultural sensibility, human insensitivity, and lack of social graces ironically reinforces her emblematic stature as the liberal legacy of an aristocratic class. While the German manages to incriminate himself, his story judges the audience as well, and the ironic social situation that unfolds is fraught with comic potential. Like the metaphorical embroidery of the speeches themselves, the comedy of the scene makes the audience conscious of their own distance from the actual history to which the fiction refers, without for a moment suggesting that the past is irrelevant, irretrievable, or unknowable. Rather, the aesthetic distance demanded is the same necessary for understanding, knowing, and using the past. The pleasure of the scene, however uneasy it may be, rests on the assurance of the playwright's point of view, rendered visible through the judgments of his comedy.

With its dark humor, contrived situation, and metaphoric excess, Scene Four of *Summer* avoids the usual focus of European Holocaust literature on the actual killing and internment processes, the horror of the camps themselves, without refusing entirely to take it up.[19] In the figure of Xenia, the play suggests that our own fascination with such a focus arises from guilt by association, that the crimes described are an extreme but logical outgrowth of a society divided by class. Thus the effect of the German tourist on Xenia *can* be read in psychological terms – as the return of the repressed, of what Xenia "knows," but cannot admit. Indeed, the recognition of herself in the eyes of the German tourist, as the cause and justification of the war, is as horrifying a *peripetia* as Oedipus' own. Xenia's furious rejection of it is likewise predictable – and fully motivates the urgency of her appeal to Marthe in the following scene.[20] The "tragic irony," however, is that Marthe's experience only corroborates the German's point of view.

As the action of Scene Five illustrates, stirring up memories of the past has a negative effect on both women – Xenia remembers the resentment she felt at Marthe's giving evidence against her father, from her point of view, an "almost unforgivable act." Marthe, however, has severed her connection with the viewpoint of her former employers. Again their differences are imaged in alternative interpretations of history. Marthe remembers Xenia's father capturing a criminal who had escaped to the island and restraining him in the boat to keep him from swimming to the open sea: "Did your father rescue him from drowning or catch a fish for dinner?" (42). Xenia's mother, taking tea on the terrace at the time, would have offered him tea and wrapped him in her stole. "Would that have made his punishment easier to bear?" (42), Marthe asks. Xenia counters with her father's liberal position – the captured man was sentenced to death, but her father used his newspaper to get him reprieved. Such a fact only supports Marthe's point of view, and Marthe has the last word: "The young man was grateful to him. When the war came he volunteered to fight for your father's world and was shot" (43). The facts are not disputed, only their interpretation. Unlike Xenia, Marthe feels neither guilty (over evidence given against Xenia's father) nor resentful (of Xenia herself and her present life): yet, pushed to defend herself, she sides with the woman whose dying wish was to spit in Xenia's face. She will not be "reconciled"; the cost is too great.

Like David's speech at the beginning of the play, the gesture of spitting in Xenia's face seems unnecessary, extreme, and difficult for the character to make. Indeed, the force of Marthe's action leaves her sprawled, vulnerable and undignified, on the floor. As in Scene Four, Xenia is as horrified at the breach of social etiquette as she is by the truth embodied in the act ("How dare you! Because you're dying you think you can be a monster! [...] You carried a dead woman's spit round in your mouth for forty years!" 45); and she leaves for a hotel. The climactic interaction between Marthe and Xenia is accompanied throughout by the pounding beat of rock music from the disco next door – somewhat irritating perhaps to the audience, but absolutely unbearable to Xenia. Perhaps nothing better measures the distance between Bond and Chekhov than this use of offstage sound. As in Chekhov's *The Cherry Orchard*, something is ended in the scene, some connection to the past severed, but the distant breaking string and its dying fall is here replaced with a dissonant, incessant, muffled pounding. Chekhov's offstage sound registers as a subtle nuance, embodying historical change as well as an emotional attitude toward it. Bond's offstage music is neither quiet nor contemplative, yet embodies in a similar way both the movement of history and its emotional repercussions. The obvious and demanding beat of technologically produced music provides a subliminal urgency and energy that moves the play to its climax, leaving the body of Marthe in its wake. In this regard, Bond offers in Marthe a contemporary version of Hecuba in *The Woman*, a woman who would also like to forget, to live out her days peacefully by the sea, but who comes to represent in her actions the force, fury, and judgment of history itself. And it nearly kills her. The next day she tells Ann of her dream the night before: "a door banged in the wind. I woke up and listened to the sea [...] This morning everything looks as if it had been in a storm. Dust and bits of paper and rubbish blown away [...] The town looks as battered and new as a child that's cried itself to sleep" (47).

Marthe is granted a far more dignified death than the one allowed Hecuba, one that befits the life she has led since the war and appropriate for a woman who has survived the camps. Yet the play suggests that such respectful treatment is owed, not to the victim of history or of terminal disease, but to the harbinger of a future that might be more just. Yet it is Xenia who survives, and her reappearance at the end of Scene Six is deeply disturbing – a thoughtless insult to the dead. "I'm sorry she's dead," Xenia remarks. "I came to tell her I wasn't angry. My presence filled her with a great rage. It was bad for someone in her condition. If I'd known, I'd never have come here" (53). Wishing she were better informed, Xenia once again passes along her own responsibility for events to others, and to the end can do nothing right. In light of the play's concerns, such persistence seems almost inhuman. At the end of the play, Ann and David must nearly push her out the door.

Despite its central image of the sea, floating with human debris, and the importance of the island as a former concentration camp, *Summer* does not focus on past destruction, the dead victims or the atrocities they endured. Rather, *Summer* asks how one can approach this history, make sense of it, atone for it, and move beyond it without violating the memory of the dead. Thus while Xenia meets a ghost on the island, Ann and David resume their affair on the island, making Xenia and the German tourist wait in the boat at the end of the scene: "They're on the edge of the island waiting to leave. We're free and told to be happy. Let's sit here a while longer" (39). Something undoubtedly occurs at the war memorial in Scene Four. But the play itself refuses to be drawn into either the past nightmare or the future vision, as they are emblematically isolated, for a moment, in the ordinary actions of two pairs of visitors. As the rest of the play makes clear, what happened there may be brushed aside, ignored, denied, or forgotten as easily as it may foster change. The real action of the play, for Ann and David, involves Marthe's death, and what she will mean to them in the future. Through it, Bond can use the psychological process of dealing with terminal illness – anger, acceptance, grieving, and letting go – as a metaphor for effectively dealing with the past. As David says, "I've seen so many deaths. I cried for them all this morning" (53). Both as individuals and as a couple, the two provide an older, more experienced version of Rose and Willy in *The Sea*. But the future they represent is as tentative, unresolved, and uncertain as Ann's possible pregnancy and its outcome: "If it grew up I'd bring it to you" (54).

CHAPTER 8

Remembering the future

Human Cannon

The more Bond writes, the more difficult the task of categorizing his plays within the critical framework of a predominant dramatic strategy. *Human Cannon* (1985), for example, combines a naturalistic concern for psychologically developed characters acting within a detailed social environment with the intention and effect of a parable or "learning play." With its situation, songs, and explicitly stated arguments, the play's debt to Brecht, especially *The Mother*, is clear. Yet the main character is based on an etching by Goya of the cannon-firing Agostina of actual historical record, who defended her city against the French in 1808.[1] Though set during the Spanish Civil War, *Human Cannon* is as much a "history play" as *Bingo* and *The Fool*. Like them, Bond's play works against sentimental, romantic, or mythologizing attitudes toward its central character. Augustina's actions are heroic in the way anyone's could be, and she herself resists becoming legendary in her own time: "What use is a legend?" she says near the end of the play. "People hear them and say: they're the big ones. We're ordinary. What do I want? A dry roof over my head and a warm blanket ... If I'm a legend, my life is wasted."[2] Though Augustina dies before a firing-squad, the play is far more celebratory than depressing in effect. At the end, Augustina's daughter holds up her grandchild, itself the consequence of the political stratagem for which Augustina was condemned; and the smile by which Augustina hopes to be remembered pays tribute to a future that gives her political actions meaning.

The restorative effect of *Human Cannon*, its "festive" celebration of social and communal values, and its "strategic" use of comic techniques make it closer in spirit to comedy than tragedy, despite its brutal (and historically accurate) end. Indeed, Augustina exploits the classic gender stereotypes of traditional farce to accomplish the major political action in the play. Using her sex, and her daughter's as well, she diverts the attention of a military guard while on cleaning detail; the soldier eventually gets caught with his pants down, while Augustina successfully blows up the munitions factory with the cannon he was guarding. As she loads the bomb shell, Augustina addresses the audience:

A woman with a bucket and mop is invisible. Today I ply the ancient trades of whoring and cleaning. The soldier follows his ancient callings of fornication and war. Inside his general unveils a plaque to the fallen. [. . .] What will the soldier do? Run back pulling up his trousers, turn and run up and down between the sheds, cursing and roaring like a wounded animal. (22)

Augustina describes her own actions and predicts what will happen. A few moments later, Juan runs onstage and fulfills Augustina's prophecy as Bond writes them into the stage directions: "*His trousers are round his ankles and he is trying to pull them up. He waves his rifle and blows his whistle. He stops for a moment and stands in the smoke and roars like a wounded animal*" (23). The farcical effect of the moment is balanced by Augustina's clear-sighted understanding of the consequences: she knows the soldier will be "court-martialled and shot," that others "will be killed or lose a leg or an arm. Or they may all be killed" (23). Throughout the play, the moral complexity of the characters' situation is simply illustrated – not to suggest the impossibility of moral action, but its necessity. Like Hecuba of *The Woman*, Augustina takes responsibility for her actions even (and especially) when she feels there is no choice.

As in *The Woman*, *The Worlds*, and *Restoration* the active, practical, and intelligent women of *Human Cannon* carry Bond's historical vision into an imaginative future, and provide the play's primary source of hope – making Bond vulnerable to the charge of using women characters in an overtly figural, emblematic fashion. Yet women's biological connection to reproduction, their historically invisible role, and their symbolic reification in the history of literature seem to render them appropriate figures through which the urgency, goals and methods of social change might best be represented. Taken together, Bond's plays give increasing credence to the belief that women's (a)historical role gives them great revolutionary potential, that any real social change, any rethinking or rebuilding of a rational society, will not be accomplished without women as crucial players.[3] In view of this symbolic trajectory, the decision made by the female refugee of *Great Peace* at the end of *The War Plays* carries greater critical weight than it otherwise might. Despite long, almost unbearable suffering as a wandering survivor of nuclear holocaust, the Woman of *Great Peace* refuses to be rescued by the emissaries of a new settlement and dies alone in the wilderness; the meaning of the trilogy rests on how the audience interprets her actions. While such use of women does not make Bond a feminist playwright, the political interpretations his plays make possible do not foreclose a feminist perspective.

The War Plays

As important and ambitious as any of Bond's earlier plays, *The War Plays* display a rich combination of dramatic strategies that likewise resists strict definition within the categories constructed for earlier chapters. Composed of three distinct, but overlapping, plays – *Red Black and Ignorant, The Tin Can People*, and *Great Peace* – *The War Plays* can be performed separately or on a single day. But the interconnected and strategic sense of the work, its dramatic methods, and its emotional and intellectual impact on an audience are linked to the trilogy form. Considered together, the plays' range of allusion, poetic style, and apparent subject-matter invoke a long history of catastrophe literature from the *Orestia* of Aeschylus to Beckett's *Endgame*. Like Bond's earlier "epic" and "literary" works, the trilogy reminds a formally educated audience of their cultural investments, playing into the belief that "great literature" reflects and transcends its own historical moment, helps shape the humanity of its audience, tackles ultimate questions, and remains open to multi-layered interpretation. But with its envisioning of nuclear disaster, the trilogy also invites comparison to more popular and political forms – to science fiction and fantasy literature since World War II, to contemporary film and television enactments, and to the agitational performance art of recent anti-nuclear movements. Set in a vaguely futuristic time after "rockets destroyed the world,"[4] one of the plays' first challenges is to render in appropriate terms what is often described as the "unimaginable" or "unthinkable" horror of nuclear destruction, its causes and probable effects – a problem exacerbated by the physical constraints of the stage compared to the purely imaginative possibilities of fiction or the technical capabilities of film.[5] Bond does not here "solve" the problems of dramatic representation inherent in the subject-matter, but rather exploits the opportunities uniquely offered by theatre – with its long, self-referential tradition, its phenomenological dependence on the human body, and its ability to make audiences more than usually aware of its functions as witness of the performance and ultimate judge. If anything, the contradictions and potential impasses of the subject-matter are rendered more apparent in the hope of moving the audience beyond them.

While acknowledging the importance and the formal difficulty of Bond's project, reviewers of the Royal Shakespeare Company's 1985 London premiere found fault with the trilogy for being, in any number of ways, excessive – too long, too wordy, too ambiguous, too simplistic, or too difficult. Despite the single cast, preferences among the three plays also varied widely. Michael Billington, reviewing for the *Guardian*, found only the second play, *The Tin Can People*, "theatrically gripping." Michael Coveney, reviewing for the *Financial Times* found the same play "the least impressive of the trilogy," and *Great Peace* "by far the best." Michael Ratcliffe of the *Observer*, found *Red Black and Ignorant* to be the "most forcefully realized of the three," the same play that Michael Billington found the weakest.[6] With few exceptions, "day-long exposure" to the plays made for a "grim and demanding experience," frequently likened by reviewers to physical or psychological torture. Francis King voiced a general feeling when he wrote of leaving the theatre at the end of the six-hour production: "As we Bond-slaves at last staggered out into the night, I was briefly filled with the euphoria experienced by victims of a hijack on their release. But then, gradually, the ghastliness of the whole experience once more overwhelmed me."[7] While no one found the viewing experience easy, many saw something to praise – riveting narrative sequences, patches of "superb writing," or moments when poetic image and subject-matter powerfully connected. But any enthusiasm for Bond's project was more than balanced by harsh criticism of his "sanctimonious" authorial stance, "befuddling blank verse," "gruelling monologues," and repetition of themes and incidents.[8] Differences in preference were more than matched by variations in the interpretation of Bond's overall intent: a few found hope in the trilogy and a muted optimism, while others saw only bleakness and despair. Though some reviewers attempted to encapsulate Bond's point in a single phrase (like "war is a bad thing," or "out of the ashes comes a new order"), Michael Ratcliffe's honest complaint that "none of it adds up" comes closest, perhaps, to describing the immediate impact of the trilogy on its audience.[9]

Clearly, the provocative stance and experimental form of *The War Plays* left questions and reservations in the minds of many. Perceiving the plays to be unnecessarily demanding, critics focused their resentment on the length, language, and variations in dramatic style – the formal qualities through which the audience's "work" is most apparent. In this regard, even the most negative comments prove instructive. For the trilogy demands not simply that the viewers contemplate nuclear disaster and its aftermath, but that they begin to *think through* the crisis as something that has already happened. Implicit in the project is a recognition that the problems addressed will not be solved in a theatre, and that any "rethinking" will be connected to the cultural forms through which the problems have been thought in the past. With the understanding that only extremity may produce (or necessitate) real change in human behavior, Bond involves the audience in a dramatic experience that is itself extreme in order to encourage an awareness of the mind-numbing ubiquity of the problem, the enormous effort involved in facing it, and the necessity of doing so if the concept of "human" is to have any meaning.

Though not new to Bond, the political ideas and dramatic strategies are affected by the magnitude of the project and its particular aims. As in earlier plays, Bond attempts to represent the dialectical relationship between historical determination and human agency, technological necessity and human freedom – pursuing a Brechtian problematic without relying heavily on Marxist categories for analysis. Though the dramatic form of each play differs, the trilogy offers itself as a "learning play," one that reflects Bond's increasing involvement in the rehearsal and direction of his own work, as well as his career-long insistence that method-trained and psychological performance styles are inappropriate for his plays. Thus *Red Black and Ignorant* can perhaps best be understood as a series of acting exercises along the lines of the original, pedagogical improvisation Bond devised for his students in Palermo. The "Palermo Improvisation" not only rehearses an incident central to the trilogy, but sets out the actors' and audience's work as the solving of a paradox. Herein lies the link to traditional (and biblical) parables – for the "truth," or meaning, of the play can only be apprehended through the surprising, apparently paradoxical turns in the narrative.[10] But in Bond's exercise, the authority of the narrative arises from the apparent authenticity of the actor's original improvised actions, not on a scripted (or "scriptural") text. Bond describes the scene assigned to be played as follows:

A soldier returns home with orders to select and kill a baby. His mother and a neighbour each have a baby. The soldier's mother welcomes him and shows him her baby. The soldier goes to the neighbour. She shows him her baby. He kills it and goes home.[11]

Once the scenario is set, the actors work through a response based on what each one, as the character, would do in the situation. Although called an "improvisation," the exercise seems closer to a controlled, scientific experiment than to the exploratory acting techniques usually associated with improvisational technique. The goal is not to write a play, present a diversity of viewpoints, share the creative experience, or to see "what works." Rather, the exercise forces the honest actor to confront his own humanity *in extremis*. If Bond's political assumptions are correct, then the spontaneous (subjective, freely taken) actions of the actors will necessarily reveal the objective (socially and culturally determined) truth about them. The basis on which the acting exercise is built provides the central contradiction of *The War Plays*: "What would the improvisation show? Airmen killed children in Vietnam and went home to be welcomed by their children. Soldiers train with nuclear weapons and go home on leave to their families [. . .] Civilians give their children a home and their armies threaten other children with nuclear death" (*PI*, 3). Rather than test the validity of the original premise, the exercise is designed to probe the actor's response and lead to further analysis.

A "paradox" emerges when the character decides to kill his own brother rather than the neighbor's child as assigned in the scenario. Bond writes that none of the actors who played the soldier "could bring themselves to kill the 'right' baby," though afterwards the actors "were surprised at what [they] had done" (3–4). While the path chosen by the characters may seem unnatural, paradoxical, or strange to the performers (and by extension, the audience as well) Bond himself, who designed the "experiment," predicted in a notebook "how the improvisation would end" (3). What is "proven" through the actors' physical enactments of the scene is not the reality of humanly engineered violence (the given), but the possibility, even under the most brutal circumstances imaginable, of human choice and resistance. Confronted with a similar dilemma in the penultimate scene of *Red Black and Ignorant*, the soldier makes an equally startling decision. Ordered to kill, the Son chooses to murder his father rather than a sick and elderly neighbor. The audience's inevitable questions about the deed are recognized and answered by the Monster, who praises his Son's actions and reiterates the lesson of the original improvisation:

Our life can be crushed as easily as an ant by an army
But at this time we could not be crushed even by the weight of the continent
    on which the army marched
We know ourself and say: I cannot give up the name of human
All that is needed is to define rightly what it is to be human
If we define it wrongly we die. (*RBI*, 18)

In both form and content, the passage directly recalls Wang's poem at the end of *The Bundle*. Just what constitutes "humanness" is the trilogy's central focus and its only source of hope.

Like the trilogy itself, the improvisation is designed to represent and thereby illuminate the unacceptable contradictions that characterize our own historical moment – the solicitude with which we protect our own children set against a murderous indifference to the children of others. The first problem for the audience is in accepting the analogy as an appropriate description of their own social situation. Twenty years earlier, viewers of *Saved* neither saw nor accepted their responsibility for the gang's murder of a child in a park; and, as several reviewers remarked, the incidents enacted in *The War Plays* seem a deliberate return to the violence of that earlier play. The opening sequence of *Great Peace*, for example, fleshes out in detail the situation described in the Palermo Improvisation: after long deliberation and with much ambivalence, a soldier smothers his mother's baby in lieu of a neighbor's entrusted to her care, and the consequences of that act reverberate through the rest of that play. Despite the nuclear devastated landscape of *Great Peace*, weapons themselves are not posited as a cause of the problem. Rather, nuclear disaster provides a specific, extreme, and historically relevant example of the violence embodied on a more ordinary (but no less acceptable) level in the murder of one child. *Red Black and Ignorant* takes the analogy further to suggest that such killing is but a form of what happens when we live our ordinary lives – eat, go to work, raise children, and express love. In a violent society, the audience may be spared the violent confrontation, but not the responsibility for it.

Indeed, Bond's improvisation, and the critical terminology ("TEs," or theatre events) that has since accompanied it, suggest a development of the questions and issues to which earlier "aggro-effects" specifically gave rise. How, for example, might viewers be urged to take responsibility for the violence depicted onstage? How can violence be "truthfully" represented without lessening the outrage and suffering involved, that is, making it more "acceptable"? How can violence be shown as a social symptom that carries consequences, rather than itself a cause? Like earlier "aggro-effects," the incident rehearsed in the improvisation gives rise to an emotionally compelling narrative and carefully choreographed stage moments that may be remembered long after the performance. Bond also notes that the acting of the improvisation became "very slow" (*PI*, 3), as if the actors were silently analyzing the incidents they played. In his commentary for *The War Plays*, he refers to the "accident time" of slowed-action sequences as important to the staging of a "TE."[12] Broader in focus than earlier "aggro-effects," Bond's newly coined term suggests a subtle shift in the text-actor-audience dynamic whereby staged violence gets reinscribed in the system of social relations that produces it. Still distinguished from Brecht's "alienation-effect" (though the political purpose is similar), "TEs" explicitly promote audience analysis of a situation that presents itself onstage as unacceptable (violent), paradoxical (estranged), unbelievable (exaggerated, understated, or absurd), or ironic.

Like Brecht's *Lehrstücke*, the audience for the Palermo Improvisation are the actors, the "learning" involved participatory and physically interactive, and the situation depicted just as extreme. *Red Black and Ignorant* provides a rehearsed sequence of such improvisations; most scenes involve a paradoxical turn of events that "tests" the audience's response, provokes questions, urges analysis and requires explanation. The brightly lit stage, sparse stage set, announcement of scene titles, epic structure, and presentational action are all self-consciously Brechtian and underscore the play's pedagogical thrust. Actors address the audience directly in an agit-prop style.[13] Here, too, the single song of the trilogy occurs in a scene vaguely reminiscent of Brecht's dressing of the pope in *Life of Galileo*.[14] As the family dresses and arms the Son for military duty, the Son sings a terrifying and triumphant rendition of the psycho-social transformation (and dehumanization) involved in becoming a

soldier ("I am the army [etc.]" *RBI*, 14). Coming where it does in
the play, the song starkly sets forth the constellation of forces that
make the military option seem both necessary ("in bad times good
cannot be done," 14) and suicidal. In *Red Black and Ignorant*, the
father who allows it to happen is a "Monster"; in *Great Peace*, the
character who understands and explains the process to a "Son" is
called "Man" (*GP*, 56).

As a warm-up exercise for the actors and audiences, *Red Black and
Ignorant* models a learning process and provides a vocabulary of
incidents and images (TEs) that serve as a prompt-book for the
whole. Like the "Palermo Improvisation," each incident (or narrative sequence) is preceded by description (the scene to be played)
and followed by explanation or analysis of what has occurred on the
stage. The credible and disturbing action is designed to provoke the
very judgments (and ideological reflexes) that the characters in turn
will challenge. *Red Black and Ignorant* thus presents itself as both a
lesson and a practice session, one that makes sense on its own, but
also arms the audience to correctly interpret and better understand
the plays that follow.

The formal simplicity of *Red Black and Ignorant* is balanced by a
more complicated dynamic arising from the "future tense" of the
trilogy that the first play introduces, but does not entirely share. The
audience's guide to the play is Monster – a charred corpse of a figure
who speaks to the audience about the unborn children of the present,
yet is himself an unborn child of the future, thrown "from the womb
into the fire" at the moment of a nuclear explosion that ends the
world (*RBI*, 5). As a narrating character, the Monster introduces
and embodies the historicizing nature of the play as it makes itself
felt through shifts in time, allusions to past cultures, action and direct
address. In the opening monologue, he invokes a series of images
(central to the trilogy) that establishes a biological, cultural, and
historical connection to the past as well as a radical break.

Alone of creatures we know that we pass between birth and death
And wish to teach each new mind to be as profound as a crystal ocean
   through which we may see the ocean bed from shore to shore

2

We speak of our children before they are born
Carry them before we can hold them
        [...]

For three seasons they grow in the womb while the world may age ten
    thousand years
When they are born the hands of mechanics housekeepers masons pilots
    designers administrators drivers gardeners are held together to receive
    them
No exiled hero could return to a land more welcoming
[. . .]
We should not wonder that in the past children thought the world was
    watched over by gods

3

But now we kill them. (5)

The Monster speaks for the author, as a member of the audience, as
an actor and chorus within scenes, and also as an individual
character. In Scene Two, he goes to school, in Scene Three, he
experiences love, in Scene Four, he behaves "like a monster" (9) to
his wife, in Scene Five he sells his child, in Scene Six he rescues a
woman trapped beneath a concrete beam, in Scene Eight he is shot
by his Son. But the play begins with our knowledge that neither the
Monster, who describes the end of the world in a powerful apocalyptic poem, nor his Mother, who "passed into death without knowing"
(5) have survived the atomic blast. Yet this Mother remembers that
"in the past there were survivors," and the Monster reminds us that
events "from the life I did not live" are strictly plausible: "If what
happens seems such that human beings would not allow it to happen
you have not read the histories of your times" (6). Such words
suggest that the actor/characters/audience are not simply victims
and witnesses, but fully responsible for events to come and for those
that have already occurred.

    With the blurring of past, present, and future, *Red Black and
Ignorant* establishes a futuristic time frame for the trilogy that
substantially alienates the action. Yet the actor-character-audience
link helps clarify the pedagogic function of the dislocation in time,
making it harder to interpret the trilogy as either utopian or
dystopian in mode. Indeed, in *Red Black and Ignorant* the characters of
the "live" performance are not only fictional, but already dead.
"Before," "during," and "after" are conflated into the playing time
of parable in order to historicize the present moment – in Brechtian
terms, playing the audience's lives as a "piece of history," historically determined yet humanly alterable.[15] Since the future both has
and has not already happened, the opening play (like the trilogy as

a whole) can alternate between the anticipatory movement of narrative and the retrospective analysis of a chorus, soliloquy, or interior
monologue – combined at times in the presentation of a single,
complex image (TE). Cause and effect is not thereby abrogated, but
freed from the constraints of a linear chronology. Such a structure
leads away from the weapons-based rhetoric of current nuclear
debate. By avoiding the "day before/ day of/ day after" sequence of
film treatments like *The War Game* (BBC, 1966), *Threads* (BBC, 1984)
and *The Day After* (1987), Bond also avoids suggesting that the cause
of disaster lies in a particular chain of events or a single button-
pressing moment. Likewise absent is any narrative of the Faustian
overreacher, of scientists as technological heroes or villains, or of
technology itself steering us toward inevitable doom. While the
specific technology assumed by the play (and audience) lies outside
the understanding or control of any of the characters, the stupidity
to which *Red Black and Ignorant* refers cannot be remedied by
knowledge of a scientific or technical nature. The education sought
is geared to those who already suffer its effects – the ultimate disaster
woven into the fabric of the everyday lives of mothers, fathers, sons,
soldiers, wives, and lovers, whose innocence cannot protect them.

Because the process whereby victims turn murderers, the innocent
are corrupted, and the good do evil is not strictly linear, the
disjunctive time of the trilogy reinforces the dialectic between
knowledge and action. Thus by the end of *Red Black and Ignorant*, the
audience understands that the Monster not only died *while* his
mother was bending her head in attention to her womb, but at some
fundamental level *because* of it. Her back turned to the blast, she lacks
the knowledge that could lead to social change. Yet the mother of
the following scenes, the Monster's Wife, is not ignorant of the
conditions in which she lives. Rather, she has learned how to survive
– by displacing her rage, controlling her fear, limiting her vision, and
accepting her fate. Indeed, surviving under such conditions is a kind
of death, as well as a kind of murder. As the narrative sequences
trace, the mother's state of stoic resignation is not easily achieved,
but difficult and actively pursued. When the Son is ordered to kill
someone on their street, the Wife works to make his job as easy as
possible, knowing that "if he didn't obey orders he'd be shot [. . .]
What can we do in the end? Fight for our own" (15, 16). She accepts
what has happened, feels guilt ("He didn't make this mess: we're the
ones who –" 16), pities her son, and tries to help. But as she fastens

the buttons to his jacket, hands him his helmet, and gives him his gun, the audience is forced to see her loving, protective gestures as murderous. When the Son leaves, she states her position more formally:

We dont own our lives
They're owned by savages: that's why we're cruel
I'll prepare the meal and first we'll wait on him and then sit down and eat
  with him to show respect
Things may happen that will make today seem so trivial we'll forget it
[. . .]
If they put a pistol to my head I'll go on washing the dishes as if they hadn't
  entered my house
How else shall we live? (17)

The question is Bond's, addressed to the audience. Here the Monster's alternative, so familiar from contemporary dystopian science fiction, is to flee "to the ruins where the people are" (18). But the Son's decision to do so at the end of the scene represents no more than the possibility of change; for none of these characters have survived. At the funeral, the actor/wife turns to accuse the audience of her own short-sightedness, of building houses "with bricks that were already on fire" (19). Such issues will be reiterated in *Great Peace* by a mother forced to live through the global consequences of the wife's (and her own) previous attitude and actions. And as foreshadowed here, the "survivor experience" makes earlier incidents look "trivial" in comparison. In both plays, the mother/child trope suggests that what might save us from our own futureless era is nothing short of a complete rethinking of our lives, a fundamental questioning of every human (ideological) reflex, a social self-education that must quite literally begin at home – the first site of ideological conditioning.

The scenes of *Red Black and Ignorant* are, strictly speaking, hypothetical and futuristic; yet the structure is grounded in the present. Tracing the arc of an individual life (the Monster's), following the destiny of a single individual (the Son's), exploring the impact of larger social institutions on individual feeling and perception within the context of a "nuclear" family – all are familiar patterns of representation that an actual nuclear holocaust would make obsolete. *The Tin Can People*, second in the trilogy, realistically envisions such a scenario, tracing the effects of "the bomb" on a group of survivors who lived in peace for seventeen years before reenacting the destruction they originally escaped. Interestingly, the story itself makes use of narrative patterns familiar from science fiction and disaster films that focus on the goals, coping strategies, successes and failures of a small group of survivors – raising expectations and desires that the parable itself will criticize.[16]

Despite the horrors they have witnessed (and to some extent because of them), the characters of *The Tin Can People* believe they have been "lucky." As the Second Man puts it:

Before the bombs we were strangers: now we're closer than children to their
     parents
All of us shared one common wound [. . .]
Now we live together in decency
Not because we're better than those who died but because when they
     destroyed each other they destroyed their problem: the conflicts that
     came of their struggle to sustain their lives: they left us their tins
Paradise was built in the ruins of hell: which is the only possible foundation.

(*TCP*, 35)

The paradise described by the Second Man is a classless society, suddenly relieved of both "exploitation" and "the need to work" (34), and with it, the "evil necessities" to which they gave rise. As such, the situation expresses a contradictory wish on the part of characters and viewing audience alike: to return to a simplified, "decent" way of life while enjoying the fruits of a technologically advanced society. In combination with an ideology of the "elect," the fantasy of unlimited consumption freed from the necessities of the production process makes for a powerfully binding myth, one shared by members of survivalist movements that actively prepare for, or passively accept, the notion of a nuclear Armageddon.[17] Likewise, the happy discovery of a fellow survivor, and the possibility he offers for biological reproduction, plays into the last (first) man and woman theme so prevalent in fictions of nuclear disaster. Together, the "garden" motifs of *The Tin Can People* help to fictionally embody, and explicitly to criticize, what Jay Lifton has called "the malignant myth of regeneration via nuclear holocaust."[18] A related motif, with an even broader hold on the popular imagination, involves the emergence of a "natural leader" among groups of disaster survivors, often in response to a threat from the outside.[19] In *The Tin Can People*, the "Second Man," who so eloquently articulates the hopes and beliefs of the group, not only reinvents (with the logic of our own political leaders) a weapon for their protection, but offers to "sacrifice" himself in their defense. The recognizable logic and emotional impulses of the members of the group, so clearly projected from our own society, eventually result in the self-destructive "tin can riots," a repetition in little of the earlier devastation from which the characters (whose needs, fears, and desires have been shaped by an obsolete social formation) were unable to learn.

Through the narrative itself, *The Tin Can People* contests a number of assumptions – most importantly, perhaps, that a better society will necessarily arise from the survivors of the old. At the end of *The Tin Can People*, for example, the First Woman's desire for change and an end to the killing seems genuinely inspired ("What we had wasn't worth saving! It was like the time before the bomb!" 50). But any romantic notions expressed in her decision to sleep with the man from whom everyone else fears disease are immediately undermined by the audience's discovery that impregnation may have already occured.

> FIRST MAN: Let me tell you!
> Have you been in an empty room – in the riot? – in a coma?
> It was you
> I fucked you. (50)

The sentimental possibilities implicit in the motif itself are thus exposed in a violation, on two levels, of audience expectation – for what the man reveals is not only a mindless, animal-like groping in the dark, but an incredible, almost comic coincidence. The tenuous hope for a different future through the regenerated offspring of this new Adam and Eve is explicitly denied in the "sequel": without parents, the child of the First Man and First Woman cannot survive; and in *Great Peace* the Woman who helps with its birth will leave the child to die in the wilderness.

The Tin Can People does not rule out the possibility of a more fully human future – but any idea of "starting over," of wiping the slate clean, is adamantly refused. When the Second Man drops dead unexpectedly, the characters' own fear of death reasserts itself in a series of hysterical, illogical, but oddly plausible reactions. The Fourth and Second Women decide to ignore death ("That's why we're dying! If someone dies we wont even look at them!" 45), eat as much as they can, and take their rightful place as the fittest to survive:

> SECOND WOMAN: We're the test
> Perhaps its not another planet: its the earth – they've cleared
> out the destructive elements – now we'll colonise it.
> We'll have the good life – our own swimming pools. (46)

Forced to rebuild the future in the image of the present, the characters' reactions are both humorous and frightening. The reverence for the dead on which the play opens is totally reversed in the stripping and humiliation of the Second Man's corpse and the dionysian food riots – a mad frenzy of waste and greed – that follow. The characters' exaggerated response encourages a critical view from the audience; yet the reasons underlying the violent episode fully implicate the audience, who have been invited by the narrative to come to a similar conclusion: "It's because there are people of his sort that bombs get dropped!" (46). Ironically, what the tin can people learn from their actions is that "We don't learn from other people's mistakes – not even from most of our own. But knowledge is collected and tools handed on. We cant go back to the beginning, but we can change the future" (51). In the final section, the Fourth Woman envisions parents showing children the place "where the tin can riots occurred" and a library that records knowledge from the past for generations for whom "bombs'll be as old [. . .] as stone axes are to us" (51). In other words, the play refuses to countenance a future envisioned as a return to a simpler, pre-industrial past. If any warning is involved, it is not "turn back before it is too late," but to learn from past mistakes, and to create a life worthy of being saved.

In retrospect, the parable of the tin can riots provides the "memorial" for which the Fourth Woman calls in the final scene, while the chorus sections offer a "library" of images directly culled from knowledge and experience of the recent past. Indeed, the viewers for whom Bond writes already represent a future – that of the survivors of particular twentieth-century holocausts from which the present generation, Bond implicitly suggests, have not yet sufficiently learned. Bombs *have* (and continue to be) deployed on civilian populations; the cost of nuclear arsenals, the reasons for which they are financed, and the physical, psychological, and environmental effects of their use are a matter of public record. Thus the scene-setting imagery of the opening chorus – the intense thirst caused by the explosion, people whose "skin hung down in knotted strips," a river writhing with the bodies of the living and the dead – deliberately recalls oral and written accounts by survivors of the first nuclear blasts.[20] In the opening burial scene, the characters likewise recount their "death immersion" in terms familiar from survivor testimonials – the overwhelming guilt at being alive, the humiliation of not being able to help or comfort the dying, the silence of the devastated landscape, the cries for help, the mothers suckling dead babies, the melted bodies and traces of human shapes, the fear of radiation sickness. The Second Chorus of *The Tin Can People*, like the first, invokes that past historical moment as the appropriate context for the futuristic situation onstage: "The world was made into a crucible for an experiment / The effects couldnt have been forseen / We called them the voice of the bomb" (40). With its extended metaphor of an archaeological discovery, years after the explosions, of fossilized ancestors in caves ("skeletons" poised "before stone buttons and stone computers", 41), the Second Chorus not only reminds the audience of the possibility of extinction involved in our nuclear "experiments," but introduces an important connection between history and humanity, scientific knowledge and self-creation. On the one hand, our own age, looked back upon from the future, may seem inhuman; the metaphor is a warning. But more importantly, the frozen relic metaphor reminds the viewer that prehistoric time is not, strictly speaking, human time; we cannot go forward by going back. Beginning with the line "Before the bombs were dropped" (46), the Third Chorus likewise addresses the audience, who pose as the seventeen-year-old past of the play's parable action. Invited to condemn themselves along with the earlier generation of the parable time (with those who blew up the world), the audience is likely to interpret the violent turn of events as a similar judgment on the characters of the play. Against such a reading, the Third Chorus issues an explicit warning: "Don't judge – but wonder the parents didn't sit on their doorsteps cursing their children and the children murder their parents as they slept at night / That they didnt burn down their neighbour's house and loot the city centre. [. . .] Wonder that not till the bombs were dropped did these people run mad" (47). What happens in *The Tin Can People* has, in fact, happened before; and the reactions of the characters in the play plausibly represent the range of responses that viewers in the present might (or have) displayed in similar situations. Differences of opinion still exist among historians regarding the United States use of the bomb in World War II, with many involved in or affected by the "nuclear experiment" subsequently questioning their former positions. The question formulated by the Fourth and final chorus – "why were the bombs dropped?" (50) – remains as relevant to the present-day audience as it is to the characters in the play.

Without the choruses, *The Tin Can People* comes closest in form to contemporary science fiction that projects into the future the needs, desires, and contradictions of the present historical moment. And as such, it holds out the littlest hope. While the need for change is clear, the means for doing so seem outside the grasp of those who might survive, just as the imaginative form in which that need is projected seems unequal to the task. As the Fourth Chorus says, "you must create justice: and what chance do you have of that, you who must eat bread baked in the bomb-factory?" (50).

In *The Tin Can People*, the direct address of *Red Black and Ignorant* is taken over by the four chorus sections that introduce the play, comment on the actions, and help articulate the meaning of the parable. In *Great Peace*, direct audience address is abandoned altogether. If any play of the trilogy can stand on its own without losing the impact of the whole, it would be *Great Peace*, for it subsumes into itself the incidents, themes, language, and experimental form of both earlier plays.[21] Though the 'great war' that connects the plays of the trilogy is never directly represented, war and its aftermath prove no less imaginable than nuclear weaponry itself; in *Great Peace*, both war and its effects are vividly recreated through the spoken memories of the refugees and the tentative interactions between them and the younger characters of the play. Once again, war is treated as historical fact, the background against which the action takes place, and a "structuring absence" that both divides and connects the two sections of the play.[22]

As in *The Woman*, *The Fool*, and *The Bundle*, *Great Peace* falls into two distinct parts and invites the audience to consider the relationship between them. Indeed, the treatment of time and the resulting pattern of movement from causes to consequences, problem to "answer," and myth to history so important to the structure of *The Woman* could be traced with equal relevance here. In rehearsals of *Great Peace*, Scenes One through Eight were in fact referred to as "the Greek play" – not least because the single-focus action is set out with such Aristotelian clarity.[23] Taking up the narrative on which *Red Black and Ignorant* ends, the son in the army and his mother alive after a limited "nuclear exchange," the situation is quickly set with the Colonel's opening remarks: limited food supplies, "famine among the civilian population," rationing, a Civil Defense recovery program, martial law. The emergency situation results in a direct order to return to the "place of civilian domicile and eliminate one child:

as young as possible and not above five years" (5). The play then returns to the identity-producing confrontation of the "Palermo Improvisation," the naturalistic style of the slightly futuristic scenario contributing to a "real time" decision-making process both harrowing and (like the choices faced by Wang and his father in *The Bundle*) deliberately drawn out for audience and character alike. Here, as before, the soldier kills the "wrong" child; and his decision is neither sudden, easy, nor without severe consequences.

Most impressive, perhaps, is the care with which Bond articulates the entirely credible psychological responses of the characters involved. Details are important and telling: the working mother's financial double bind, for example, is exposed and strained by the care-giver's own economic needs ("What with the cost of food, runnin the 'ouse – lightin an 'eat – an its gettin colder – I dont mind 'er for a profit but I cant be out of pocket," 7). Likewise, the Son's humane hesitation is set against the murderous efficiency of the street-wise Pemberton, who finishes his own job a full four scenes before his friend:

PEMBERTON: You come round our place t' pick me up I'd've give yer a
  copy of the post mortem not stand there like a corpse wonderin if its
  got BO.
  Two! – it ain as if yer 'ad t' go out lookin.
SON: 'Ow did I know yer'd be round so soon?
PEMBERTON: This ain soon!
  What's the matter? – give it time t' write its memoirs?
  Pity the poor bleeder in your 'ands – shouldn't let you loose on a fossile
  chicken.
SON: Corpse off!
  Me mum was 'ere – I'm supposed t' ask 'er t' old it? (9)

The only soldier in the play with a name, Pemberton is a direct descendant of the gang members of *Saved*, and like them, a character whose language and actions reveal his cultural determinants – here represented as self-destructive, immersed in death, and headed for oblivion. A product of the system, Pemberton makes it work for him, thus earning from the viewers a kind of odd respect:

Crep in the back window. 'E's stood there. Told 'im why I'd come. 'Is class dont panic: read the papers with no pictures [...] Twenty thousand US dollars. Says I get the rest when 'e sees the body. Got it all sussed: 'e sees the body 'e knows 'is kid's safe. I dont kill two. 'Is sort know 'ow t' 'andle money. 'E as good as put me under contract. (9)

Hardly an evil character, Pemberton shows real concern over his friend's behavior later in the play, and tries to prevent the serio-comic train of events that leads to the Son's execution for dereliction of duty. Unlike the Son, who thinks through the consequences of his actions, tries to do the right thing, and finally proves his "humanity" by resisting the mindless orders of his superiors, Pemberton manages to survive by feigning death – that is, assigning responsibility for his actions to others, aping the manners and mores of his leaders, and becoming an excellent soldier. Indeed, his quick wit, personal initiative, pragmatic stance, and basic class consciousness give him the very "leadership potential" he mocks in the opening scene ("'Oo's interested in your potential / You ain the broom you're the shit on the bristles," 5); and through him Bond indicts the social system that fosters his identity.

When the Woman stumbles upon the soldiers' camp seventeen years later, Pemberton has literally "taken charge," the very characteristics that have allowed him to survive the same that prevent him from being fully human. In Scene Twelve, the longest of the play, the audience gradually realizes that the soldiers have outlived the social system that created them. Having witnessed "the end of the world" while they were "corpsin civvies in a quarry" (32), Pemberton and his redundant soldiers now cannibalize skeletal human remains and fully believe they are dead. For them, that "end" was experienced in apocalyptic terms, a nightmare vision of Ezekiel's dancing bones that lands them in a horrific landscape, the details of which rival medieval representations of Hell: "All the bodies – livin an dead, army an civvie – shot up in the sky / It was full of bodies whirlin round in circles like a painted ceilin / The wind blew em up there / Whirlin round over our 'eads like a dance" (32). Later they dig their way through dead bodies and see tower blocks with people "squashed flat on the glass [...] like specimens on a microscope slide" (33), humans with limbs hung awry, babies falling to pieces, a "mouth floatin' in a puddle of blood," a soot-covered woman crawling like a spider into the crack of a rock, and so on (33–34). The Woman does not deny the physical accuracy of their memory – we are led to believe it – but rather she challenges the conclusions to which they have come. However described, the soldiers have not witnessed the Apocalypse in its biblical, relevatory sense: as a sudden intervention by God, a stopping of worldly time, the future breaking into the present by the force of some outside agency. The play suggests that such an understanding of history is a way of denying responsibility, and of rendering meaningful an irrational (however plausible) train of events. What the soldiers see may or may not have occurred, may or may not be real, the blurring of "reality" a metatheatrical gesture that reminds the audience of the imaginative work the play itself is demanding of its viewers.

Another "paradox" emerges as Pemberton proceeds to "prove" he is dead. He does so by questioning the reality of the Woman's illusions, primary among them the child she carries. The challenge gradually escalates to the actions on which the scene ends, the soldiers violating the "wound sheet" the Woman believes is alive, Pemberton firing at the Woman with ammunition that has gone bad, and finally gunning down his own tortured soldiers. The scene in which an imaginary child is tossed about and ripped in half is as violent and emotionally harrowing as the original baby-stoning sequence of *Saved*, and the characters' actions and beliefs bespeak the limits of their own social situation, even as they did in the earlier play. But the Woman sees their hopelessness clearly:

Yer saw somethin yer dont like t'remember an that's 'ow yer forget
Look at your poor faces
I dont know what you've been through or what yer got up to – things yer
     shouldnt
But you're good people [. . .] they [the tin can people] died out – but *you'd*
     stand a chance – you're as tough as this kid
Is it so terrible t'be alive? (37)

Yet the Woman's insistence on their humanity, her very willingness to forgive, goads Pemberton and his soldiers to the most brutal acts of the play. Indeed, without her presence and the questions she evokes, the soldiers might have survived. In this regard, Soldier 4's initial misgivings prove accurate: "Chuck 'er out – we're dead – we 'ad enough rows before we settled that / We dont wanna go through that again" (34). To the end, Pemberton acts like the soldier he has become, unwittingly revealing to the audience a fundamental truth about himself and the society he represents.

Despite the "before/after" structure implied by the play's two parts, *Great Peace* unfolds as an extended sequence of "afters" – of consequences that shape the characters and that characters in turn create. The suspenseful, traumatizing, and impossible choices of Part One thus give way to the equally difficult consequences envisioned in the twelve wilderness scenes of Part Two. Here the action slows to

accommodate the reflective pacing and imaginative working-
through of the disaster aftermath, with the wandering Woman (the
suffering survivor of the first eight scenes) as our guide. Fundamentally conditioned by the irrationality of her old way of life, the
Woman can neither start over nor return to her former way of life.
The problem is articulated in Scene Ten when, like Basho of *The
Bundle*, she leaves a living child to fend for itself in the wilderness,
keeping faith with the bundle of rags she calls her own. Only the
vaguest memory of any ordinary past remains for the surviving
characters; yet they go on, actively creating the meaning for which
they search. Against the vast Beckettian landscape, the length and
language of *Great Peace* bespeak the possibility of life after *Endgame*.
With her struggle to survive, practical knowledge, wry sense of
humor, and murderous relationship to her own children, the
Woman of *Great Peace* offers an updated, more shocking, version of
Brecht's *Mother Courage*, even to the pram-like cart she pushes
through the scenes.[24] As in Brecht's play, the process of enlightenment that the audience traces is not identical to the characters' own;
and however sympathetic the central figure, she is not one with
whom the audience easily identifies. Here too the most heavily
alienated actions, those Bond would call "TEs," invoke and question
the "natural" mother–child relationship – introduced in Part Two
with the bundle of rags that the Woman nurtures and the First
Woman, who has never seen a child, accepts as real in Scene One.[25]

> WOMAN 1: That came out of you . . .?
> WOMAN: O yes
>   Its a good child – not always cryin
>   Tries to comfort me
>   Its older than its years
>   Uh – if yours is as good you'll be lucky
>   Some children cry
>   Mine knows Ive 'ad a lot t' bear – it doesnt burden me
> WOMAN 1 (*stares at the bundle*): Is that inside me? (26)

The irony of the Woman's lines strikes a comic chord in the
audience, though the situation in which a woman might realistically
mistake a puppet for a real child is shocking in the extreme. A similar
interaction occurs later between the Woman and Mother 2: "My
dear you've 'ad your baby since the war? [. . .] Why hasn't it grown?"
Here the Woman claims "it 'as but its slow / The bombs stunted it or
I couldn't feed it properly / I loved it but that wasnt enough" (46).

Given the traumatizing events of earlier scenes and the Woman's present living conditions, the psychological credibility of the Woman's madness is hardly at issue. But within the parabolic landscape of the play, the ability to accept the Woman's child as real becomes an act by which imagination, kindness, hope, and innocent play combine as a measure of basic humanity. The First Woman, Mother 2 and her Daughter each prove capable of the leap.

The tentative hope on which the wilderness scenes begin, with an unspoken pact between an older and a younger woman, is quickly dashed. The First Woman dies in childbirth, and though the Woman may have helped her, she astonishes the audience by leaving the First Woman's child to die. The situation directly recalls the opening scenes and the Woman's readiness to sacrifice her neighbor's child to protect her own; but in the replayed version, the Woman's decision seems mad, not rational. As she draws a picture in the dust "to pay" for the bundle she takes from it ("There's a 'ouse – with two doors – an a pond – a tree – these dots are the apples – a sun with a cloud – a car – an a boat on the lake – all ready for when you're big – an a matchstick lady in an apron t'feed you an teach yer lessons," 29), the audience is forced to consider far more than the Woman's culpability and her earlier words to its mother, "Per'aps it'd think it was best not t' be born? / We didnt ask that when I 'ad mine, but now its different" (27). The moment is equally heavy with the viewer's recognition of a shared biological past, of their own early childhood (when imagination and reality were not yet clearly distinguished), of an innocence that must be violated, and of a desire for things to be otherwise.

Once the Woman's insanity has been fully established and the audience has accepted that her child does not exist, the Bundle actually speaks – and viewers must once again adjust to the shock. With an interesting reversal of Katrin's mute presence in *Mother Courage*, Bond's Bundle gains her voice after being violated by the soldiers: "Now yer know: yer've 'ad your education – that's what people are: wicked or mad or in uniform [. . .] When you get better you'll still 'ave a limp" (41); and her speech gives the Woman strength, however briefly, to go on ("T'night all the walkin and pain is worth it [. . .] Yes talk my precious an all the world can sleep," 42). In the next scene, "some years later," we find the Bundle has not spoken a word since, nearly driving her mother mad. When the Woman hits her baby, as when the soldiers abused it, the shock is as

11 The rag-child speaks to its mother, the Woman refugee of *Great Peace*

great as when the Bundle actually spoke. The Woman's development in the wilderness scenes, her movement from insanity to reason,
is in fact marked by the gradual understanding that her child is dead
(but should not be so) and the doll she carries mere rags. Yet the
audience's understanding is marked by a growing awareness that the
rags are real, the representation "truthful," that this manifestation
of insanity is more rational than the society from which such
protective denial originally grew. The Bundle speaks once more
when the Woman uses her for a pillow for Mother 2, and the
forgiveness offered seems a turning-point in the Woman's own quest
for sanity – a quest that, like Lear's and Hecuba's before her,
involves remembering the past and basing her actions upon what she
has learned from it. Thus she intermittently mistakes the characters
she meets for those of her earlier life, quite literally shades from the
past who both bind her to the landscape and provide her the means
for human reconnection. Like her rituals with the rag doll, the
mistakes prove therapeutic. As she later explains to the Daughter:

When you dumped your mother on me – its all right, Im glad you did – I
    started t'remember: yer see, you gave me a new life too
I thought you an your mother'd been my neighbours when you were a kid
Then I realised you 'adnt: I'd made a mistake
                [. . .]
I pretended about you an your mother – but that man *is* my son. (54)

The Woman's insistence, at the very moment she seems most sane,
that this character is her son further complicates the issues of truth
and appearance; and double-casting the Son and the Man, as in the
original production, unsettles the certainty of viewers who witnessed
the Son's death seven scenes earlier. Though the Man proves
capable of pretending anything in order to "save" the Woman from
the wilderness, he is no more her son than the daughter and mother
were her former neighbors.

    As the play's title ambiguously suggests, in the "after-world" of
Great Peace, the line between the living and the dead, sanity and
reason, human and inhuman, hope and despair is forever being
crossed; and in the end, the questioning process that such radical
uncertainty has provoked supplants the traditional "enlightenment"
that didactic plays are expected to deliver. While the action of *Great
Peace can* be interpreted allegorically, the "texts" to which the
parable refers are historical and scientific, not sacred. The Woman,
for example, traces a recognizable psychological arc described by

Jay Lifton in his study of Hiroshima survivors.[26] Indeed, the Woman's status in *Great Peace* is that of an *hibakusha* for whom the barrier between fact and fiction, life and death, madness and sanity has for all practical purposes broken down. The audience can understand the character's "psychic closing-off" as the consequence of a "death immersion," an experience of virtual annihilation unprecedented in the personal history of the victim – and in the fictive future of *Great Peace*, globally unprecedented as well. The characters the Woman comes to "recognize" are those who reanimate the mourning process necessary to healing and recovery, a process not yet completed by the end of the play.

As Bond notes in the commentary, however, the Woman "does not return to the past to find she is innocent but to find what crimes her innocence drove her to."[27] In this regard, she shares the survivor status of the viewing audience – unwitting accomplices of the crimes committed in the opening eight scenes, and responsible for the world that is already destroyed before the play opens. As in earlier plays, however, the pessimism implied by such a view of history is more than balanced by the hope vested in the process of confronting it. The interactions among the refugees of *Great Peace* thus corroborate the insights of Lifton's psychological studies: of survivors' capacity (especially those who have colluded at a distance with killing) to "confront their own psychological experience and its moral consequences."[28] Even the soldiers who commit suicide provide an illuminating exception to the rule. Rather than resign oneself to a state of "psychic numbing" in which the painful experience is repressed at a considerable expenditure of psychic energy, the survivor may have "a more constructive response: opening oneself up to the pain of the experience in order to derive from it various forms of insight," including what Lifton calls "survivor illumination."[29] Such a process is precisely what the Woman of the play, and by extension the audience, are called upon to undertake. Indeed, *Great Peace* invests all its hope in the process of questioning that the Woman's behavior invites.

At the end of the play, the Woman of *Great Peace* rejects the hope offered by the Man from the settlement community. The Man's desire to help the Woman – to give her "peace," to assuage his guilt, to heal and give shelter, and to remember the past – is genuine; and the similar desires he evokes in the audience Bond leaves deliberately unsatisfied. As a measure of the Man's humanity, the

rescuing gesture means everything; as a measure of political effectiveness, it means little. We are back to Wang's question in *The Bundle*,
"what does it mean to save one?" The meaning of the Woman's
refusal is left open for the audience to contemplate. In Scene Eight,
the Son's silent refusal to pick up the Colonel's crumpled cigarette
packet evokes similar questions from the audience. Should we read
such resistance as a subversive act, as suicide, as evidence of a guilty
conscience, or as simply insane? By choosing isolation over reinte-
gration, the Woman likewise enacts her basic freedom in the form of
resistance: "This may be my last winter – I'll choose 'ow I live it"
(62). She may not be sane, but neither is the world for which she
remains, at the end, a figure: "if they took me back t' their place
they'd 'ave t'build a mad 'ouse t'keep me in" (54). Not simply
mistrustful, the Woman's experiences necessarily isolate her from the
younger, recovering community.

While the Woman's act of refusal demands audience interpretation, her death does not. Like Bond's Lear, the Woman of *Great
Peace* travels far, suffers much, and seems to deserve a peaceful death;
and the play refuses to burden her final moments with special
significance. As in both *Lear* and *The Woman*, the death of the main
character provides narrative resolution without solving the problems
raised. In the penultimate scene of *Great Peace*, the Woman simply
stops in her tracks – "drops dead" – and adds her bones to the ashes
(63). Yet the journey she represents is not over. If anything, the play
has gradually stripped the Woman of the ways in which she might be
understood as something other than what she is – a fictional
character. She cannot be placated, framed, brought in from the
wilderness, given "new life," or remain entirely symbolic of loss. Her
death does not confer new meaning on what comes before. Like the
jacket left by the Man, the Woman is "useful" in the same way that
Bond's play might be for the audience. In the final analysis, *The War
Plays* trilogy is not an extended political parable, but rather an
opportunity for interpretation that exercises the meaning-making
powers of the viewing audience.

Bond's trilogy reminds viewers, as forcefully as any earlier work, of
the challenge faced by writers in the current cultural situation. If
strictly realistic and naturalistic modes of address seem outmoded,
their conventions too visible, so too do the modernist experiments
that have fueled the aesthetics of late consumer capitalism. That
Bond's work attempts to negotiate this difficult historical moment is

hard to deny: the issues are imprinted in the content of the plays, the formal strategies and techniques through which they are mediated, Bond's own critical writing and direction of development, and the kind of success he has been accorded so far. Whether Bond's plays will provide a productive model, and a way out of the impasse, for a younger generation of politically committed artists, or whether they will remain no more than an illustration of the historical contradictions they embody, is important work for future audiences to decide.

Notes

I INTRODUCTION

1 For a cultural overview, see Alan Sinfield, *Literature, Politics and Culture in Postwar Britain* (Berkeley, CA: University of California Press, 1989). For Bond's relationship to the Royal Court, see Philip Roberts, *The Royal Court Theatre, 1965–72* (London: Routledge, 1986).

2 Bond puts it simply: "I try to tell the truth" (personal interview, Royal Court Theatre, 6 Dec. 1979). The "truth-telling" agenda is familiar to readers of Brecht: see Bertolt Brecht, *Brecht on Theatre*, ed. and trans. by John Willett (New York: Hill and Wang, 1964), p. 107.

3 The extensive use of quotation from interviews etc. is most useful in a study like Malcolm Hay and Philip Roberts, *Bond: A Study of His Plays* (London: Methuen, 1980).

4 The label "A Rational Theatre" titles Bond's preface to *Plays: Vol. 2* (London: Methuen, 1978), p. ix. For a fuller account of what follows, see Jenny S. Spencer, "Edward Bond's Dramatic Strategies," *Contemporary English Drama*, ed. by Christopher Bigsby (London: Edward Arnold, 1981), pp. 124–134.

5 See Colin MacCabe, "Realism and Cinema: Notes on Some Brechtian Theses," *Screen*, vol. 15, no. 2 (1974), pp. 7–27, and Tony Stevens, "Reading the Realist Film," *Screen Education*, no. 26 (Spring, 1978), pp. 13–34.

6 *Brecht on Theatre*, pp. 109–110.

7 The problematic nature of "audience" itself – as a conceptual space (implied by dramatic form), an historical presence (recorded by reviewers), an aesthetic construct (formulated through literary criticism), or a virtual reality (hypothesized by critical discourse) – is an issue that needs a more careful articulation than is possible in the chapters that follow. On a number of levels, my reading of Bond's plays "gives audience" to the drama in ways that necessarily shift between collective and individual responses, subjective and institutional spaces, historical and hypothetical realms.

8 See *The Messingkauf Dialogues*, trans. by John Willett (London: Methuen, 1977), pp. 32–33.

9 "Letter to Tony Coult," in Malcolm Hay and Philip Roberts, *Edward Bond: A Companion to the Plays* (London: T Q Publications, 1978), p. 74.
10 Terry Eagleton, "Nature and Violence: the Prefaces of Edward Bond," *Critical Quarterly*, vol. 26 (1984), pp. 127–135. Fredric Jameson's afterword to *Aesthetics and Politics* (London: Verso, 1977), pp. 196–213, offers an important perspective on many of the issues that have informed this chapter.

2 VIOLENCE AND VOYEURISM

1 For historical accounts, see Richard Scharine, *The Plays of Edward Bond* (Lewisburg, PA: Bucknell University Press, 1976), pp. 47–54, Ann S. Jenkins, "The Reactions of London's Drama Critics to Certain Plays by Henrik Ibsen, Harold Pinter and Edward Bond," diss., Florida State University (Ann Arbor, Michigan: University Microfilm, 1973), and Philip Roberts, *The Royal Court Theatre, 1965–72* (London: Routledge, 1986), pp. 29–43.
2 Herbert Kretzmer, *Daily Express* (4 Nov. 1965) and Penelope Gilliatt, *Observer* (14 Nov. 1965) both excerpted in Philip Roberts, *Bond on File* (London: Methuen, 1985), p. 16.
3 An exception is Frances Rademacher, "Violence and the Comic in the Plays of Edward Bond," *Modern Drama* (Sept. 1980), pp. 258–268, who uses Freudian paradigms to describe and categorize the kinds of humor found in Bond's early plays.
4 For example, Bernard Levin of the *Daily Mail* wrote: "This bizarre and unclassifiable piece is an astonishing tour de force for a first play, and if it comes to that, would be an astonishing tour de force for a fifty-first" (10 Dec. 1962), in Roberts, *Bond on File*, p. 14. See also Kenneth Tynan, n. 6 below.
5 *Jewish Chronicle* (14 Dec. 1962), p. 35.
6 *Observer* (16 Dec. 1962). For a discussion of Bond's early reception and some of its consequences, see Christopher Innes, "The Political Spectrum of Edward Bond: From Rationalism to Rhapsody," *Modern Drama*, vol. 25 (June 1982), pp. 190–191.
7 In its anti-Shavian feeling, Bond's early work is similar to those of his contemporaries at the Royal Court. See Roberts, *The Royal Court*, p. 124.
8 M. Hay and P. Roberts, *Bond: A Study of His Plays* (London: Methuen, 1980), p. 31.
9 *Ibid.*, p. 26.
10 *Ibid.*, p. 23.
11 *Bond: Plays One* (London: Methuen, 1977), p. 228. Quotations from *The Pope's Wedding* and *Saved* hereafter cited in the text refer to this edition.
12 Hay and Roberts, *Bond: A Study*, p. 24.
13 Sigmund Freud, *Sexuality and the Psychology of Love* (New York: Mac-

millan, 1972), pp. 172–173. See also Freud, *Three Essays on the Theory of Sexuality* (New York: Avon, 1962), pp. 88–93.

14 Laura Mulvey, "Visual Pleasure and Narrative Cinema," *Screen*, vol. 16 (Autumn 1975), p. 14.

15 See Freud, *Sexuality and the Psychology of Love*, p. 103.

16 Such a reading of the play does not contradict Bond's own sense of the play being about the identity of opposites: "What you see in *The Pope's Wedding* is a sort of identity of opposites, I think. You see two completely different worlds, and then, when they are brought together, they are the same world" (Hay and Roberts, *Bond: A Study*, p. 31). Elsewhere, Bond notes, "At the time there were a lot of rather metaphysical plays with sort of tramps in them who just sort of came on and said strange things [. . .] and I think it was an attempt to humanize that image, which I felt was very powerful," "Drama and the Dialectics of Violence," *Theatre Quarterly*, vol. 2 (Jan. – Mar. 1972), p. 7.

17 Georgina in *Narrow Road to the Deep North* (1968), Hatch in *The Sea* (1973), Bodice and Fontanelle in *Lear* (1971), and the Son in *Bingo* (1973) provide the clearest examples of such proto-fascistic types.

18 See Freud, *General Psychological Theory* (New York: Macmillan, 1963), p. 91.

19 *Jewish Chronicle* (14 Dec. 1962), p. 35.

20 See the *Birmingham Post* (23 Nov. 1973) review of the Northcott Theatre production at the Bush Theatre in London.

21 As such, Bond's technique shares characteristics of British New Wave filmmaking in the 1950s as described by John Hill, *Sex, Class and Realism* (London: British Film Institute, 1968), p. 129.

22 Christian Metz, "A Note on Two Kinds of Voyeurism," *The Imaginary Signifier: Psychoanalysis and the Cinema* (Bloomington, IN: Indiana University Press, 1977), p. 95.

23 *Ibid.*, p. 94. Metz describes film as "unauthorized scopophilia" in a chapter entitled "The Passion for Perceiving," *ibid.*, p. 63.

24 See Freud, *Sexuality and the Psychology of Love*, pp. 107–132. Of the five cases Freud uses for his analysis, one sounds close to Len's own situation: not ill, he came "to be analysed merely on account of lack of decision in life" (p. 111). In all the various transformations of the fantasy, the child is being beaten *by the father*.

25 See Metz, *The Imaginary Signifier*, pp. 105–108, for an analogous discussion of the function of dream censorship and its relation to filmic pleasure.

26 Without mentioning repression, Bond writes of the "Oedipus, atavistic fury" in almost Freudian terms as that which is "kept under painful control by other people in the play, and that partly accounts for the corruption of their lives," in the "Author's Note" to *Saved, Plays: One* (London: Methuen, 1977), p. 310.

27 *Ibid.*

28 Bond himself finds Len a more active and positive character than my analysis may imply (letter to the author, Feb. 1991). See Hay and Roberts, *Bond: A Study*, pp. 55–57, for further discussion of the play's ending.

29 Bond, *The Sea*, in *Bond: Plays Two* (London: Metheun, 1978), p. 148. The Monster of *The War Plays* follows this advice quite literally as he looks back through the howling flames of a nuclear holocaust in order to trace its causes.

30 Quotations from *Blow-Up* (1966) transcribed directly from the film distributed on video by MGM/United Artists. On Bond's reluctance to talk about his film work see Scharine, *The Plays of Edward Bond*, p. 159.

3 REREADING HISTORY

1 John Osborne's *Luther* (1963) and *A Patriot for Me* (1966), Robert Bolt's *A Man for All Seasons* (1961), Tom Stoppard's *Travesties* (1975), Peter Shaffer's *The Royal Hunt of the Sun* (1965) and *Amadeus* (1980) (to name but a popular few) are all Brechtian-like history plays that share little affinity with Brecht's politics. For further contextualization of Bond's use of history, see Richard Cave, *New British Drama in Performance, 1970–1985* (New York: St. Martin's Press, 1988), pp. 249–302.

2 Christopher Bigsby, "The Language of Crisis in British Theatre," in *Contemporary English Drama*, ed. Bigsby (London: Edward Arnold, 1981), p. 38.

3 See Edward Bond, "The Romans and the Establishment's Fig Leaf," *Theatre*, vol. 12 (Spring, 1981), pp. 39–42. For a summary of Brenton's play and the vociferous critical response it aroused, see Richard Beacham's essay in *ibid.*, "Brenton Invades Britain: *The Romans in Britain* Controversy," pp. 34–37.

4 More than two years before his wish came true, Brenton was calling for a theatre "as loud as parliament," and big enough "to begin to reverberate, for it to be discussed, for it to be a national event, for it to be news," in Catherine Itzen, *Stages of the Revolution* (London: Methuen, 1980), p. 192.

5 Malcolm Hay and Philip Roberts, *Bond: A Study of His Plays* (London: Methuen, 1980), p. 183. The first performance was directed by Jane Howell and John Dove in the Northcott Theatre, Exeter.

6 For the factual records of Shakespeare's life with which Bond is undoubtedly familiar, see S. Schoenbaum, *William Shakespeare: A Documentary Life* (New York: Oxford University Press, 1975), pp. 161–253.

7 See Ronald Hayman, *British Theatre Since 1955: A Reassessment* (Oxford: Oxford University Press, 1979), pp. 22–25; Albert Hunt, "A Writer's Theatre," *New Society* (11 Dec. 1975), pp. 606–607; and Simon Trussler, *Edward Bond* (Harlow: Longman, 1976), pp. 26–33.

8 *Bond: Plays Three* (London: Methuen, 1987), p. 4. Quotations from *Bingo* hereafter cited in the text refer to this edition. Bond replaces

Shakespeare's real daughter Susannah with the Old Woman servant; the drinking scene with Jonson, from *Ben Jonson's Conversations with William Drummond of Hawthornden*, ed. by R. F. Patterson (Folcraft, PA: Folcraft Press, 1923), eliminates Drayton; Shakespeare's suicide is Bond's own invention.

9 Personal interview, Trevor Griffiths, International Film Festival, Toronto, 1982. Griffiths was the major screenwriter for *Reds* (US: Paramount, 1981).

10 Bertolt Brecht, *Brecht on Theatre*, ed. and trans. by John Willett (New York: Hill and Wang, 1964), pp. 190–191.

11 *Ibid.*, p. 191. Bond's use of dialect within the play further distances (and situates) the characters from our own time.

12 In characteristically overstated fashion, Bond writes in the preface to *Bingo*, "A consumer society depends upon its members being avaricious, ostentatious, gluttonous, envious, wasteful, selfish and inhuman. Officially, we teach morality but if we all became 'good' the economy would collapse" (p. 7).

13 From the poor (like the Old Man), the beggar-woman receives bread and love; from the rich (like Shakespeare), money and death – a fact underscored by the play's subtitle, *Scenes of Money and Death*. Shakespeare's reputed generosity provides a basis for bringing out the purse; he does nothing to prevent her hanging.

14 Bond increasingly cedes the voice of reason, justice, and progressive historical change to women. Hecuba and Ismene of *The Woman* (1978), Rose in *Restoration*, and Augustina in *Human Cannon* all play roles more important than might otherwise be expected, given the historical period of the play. Whether Bond bypasses complicated issues of gender and power by simply designating women as the most appropriate subjects to carry on class struggle is open to question.

15 The inability to see cause and effect is comically underscored in Scene Four when he laments with Jonson that "such coincidences are possible." The basis for the episode may be found in *Ben Jonson's Conversations with William Drummond of Hawthornden* (n. 8 above).

16 See especially "The Relation of the Poet to Day-Dreaming" (1908), *Character and Culture* (New York: Macmillan, 1963), pp. 34–43. The essay "Character and Anal Eroticism," with its connection between money and feces in the same text, pp. 27–33, is also central to the metaphoric field of *Bingo*.

17 Bond has encouraged this view, adding *The Woman, Scenes of War and Freedom* to a sequence that "deals with society at three important stages of cultural development" (Hay and Roberts, *Bond: A Study*, p. 179). Although Hay and Roberts offer distinct analyses of *Bingo* and *The Fool*, both appear in a single chapter. The plays' similarities may have led to Albert Hunt's complaint that Bond seemed self-indulgently preoccupied with "writers' problems": "A Writer's Theatre," pp. 606–607.

18 Clare's life, as opposed to his art, has provided a focus of interest since his death in 1864. See Frederick Martin, *The Life of John Clare* (London: Macmillan, 1865), and the standard biography by J. W. and Anne Tibble, *John Clare: A Life* (London: Michael Joseph, 1932), who edited the first complete editions of Clare's work for publication. See also Mark Storey, *John Clare: The Critical Heritage* (London: Routledge, 1973). For a collection of Clare's autobiographical writings, on which many of the factual details of Bond's plays depend, see *John Clare's Autobiographical Writings*, ed. by Eric Robinson (Oxford: Oxford University Press, 1983).

19 See Storey, *John Clare: The Critical Heritage*, p. 248. For Clare's own accounts of the characters and situations that arise in the play see *The Letters of John Clare* and *The Prose of John Clare*, ed. by J. W. and A. Tibble (New York: Barnes and Noble, 1951).

20 In general, reviewers perceived a lack of coherent structure in the play, especially in relating the social background to Clare's own life and art. Robert Cushman found "the play halts; nothing binds it" (*Observer*, 23 Nov. 1975); Julius Novick, reviewing an American production, found it "flaccid" and "sprawling [...] the connections Mr. Bond is presumably trying to make do not get made," *Village Voice* (15 Nov. 1976), p. 115. For similar complaints, see Kenneth Hurren, "Poets, Peasants and Nuts," *The Spectator* (29 Nov. 1975), p. 707; Richard Eder, *New York Times* (4 Nov. 1976); and John Elsom, the *Listener* (27 Nov. 1975), p. 735.

21 That previous knowledge of Clare's life may be necessary for the play to make its full impact is supported by Irving Wardle's comment, "I know little of Clare's life [...] But apart from recognizing the now familiar landmarks of Bond's bleak territory, I have no clear impression of what the play is saying," *The Times*, 19 Nov. 1975. In general, the more familiarity reviewers showed about the life of John Clare, the more favorable their evaluation of Bond's play.

22 Raymond Williams, *The Country and the City* (New York: Oxford University Press, 1973), pp. 134, 141.

23 The two-act division, usually divided by an interval, is used here as a convenience to the reader; Bond uses only scene divisions in the published playscript. Quotations from *The Fool* hereafter included in the text refer to the *Bond: Plays Three* (London: Methuen, 1987) edition.

24 Hay and Roberts, along with most reviewers, note the important shift in focus between the play's two parts in *Bond: A Study*, p. 204.

25 In a theatre poem accompanying the published script, Bond writes: "Clare, you created illusions / And they destroy poets" (160), a line that works against the Clare myth in an interesting way, suggesting that his obsession with Mary is one measure of his blindness. See also Raymond Williams' analysis in *The Country and the City*, pp. 127–141.

26 Clare did in fact travel to London, observe a boxing match there, and

meet the infamous Mary Lamb. See J. W. and A. Tibble, *The Prose of John Clare*, pp. 79–96.

27 Williams, *The Country and the City*, p. 128. In fact, Lamb is the artist who suggests Clare "transplant Arcadia to Helpstone" (p. 141).

28 J. W. and A. Tibble, *The Prose of John Clare*, p. 215.

4 REWRITING CLASSICS

1 In the program note to the 1975 Liverpool Everyman Theatre production of *Lear*, Bond defends himself as follows: *"King Lear* is a play for which (it's a stupid thing to say) I have tremendous admiration, and I've learned more from it than any other play. But the thing is I'm afraid we use the play in the wrong way; as a society we use the play in the wrong way. And it is for this reason that I would like to rewrite it, so that we now have to use the play for ourselves, for our society, for our problems." Quoted in Malcolm Hay and Philip Roberts, *Bond: A Study of His Plays* (London: Methuen, 1980), pp. 105–106.

2 See Bond's letter to Tony Coult in Malcolm Hay and Philip Roberts, *Bond: A Companion to the Plays* (London: TQ Publications, 1978), p. 75.

3 Tynan's brief but favorable review of *The Pope's Wedding* and Charles Marowitz's "Grappling with a Masterpiece," a full-page commentary on the Brook production, both appear in the *Observer*, 16 Dec. 1962.

4 See "King Lear or Endgame," *Shakespeare Our Contemporary*, trans. by Boleslaw Taborski (Garden City, NY: Doubleday & Co., 1964). Brook read the French edition of Kott's book, which appeared in 1962.

5 For A. C. Bradley's "redemptive" interpretation of *King Lear*, see *Shakespearean Tragedy* (London: Macmillan, 1908), p. 279. See also Ruby Cohn's discussion in *Modern Shakespeare Offshoots* (Princeton, NJ: Princeton University Press, 1974), pp. 238–250.

6 Hay and Roberts, *Companion*, p. 53.

7 Most early studies of *Lear* involve comparative analysis of Bond and Shakespeare. My analysis is indebted to the work of Ruby Cohn in "Lear Come Lately," *Modern Shakespeare Offshoots*, pp. 255–266, Katherine Worth in *Revolutions in Modern Drama* (London: G. Bell & Sons, 1972), pp. 168–187, Horst Oppel and Sandra Christenson in *Edward Bond's "Lear" and Shakespeare's "King Lear"* (Mainz: Akademie des Wissenschafften und des Literatur, 1974), and Perry Nodelman in "Beyond Politics in *Lear*," *Modern Drama* (23 Sept. 1980), pp. 269–276.

8 For a useful description of these concurrent productions see Richard Findlater, "King Lear/Bond Lear," *Plays and Players* (18 Sept. 1982), pp. 18–20.

9 Bond contributed to the making of this critical issue with his prefatory remarks to the play. See *Bond: Plays Two* (London: Methuen, 1978), p. 3. References to *Lear* hereafter cited in the text refer to this edition.

10 *Shakespeare's Imagery and What It Tells Us* (Cambridge: Cambridge University Press, 1966), pp. 338–339.

11 "Production Casebook No. 5: Edward Bond's *Lear* at the Royal Court," *Theatre Quarterly*, vol. 2 (Jan.–Mar. 1972), p. 25.

12 *Modern Shakespeare Offshoots*, p. 96.

13 See Tony Coult's perceptive study *The Plays of Edward Bond* (London: Methuen, 1977) on Bond's use of metaphor in *Lear* and other plays.

14 *The Territorial Imperative* (New York: Atheneum Press, 1966). See also Ardrey's *The Social Contract: A Personal Inquiry into the Evolutionary Sources of Order and Disorder* (New York: Atheneum Press, 1970). In his introductory remarks, Ardrey refers to both the symposium and the general public interest in biological theories of aggression.

15 Perry Nodelman makes a similar point in *Lear* in "Beyond Politics in *Lear*," pp. 269–276, that nearly every event in Shakespeare's play is indirectly alluded to or caricatured in Act I.

16 Hay and Roberts, *Companion*, p. 53.

17 Northrup Frye, *Anatomy of Criticism: Four Essays* (Princeton, NJ: Princeton University Press, 1957), p. 96.

18 Using Aeschylus and Shakespeare, who go out of their way to show how catastrophe might have been avoided, in addition to Aristotle's original definition, Walter Kauffman argues in *Tragedy and Philosophy* (Princeton, NJ: Princeton University Press, 1968) that literary critics like George Steiner, who equate tragedy with inevitability, define tragedy in a way that would eliminate most tragedies from the very genre they would define.

19 "Edward Bond: Us, Our Drama and the National Theatre," *Plays and Players* (26 Oct. 1978), p. 8.

20 See *The Woman* (London: Methuen, 1979), p. 68. References to the play hereafter included in the text refer to this edition.

21 Walter Kauffman persuasively argues this position in *Tragedy and Philosophy*, pp. 82–100, 204–227.

22 Euripides' plays *The Trojan Women* and *The Hecabe* were urgently topical in their own time. Two years before the first production of *The Trojan Women*, the Greeks had captured and annihilated the islanders of Melos in reprisal for their wish to remain neutral in Athens' sixteen-year war. The men were murdered, the women and children enslaved; and the barbarity of the action was a controversial topic in Athens.

23 The statue may further allude to that of Athena herself, who, at the end of Aeschylus' *Oresteia*, promises military victory in exchange for the foundation of a new legal system.

24 Personal interview, Royal Court Theatre, 6 Dec. 1979.

25 For discussion of the differing verbal behavior of Heros and the women, see Jenny Spencer, "Bond's *The Woman*," *Modern Drama*, vol. 32 (Dec. 1989), pp. 569–570.

26 Fredric Jameson, *The Political Unconscious* (Ithaca, NY: Cornell University Press, 1981), pp. 116–117.
27 *Ibid.*, p. 84.

5 POLITICAL PARABLES

1 In one interview, Bond said he "knew the critics would like it [*Narrow Road*], and they did. [It was] critic fodder, really." BBC Broadcast, 26 March 1969, British Library National Sound Archive, London. He goes on to say: "It's a very easy, light little play. In a sense [the critics] just hadn't understood a word of the performance of *Early Morning*."
2 Most reviewers read *Narrow Road* as a parable influenced by both Brecht and by Japanese Noh, though many were confused about its meaning. See Irving Wardle, *The Times* (20 Feb. 1969); Herbert Kretzmer, *Daily Mail* (20 Feb. 1969); Anthony Seymour, *Yorkshire Post* (21 Feb. 1969); Deryck Harvey, *Cambridge Evening News* (21 Feb. 1969) and the *Oxford Mail* (22 Feb. 1969).
3 *Bond: Plays Two* (London: Methuen, 1978), p. 172. Quotations from *Narrow Road to the Deep North* hereafter cited in the text refer to this edition.
4 Bertolt Brecht, *The Messingkauf Dialogues*, trans. by John Willett (London: Methuen, 1977), p. 89.
5 For the recent critical reassessment of Brechtian *Lehrstück*, see the groundbreaking work of Reiner Steinweg, *Das Lehrstück* (Stuttgart: J. B. Metalersche Verlagsbuchhandlung, 1972). See also Rainer Nagele, "Brecht's Theatre of Cruelty," *Reading After Freud* (New York: Columbia University Press, 1987), pp. 111–134, and Timothy Wiles, *The Theatre Event* (Chicago: University of Chicago Press, 1980), pp. 69–107.
6 Review of *Narrow Road to the Deep North*, *Punch* (26 Feb. 1969).
7 *Narrow Road* shares with *Bingo* and *The Fool* the implicit connection between sexual repression and fascist tendencies as explored in the Frankfurt School's studies of the authoritarian personality and formulated by Wilhelm Reich in *The Mass Psychology of Fascism*, trans. by Vincent Carfagno (London: Penguin Books, 1970).
8 Bond later commented that the entire play "poured out of my indignation at this man ... I turned Basho into a sort of monster, a hollow zombie. One of those people who appear immensely cultured, with all the filigree of culture, all the outward show, but as hollow as can be ..." M. Hay and P. Roberts, *Bond: A Study of His Plays* (London: Methuen, 1980), p. 91.
9 See n. 2 above.
10 Although Brecht is associated with almost anyone who breaks the illusion of the naturalistic stage, his direct influence on British theatre has been limited in specific ways. See Maro Germanou, "Brecht and the

English Theatre," *Brecht in Perspective*, ed. by Graham Bartram and Anthony Waine (London: Longman, 1982), pp. 208–224.

11 In his notes on the play, Bond writes that because *Narrow Road* is about "cities, groups and organizations, the temptation is to use 1920s expressionism – putting a machine on the stage. This mustn't be done. Need a simple, expressive, perhaps not elegant, but certainly cogent story – which contains all the drama *in itself*, and doesn't use expressionism to refer outwards," Hay and Roberts, *Bond: A Study*, p. 90.

12 Whereas *Narrow Road* was written for an international "People and Cities" conference held at Coventry Cathedral, *Black Mass* originally formed part of the "Sharpeville Sequence: A Scene, a Story and Three Poems" written for the Sharpeville Massacre Tenth Anniversary Commemoration Evening held by the Anti-Apartheid Movement on 22 March 1970. *Passion* formed part of the Campaign for Nuclear Disarmament Festival of Life on Easter Sunday, 11 April 1971. Both plays are reprinted in *Plays: Two*.

13 Ending with the image of a beggar, holding out to the audience an empty alms can with a gun poised at his side, *September* supports the cause and self-consciously critiques the methods whereby funds must be raised to save the environment. See Bond, *Two Post-Modern Plays* (London: Methuen, 1990), pp. 197–210.

14 See Hay and Roberts, *Bond: A Study*, pp. 225–230, 228.

15 *A-A-America! & Stone* (London: Methuen, 1976), p. 61. Quotations from *Stone* hereafter included in the text refer to this edition.

16 Hay and Roberts, *Bond: A Study*, p. 228.

17 *Ibid.*, p. 227, for Bond's insistence on leaving open the cause of the Tramp's death.

18 The entire sequence recalls Brecht's cabaret scene in *The Seven Deadly Sins*. As Anna reminds her sister: "It wasn't art that sort of people came for / That sort of people came for something else; And when a man has paid for his evening / He expects a good show in return. So if you cover up your bosom and thighs like you had a rash / Don't be surprised to see them yawning," *Bertolt Brecht: Collected Plays*, vol. II Part 3, ed. by John Willett and Ralph Manheim (London: Methuen, 1979), p. 73. The perils of life, in the form of one's own natural inclination to behave virtuously, is an informing idea of both plays.

19 Directly or indirectly, *Stone* alludes to Beckett's *Waiting for Godot* (Bond's Tramp introduces himself with complaints about his boots), the myth of Sisyphus, *Everyman*, and *Pilgrim's Progress* in addition to Brecht and the Bible. Insofar as a fable embodies a moral precept, idea, or proverb into an *action*, the term seems appropriate to Bond's parables.

20 See Luke 8:9–10, Matthew 13:11–14, and Mark 4:12 on Christ's parables and how they were received.

21 The Brecht plays most germane to the issues and situations in the *Bundle* include *The Yea Sayer and the Nay Sayer*, *The Exception and the Rule*, *The*

Seven Deadly Sins, *The Measures Taken*, *The Good Person of Setzuan* and *The Caucasian Chalk Circle*. Useful comparison could fuel a separate study.

22 *The Bundle* (London: Methuen, 1978), p. 78. Quotations from the play hereafter included in the text refer to this edition.

23 Eric Bentley, *The Brecht Commentaries, 1942–1980* (London: Methuen, 1981), p. 295.

24 The alternatives pose other problems: a play based on current events risks being overtaken by changes in the political situation; more fully "rounded," naturalistic theatre resists the abstraction necessary for conceptual thinking; and history plays are often limited by the analogous contemporary situations on which they may usefully comment. As Steinweg notes, Brecht divided his own *Lehrstücke* into several types – experimenting with biographical, historical, and parable forms for his pedagogical ends. At times Brecht saw the *Lehrstück* as central to epic theatre; at others, he suggested that parables might no longer be suitable for it. See *Das Lehrstück*, p. 83.

25 *Brecht: Collected Plays*, vol. II, pp. 296–297.

26 See Paul Ricoeur's description of parable form in "The Specificity of Religious Language," *Semeia: An Experimental Journal for Biblical Criticism*, vol. 4 (1975), pp. 107–145. See also David Tracy, "Metaphor and Religion," *Critical Inquiry* (Autumn, 1978), pp. 99–101.

27 Michael Billington notes, "The parable itself is clear and specific: it's only when you start applying it to the world outside that doubts arise," the *Guardian* (16 Jan. 1978). John Peter voices similar reservations about the Marxist–Leninist ideology of "armed revolt" he finds in the play, *The Sunday Times* (1 Jan. 1978).

28 See *The Messingkauf Dialogues*, pp. 32–33.

29 Karl Marx, "The Eighteenth Brumaire of Louis Bonaparte," *Selected Works* (New York: International Publishers, 1965), p. 95.

30 Bertolt Brecht, *Brecht on Theatre*, ed. and trans. by John Willett (New York: Hill and Wang, 1964), p. 55.

31 *Ibid.*, p. 36. For Brecht's descriptions of the *gestus*, a notion as central to epic theatre as the alienation-effect, see also pp. 42, 86, 104–105, 115–116, 198–201.

32 Hay and Roberts make similar points about this play in *Bond: A Study*, pp. 266–287.

33 *Messingkauf Dialogues*, pp. 88–89.

6 SOCIAL PLEASURES

1 Bond introduces the term "TE" with the "Palermo Improvisation," included in a recent edition of *Part One: Red Black and Ignorant* (Woodstock, IL: The Dramatic Publishing Co., 1989). The term refers to startling moments in a play based on credible human responses to extreme situations that need to be socially analyzed and explained.

Though similar to Brechtian alienation-effects, TEs are generated from *inside* the experience, rather than from a detached point of view. See chapter 8 for further discussion.

2 The chapter title, "Social pleasures," is from Terry Lovell's *Pictures of Reality* (London: British Film Institute, 1980), p. 95. Lovell writes of desires essentially public and social in nature that Marxist aesthetics ignores at its peril. Issues of audience pleasure are clearly relevant to any theorizing of Bond's comic strategies.

3 A.J.M., *London Theatre* (Nov. 1965). However "revolted," critics and reviewers almost uniformly picked up on the play's humor, an observation supporting Frances Rademacher's contention that Bond's comedy intensifies the violent effect of the action. See "Violence and the Comic in Bond's Plays," *Modern Drama* (Sept. 1980), pp. 258–268.

4 Surely in response to the tenor of charges against *Saved*, Bond writes in the first Author's Note that "Saved is almost irresponsibly optimistic" (*Plays: One* [London: Methuen, 1977], p. 309). Quotations from the play hereafter cited in the text refer to this edition.

5 The alternating pattern is not necessarily an oscillating one – such dramatic variations in tempo, blocking, and sound are essential to aesthetic pleasure and one gauge of the successful playwright. Malcolm Hay and Philip Roberts find such patterns as evidence of Bond's masterful play construction in *Bond: A Study of His Plays* (London: Methuen, 1980), pp. 39–64.

6 See Freud, "Wit and its Relation to the Unconscious," *The Basic Writings of Sigmund Freud*, trans. by A. A. Brill (New York: Modern Library), pp. 762–803. In the following analysis, "wit" refers to identifiable joking or word-play in the German sense of *Witz*, rather than to the more particular and literary meaning "wit" assumes in common English parlance.

7 Steve Neale, "Psychoanalysis and Comedy," *Screen*, vol. 22, no. 2 (1981), p. 33.

8 Freud, "Wit and its Relation to the Unconscious," pp. 693, 688. Freud's technical vocabulary proves useful for demonstrating the complexity and variation of the play's wit, examples of which will not be labored here.

9 Providing another link to Len and the play's domestic scenes, such clichés mirror the more naively expressed sentiments of Len: "This is the life" (23, 29), "Kids need proper 'omes" (50), "One a them things. Yer can't make too much a it" (98), and so on.

10 One wonders about the reactions that an audience of working-class youths, similar to those portrayed in *Saved*, might have toward the play. In some sense, the play seems written for them as much as for the audience who see, read, and study it now.

11 Freud, "Wit and its Relation to the Unconscious," pp. 732, 737.

12 Jeremy Kingston, *Punch* (10 Nov. 1965).

13 *Bond: Plays One* (London: Methuen, 1977), p. 136. Quotations from the play hereafter cited in the text refer to this edition. See also Hay and Roberts, *Bond: A Study*, pp. 67–69. Philip Roberts takes up the censorship battle and its effect on the Royal Court in more depth in *The Royal Court Theatre, 1965–1972* (London: Routledge, 1986), pp. 62–68, 83–88.

14 Freud, *The Interpretation of Dreams* (New York: Random House, 1938), pp. 483–484. In context, Freud's comment is intended to remind the dream analyzer of the result of censorship upon the dream work. In an odd way, Bond's script exposes the superficiality of the Lord Chamberlain's office by exposing its profound connection to nineteenth-century attitudes toward sexuality that Freud's theory documents.

15 William Gaskill, on the other hand, felt only a realistic acting style would evoke the effect of a dream. See Hay and Roberts, *Bond: A Study*, p. 86.

16 *Ibid.*, p. 88.

17 The play's revival a year later evoked the same divided response. For Irving Wardle, *Early Morning* was a "solipsistic muddle; confusingly plotted and projecting a wrathfully infantile view of existence" ("Upsetting Our Idols," *The Times*, 14 Mar. 1969). Jeremy Kingston, "At the Theatre," *Punch* (21 Nov. 1969), J. C. Trewin, *Illustrated London News* (23 Nov. 1969), and the reviewer for *The Sunday Times* (16 Mar. 1969) were equally dismissive. For positive reviews, see Ronald Bryden, "Bond in a Wild Victorian Dreamworld," *Observer* (16 Mar. 1969) and Martin Esslin, *Plays and Players* (May 1969), pp. 25–26.

18 Freud, "Wit and its Relation to the Unconscious," pp. 760–761, 737–739, 752.

19 Niloufer Harbinger presents a different point of view of *Early Morning*'s relation to history in *Twentieth-Century English History Plays* (Totowa, NJ: Harper and Row, 1988), pp. 213–252. Although historical documents may have influenced Bond's work, what Harbinger most convincingly shows, albeit unwittingly, is the impossibility of reading them in quite the same way after reading Bond's play. The same dynamic is at work in scripts more obviously influenced by specific sources, such as *Lear* and *Restoration*.

20 Lovell, *Pictures of Reality*, p. 87.

21 Bakhtin, *Rabelais and His World*, trans. by Hélène Iswolsky (Bloomington, IN: Indiana University Press, 1984), p. 474.

22 *Ibid.*, p. 19.

23 *Ibid.*, p. 25.

24 *Ibid.*, pp. 89, 34. Interestingly, Bond has called *Early Morning* his "freedom play" (Hay and Roberts, *Bond: A Study*, p. 88).

25 Bakhtin, *Rabelais*, p. 94.

26 *Ibid.*, p. 49.

27 In a 1972 interview in *Theatre Quarterly*, Bond makes a similar point: "I

think *Early Morning* is essentially about working-class life. I mean, the plays that I am told are based on social realism very often seem to me the wildest fairy stories, and setting them against an immediately recognizable background doesn't make them any truer" (quoted in Philip Roberts, *Bond on File* [London: Methuen, 1985], p. 19).

28 The aggressive politics, use of songs, and "plain fun" make *Stone* and *Derek* close to fulfilling the demands of working-class audiences that John McGrath so carefully describes in *A Good Night Out* (London: Methuen, 1981). The popularity of *Derek* with young audiences has led to its inclusion in several successful Royal Shakespeare Company school tours.

29 *Derek* (London: Methuen, 1983), p. 15. References to the play hereafter are included in the text.

30 In the "Author's Note" to *Derek*, Bond writes: "The play is a farce. In conventional farce reality is not allowed to interfere with the energy of the play. But in this play energy is produced from the reality of the farce. So the play should be performed with farcical energy. But to produce this energy the director and performers must base their work on the realism – social realism – of the play's actions and characters" (p. 6). See also n. 15 above.

31 In other words, Bond's plays acknowledge the "structure of feeling" of our own cultural moment, including those of "failed revolutions" that Raymond Williams identifies and discusses in *Modern Tragedy* (Stanford, CA: Stanford University Press, 1966).

32 Susanne K. Langer, *Feeling and Form: A Theory of Art* (New York: Charles Scribner's Sons, 1953), pp. 326–350.

33 The existence of a unifying and inclusive "worldview" of comedy is persuasively argued by Robert B. Heilman in *The Ways of the World: Comedy and Society* (Seattle, WA: University of Washington Press, 1978).

34 For Bond's comments on *The Sea*, see Hay and Roberts, *Bond: A Study*, p. 139.

35 *Bond: Plays Two* (London: Methuen, 1978), p. 124. Quotations from *The Sea* hereafter included in the text refer to this edition.

36 See Hay and Roberts, *Bond: A Study*, pp. 159–160, for a more detailed elaboration of this point.

37 Hay and Roberts, *ibid.*, argue the opposite, making an excellent case for the subtlety with which Bond develops Willy's character without relying on conventional subtextual cues, pp. 150–164.

38 For Bond's comments on *Restoration* see the *Guardian*, 31 July 1981, excerpted in Roberts, *Bond on File*, p. 49. Katherine Worth also comments on the differences between *The Sea* and *Restoration* in her critical review, "Bond's *Restoration*," *Modern Drama*, vol. 24 (Dec. 1981), pp. 479–493; much that follows is indebted to Worth's informed and enthusiastic response to the play.

39 Reviews cited: Benedict Nightingale, "The Grim World of Edward Bond," *New Statesman* (31 July 1981); Jane Bryce, "Rehearsing Opti-

mism," *The Leveller* (10–24 July 1981); John Russell Taylor, "The Worlds/Restoration," *Plays and Players* (Oct. 1981); Worth, "Bond's *Restoration*." The same deep division reappears in reviews of the Royal Shakespeare Company's production, collected in *London Theatre Record* (26 March – 8 April 1989), pp. 386–389.

40 Letter from Edward Bond, dated 10 Feb. 1990 (original addressee unknown).

41 Worth, "Bond's *Restoration*," p. 479.

42 *Restoration* (London: Methuen, 1982), pp. 7, 8. Quotations hereafter included in the text refer to this edition.

43 See *The Works of George Farquhar*, vol. i (Oxford: Clarendon Press, 1988), p. 308. Ann's abuse of her servants in *Restoration* also recalls that of Lurewell (ii.i) of the same Farquhar play. While some reviewers unfavorably compared Bond's attempt at wit with Congreve, Bond (like Brecht) is clearly more drawn to the later playwright.

44 Maurice Charney, *Comedy High and Low: An Introduction to the Experience of Comedy* (New York: Peter Lang, 1987), p. 62. Charney's description of the comic pretender, deflated by comedy almost against the will of the spectator, is precisely the structure upon which Bond's play works.

45 Simon Callow, *Being an Actor* (New York: Grove, 1984), p. 112. Later, Callow quotes from his journal: "today I've arrived at my new performance: eighteenth-century man, genial, agreeable, reasonable, rational, with his fixed and highly satisfactory world view" (p. 165). Most reviewers of Callow's performance agreed that despite his despicable actions, Lord Are is a thoroughly likeable character.

46 See "A Short Organum for the Theatre," Bertolt Brecht, *Brecht on Theatre*, ed. and trans. by John Willett (New York: Hill and Wang, 1964), pp. 197, 195.

47 Bob is neither as innocent nor as stupid as such a summary of his character might imply. He could leave England, but he doesn't want to; he longs for the day when he can, as "a freeborn Englishman," denounce Are from the rooftops. When Rose leaves, he admits the truth – "I know well enough [...] But I've left it too late" (78). Having invested so much of his life working for others, he keenly feels the bind: "I must trust the clown an' hope for my reward" (79).

48 This idea is not only suggested by the shift from Restoration comedy to more sentimental and melodramatic forms, but in Are's own development from an amoral opportunist to something more frightening and evil. In a letter, Bond makes the point directly: "Consider the way Are develops from a restoration character into a nineteenth century character. Surely Balzac would understand the latter Are?" (10 Feb. 1990).

49 *Brecht on Theatre*, p. 89.

50 About the importance of dividing the elements of theatre, Brecht writes, "Some exercise in complex seeing is needed – though it is perhaps more important to be able to think above the stream than to think in the stream," *ibid.*, p. 44.

51 Bond introduces the term in *The Activist Papers*, published with *The Worlds* (London: Methuen, 1980), pp. 134–143. In *The Worlds*, it applies to a spoken monologue; yet the concept extends here to song and helps to identify how Bond's use differs somewhat from Brecht's. Elsewhere Bond writes, "the songs [*of Restoration*] are an exercise in public soliloquy: privileged insights by the characters into their own condition. Most of the songs are set between scenes and the character is – for these songs – converted into a contemporary counterpart: some of them are revolutionary – some of them are tragic ('My Mate Was a Hard Case,' for example)." Bond goes on to point out that not all the songs work in the same way, that tensions exist within and across songs, that different songs serve to comment on each other as well as the action, and that the songs are not intended to simplify or "usurp" the work of the audience. Song is privileged, but not "too privileged" (letter, 10 Feb. 1990).

52 See Roger Sales, "The Politics of Pastoral," in *Peasants and Countrymen in Literature*, ed. by Kathleen Parkinson and Martin Priestman (London: Roehampton Institute, 1982), p. 97.

53 William Empson, *Some Versions of Pastoral* (London: Chatto & Windus, 1966), p.196.

54 Roger Sales, "The Politics of Pastoral," p. 97; see also Raman Seldon, "Realism and Country People," *Peasants and Countrymen*, pp. 39–58.

55 Worth, "Bond's *Restoration*," p. 492.

7 READING THE PRESENT

1 Writing about a production of *The Mother* in 1932, Brecht recorded wide differences in reception along class lines that might apply to Bond's own production of *The Worlds*: "The worker [. . .] was not at all put off by the extreme dryness and compression with which the various situations were sketched, but at once concentrated on the essential, on how the characters behaved in them. His reaction was in fact a political one from the first. The West-ender sat with so bored and stupid a smile as to seem positively comic; he missed the emotional embroidery and embellishment he was used to" (Bertolt Brecht, *Brecht on Theatre*, ed. and trans. by John Willett [New York: Hill and Wang, 1964], p. 62). Here and elsewhere, Brecht suggests that audiences of epic theatre are rewarded for the political interest they bring to the theatre. Bond likewise writes in a poem "To the Audience": "you use the values by which you live / And show who you are – it is inescapable," *Summer and Fables* (London: Methuen, 1982). In this sense, Bond's plays judge the audience.

2 A similar prophetic note was struck with the production of Bond's *Jackets II* at the Bush Theatre, which closed a mere two weeks before the April 1990 "poll tax riots" in Trafalgar Square, an incident with striking similarities to the backdrop of the play.

3 Michael Leapman, "Terrorism is a Fashionable Study Field in West," *The Times*, 19 Nov. 1979, p. 6.

4 *The Worlds and The Activist Papers* (London: Methuen, 1980), p. 83. References to the play and the *Papers* hereafter included in the text.

5 The scripted labels were not made available to the audience of Bond's own production of the play, but served as rehearsal cues for the actors and signal to the reader Bond's experiment with form.

6 See John Russell Taylor, "The Worlds/Restoration," *Plays and Players* (Oct. 1981) and the *Guardian* review quoted in "Rehearsing Optimism," *The Leveller* (10–24 July 1981).

7 Karl Marx, "The Eighteenth Brumaire of Louis Bonaparte," *Selected Works* (New York: International Publishers, 1974), p. 97. Bond's dramatic strategies in *The Worlds* directly relate to Brecht's comments on the need for a new kind of theatre: "today's catastrophes do not progress in a straight line but in cyclical crises [...] the graph of people's actions is complicated by abortive actions; the power groups themselves comprise movements not only against one another but within themselves, etc., etc. Even to dramatize a simple newspaper report one needs something much more than the dramatic technique of a Hebbel or an Ibsen," *Brecht on Theatre*, p. 30.

8 The scenes of *The Worlds* are numbered from one to six in each part. For easier identification, however, Scenes One through Six of Part Two will be referred to hereafter in the text as Scenes Seven through Twelve.

9 Ian McDiarmid, who led the cast in the 1981 production at the Half Moon Theatre, speaks of trying "to get rid of naturalistic detail," "Rehearsing Optimism," *The Leveller* (10–24 July 1981). A similar effort informed Bond's rehearsals of the 1979 production at the Theatre Upstairs.

10 In *The Activist Papers* Bond writes, "We haven't done much when we've abused the stupid and presumptuous people in power. Abuse won't take away their power" (pp. 106–107). Earlier, Bond writes that the ruling class does not act conspiratorially, or even consciously, which makes problems harder to "detect and describe. The ruling class doesn't know what it's doing. That's why it's always losing its temper" (87).

11 John Russell Taylor notes that Trench ends up "railing against the world and siding happily, if a little ineffectually, with the terrorists," *Plays and Players* (Oct. 1981). Much would depend on how Trench is played, both early in Part Two and at the end. Bond's stage directions to Trench's final speeches note he is *"in his own world"* (79).

12 In *The Activist Papers*, Bond states that all of Scene Four "could be acted as a group public soliloquy," p. 141. The term is first mentioned in reference to Terry's "If We Were Here" speech in Part Two, a soliloquy that moves beyond the limits of naturalistic plausibility.

13 The internal dissonance between the three worlds of the play, their

differing temporality, and their absent (but structuring) relationship to each other find clear analogues in Louis Althusser's discussion of Bertolazzi's *El Nost Milan* in "The 'Piccolo Teatro': Bertolazzi and Brecht," *For Marx* (New York: Random House, 1970), pp. 129–151.

14 Charles Marowitz found Bond's translation of Chekhov's *Three Sisters* excellent, "the best [he'd] ever read or heard" (*Confessions of a Counterfeit Critic* [London: Methuen, 1973], p. 128). Discussion of the production, however, has generally focused on Gaskill's casting of pop singer Marianne Faithfull in the leading role.

15 The lack of precise location irritated several reviewers. Certainly a more factual, historically located plot would have made Bond's analysis easier to dispute. Bond's play is self-consciously fictional, literary, metaphoric, "written," and thus lends itself to an emblematic reading of history. That historical events since 1982, including the recent "opening up" of Eastern Europe, have not undermined or deflected the play's issues pays tribute to its political analysis.

16 *Summer and Fables* (London: Methuen, 1982), pp. 1–8. Quotations from the play hereafter included in the text refer to this edition. Although Xenia can easily be played as a caricatured figure from drawing-room comedy, the play's impact depends, in part, on a sympathetic and fully rounded portrayal of her character. In this sense, Chekhov's example proves instructive – Madame Ranevskaya, for example, need be no less "forgivable" for being sympathetically portrayed, nor do the farcical moments reduce the humanity of Chekhov's characters. Played with irony, Xenia provides her own best criticism.

17 Thematic concerns of some importance to *Summer* appear in *The Cherry Orchard*, especially in Trofimov's speech about the orchard itself. See *Chekhov: The Major Plays* (New York: Signet Classic, 1964), pp. 350–351. Bond's approach to Chekhov is similar to his approach to Shakespeare as described in chapter 3 of this book.

18 The term "texture of memory" was suggested by James E. Young's chapter on Holocaust memorials in *Writing and Rewriting the Holocaust* (Bloomington, IN: Indiana University Press, 1990), p. 172.

19 Such a focus is noted by James Young, "Review of *Facing the Holocaust*," *Modern Judaism*, vol. 7 (May 1987).

20 Xenia's response has also been that of many audience members. As one reviewer put it, Bond's "is not a liberal argument, and the broadly liberal audience were bristling with objections." Mark Armory, *Spectator London Theatre Record* (28 Jan. – 10 Feb. 1982), p. 38.

8 REMEMBERING THE FUTURE

1 *Human Cannon* was commissioned by the National Theatre, but not produced. For the etching that inspired the play, see *The Disasters of War* (New York: Dover Publications, 1967), plate no. 7.

2 *Human Cannon* (London: Methuen, 1985), pp. 33–34. Page references hereafter included in the text refer to this edition.

3 In "Beyond Actually Existing Socialism," Raymond Williams puts it more strongly: "The outstanding case is that of women, who as workers, share one kind of subjection but who more generally, as women, are still profoundly subject to kinds of appropriation deeply rooted in the whole mode of production (and especially the appropriation of their full, as distinct from wage-earning productive forces). The cultural revolution, as distinct from incentives and reforms to permit their inclusion in 'the plan', will be deeply sited among women or it will not, in practice, occur at all." *Problems in Materialism and Culture* (London: Verso, 1980), p. 272.

4 Edward Bond, *The War Plays, Parts One and Two* (London: Methuen, 1985), p. 5. This edition contains *Red Black and Ignorant* and *The Tin Can People*, hereafter abbreviated in the text as *RBI* and *TCP*. Page references to *Great Peace*, hereafter abbreviated *GP*, come from *The War Plays, Part Three* (London: Methuen, 1985).

5 Comparison to fiction and film may be instructive since unlike them, theatre simultaneously negotiates two terrains – the linguistic and the specular – in a form vitally connected to the human body. Though fictional and imaginative, a dramatic performance cannot, like fiction and film, be mechanically reproduced and distributed as a commodity. Though Bond's choice of the stage might seem inappropriate to the demands of his subject-matter, theatre offers a uniquely "human" artistic opportunity; relatively autonomous in economic terms, it may avoid the inherent political complicity of more popular forms.

6 *London Theatre Record*, vol. 5, no. 15 (15–30 July 1985), pp. 717–723.

7 The *Sunday Telegraph*, 28 July 1985, p. 16.

8 In addition to the reviews cited in n. 8 above, see Martin Cropper, *The Times* (27 July 1985) and Keith Colquhoun, *The Times Literary Supplement* (9 Aug. 1985). The general criticism of the trilogy returns full circle to the early reviews of *The Pope's Wedding* and the impatience of reviewers with sections of the play deemed irrelevant to the narrative. From the very first, Bond has insisted on staging, in any number of ways, *more* than the audience feels necessary.

9 "Egg-bound Bond," *Observer* (28 July 1985).

10 See chapter 5, "Political parables," for a discussion of Bond's use of the parable form. If *The Bundle* can be understood as a parable about parables, so too can *The War Plays* be grasped as a "learning play" about learning.

11 "Palermo Improvisation," *The War Plays: Part One* (Woodstock, IL: Dramatic Publishing Co., 1989), p. 3. Hereafter abbreviated as *PI*, with page references included in the text.

12 "Commentary on the War Plays," unpublished draft, p. 74.

13 Bond writes in the "Commentary" that *Red Black and Ignorant* "is derived from agitprop," p. 70.
14 Brecht, *Collected Plays*, vol. v (New York: Random House, 1972), pp. 81–85.
15 Bertolt Brecht, *Brecht on Theatre*, ed. and trans. by John Willett (New York: Hill and Wang, 1964), p. 86. Brecht writes that the "historicizing theatre [...] concentrates entirely on whatever in this perfectly every-day event is remarkable, particular and demanding inquiry [to] show the incident as a unique, historical one: if they want to demonstrate a custom which leads to conclusions about the entire structure of society at a particular (transient) time," *ibid.*, pp. 97–98.
16 See Raymond Williams' discussion of "Utopia and Science Fiction" in *Problems in Materialism and Culture*, pp. 196–212.
17 Jay Lifton, "The New Psychology of Human Survival," *The Future of Immortality* (New York: Basic Books, 1987), pp. 123–124. See also David Dowling, *Fictions of Nuclear Disaster* (New York: Macmillan, 1987), pp. 43–113.
18 Lifton, in *The Future of Immortality*, p. 124.
19 In this, science fiction and disaster films share similar patterns. See Nick Roddick, "Only the Stars Survive: Disaster Movies in the Seventies," *Performance and Politics in Popular Drama*, ed. by David Bradby *et al.* (Cambridge: Cambridge University Press, 1980), pp. 254–257.
20 Jay Lifton, *Death in Life: Survivors of Hiroshima* (New York: Simon & Schuster, 1967). "Death immersion" is a term coined by Lifton to describe the first phase of experience of a nuclear holocaust; more recently, Lifton has extended his analysis of Hiroshima survivors to the survivors of other genocidal holocausts. Lifton's interview material, gathered seventeen years after the event, is further corroborated by written testimonials, such as *Hiroshima Diary; the Journal of a Japanese Physician Aug. 6 – Sept. 30, 1945*, trans. by Warner Wells (Chapel Hill, NC: University of North Carolina Press, 1955).
21 *Great Peace*, like *Lear* and *The Woman* before it, come close to offering what Peter Szondi describes as a form no longer available to modern playwrights – that of "absolute drama." See Szondi, *Theory of the Modern Drama*, trans. by Michael Hays (Minneapolis: University of Minnesota Press, 1987), pp. 7–10.
22 *Great Peace* (London: Methuen, 1985) is divided into twenty scenes with no act divisions between them. However, Scenes One through Eight not only differ in form from the later scenes, but occur seventeen years earlier, presumably before the massive nuclear attack that has de-stroyed the world. For the reader's convenience, the first eight scenes will be referred to in the text as Part One, the twelve scenes following as Part Two.
23 Bond writes that "the events of the first seven or eight scenes of the third play occur before the events of the second play. These scenes make up a

forth play, a political-military-family drama. In rehearsals it came to be called the Greek Play. It could be played in its position in the text or separately on its own. Or it could be played after the first play," "Commentary on the War Plays," unpublished draft, p. 69.

24 In a section entitled "Pram," Bond makes the connection to *Mother Courage* explicit: "The Woman's pram is a psyche-x-ray of Mother Courage's wagon." Like Brecht, Bond understands, and elaborates, upon, the situation in which a woman cannot be both a good mother and a good neighbor. The contradiction of Brecht's play is startlingly, but accurately, stated in Bond's interpretation: "When Katherine beats her drum she is beating her baby to death. That, at least, is what we ask of the Woman – and of those who make bombs. Fictional characters show us what we do but cannot live our lives for us. So Katherine beats out her baby's brains. How else can the town be saved?" ("Commentary on the War Plays," unpublished draft, p. 84).

25 The pregnant woman who seeks help from the Woman is the First Woman from *The Tin Can Riots*, named Woman 1 in *Great Peace*. For the reader's convenience, Woman 1 is referred to as First Woman hereafter in the text. Mother 2 appears with her daughter in Scene Fourteen. Although distinguished from Woman 1 (the Woman's neighbor) in the text, the part was doubled in the first production.

26 See Jay Lifton, *Death in Life*. Lifton interviewed survivors of Hiroshima seventeen years after the bomb was dropped, the precise break envisioned by the play; nearly all of the "indelible images" of death that Lifton encountered appear in some form in *Great Peace*.

27 "Commentary on the War Plays," unpublished draft, p. 87.

28 Jay Lifton, *The Future of Immortality*, p. 104.

29 *Ibid.*, p. 105. See also Lifton's essays on "The Concept of the Survivor," and "The Survivor as Creator," *The Future of Immortality*, pp. 231–256. The pattern Lifton traces involves five concepts – "death imprint" or "death anxiety" (involving indelible images of death from the original traumatizing experience), "survivor guilt," "psychic numbing" (a mental impairment that involves an essential separation of image and associated feeling), "the suspicion of counterfeit nurturance" (often following from the sense of a counterfeit universe, the witnessing of complete moral inversion), and finally the "struggle for meaning," that can readily extend into a "survivor mission" (240–241). Such a psychological pattern can be traced for the refugees in *Great Peace*.

Index